AF352594

Verbal Art and Systemic Functional Linguistics

Key Concepts in Systemic Functional Linguistics

Series Editors
Gerard O'Grady, Cardiff University
Rebekah Wegener, University of Salzburg
Tom Bartlett, University of Glasgow

Books in this series provide monographic treatments of core theoretical concepts within Systemic Functional Linguistics, together with coverage of more recent concerns in Systemic Functional Linguistic theory and important areas of application and trans-disciplinary collaboration.

Each monograph is organized around a description of the historical factors that led to the emergence of the concept within Systemic Functional Linguistics and a detailed theoretical description of the concept within the overall architecture of the theory.

Published

Systemic Functional Translation Studies: Theoretical Insights and New Directions
Bo Wang and Yuanyi Ma

Neo-Firthian Approaches to Linguistic Typology
William B. McGregor

Verbal Art and Systemic Functional Linguistics

Donna R. Miller

SHEFFIELD UK   BRISTOL CT

Published by Equinox Publishing Ltd.

UK: Office 415, The Workstation, 15 Paternoster Row, Sheffield, South Yorkshire S1 2BX
USA: ISD, 70 Enterprise Drive, Bristol, CT 06010

www.equinoxpub.com

First published 2021

© Donna R. Miller 2021

All rights reserved. No part of this publication may be reproduced or transmitted in any form or by any means, electronic or mechanical, including photocopying, recording or any information storage or retrieval system, without prior permission in writing from the publishers.

ISBN-13   978 1 78179 533 0 (hardback)
           978 1 78179 534 7 (paperback)
           978 1 80050 068 6 (ePDF)
           978 1 80050 107 2 (ePub)

British Library Cataloguing-in-Publication Data

A catalogue record for this book is available from the British Library.

Library of Congress Cataloging-in-Publication Data

Names: Miller, D. R. (Donna R.) author.
Title: Verbal art and systemic functional linguistics / Donna R. Miller.
Description: Bristol, CT : Equinox Publishing Ltd, 2021. | Series: Key
   concepts in systemic functional linguistics | Includes bibliographical
   references and index. | Summary: "This book provides an overview of the
   dialectic of theory and practice through which SFL positions itself as
   an appliable linguistics with reference to the theory of Verbal Art"--
   Provided by publisher.
Identifiers: LCCN 2021011879 (print) | LCCN 2021011880 (ebook) | ISBN
   9781781795330 (hardback) | ISBN 9781781795347 (paperback) | ISBN
   9781800500686 (pdf) | ISBN 9781800501072 (epub)
Subjects: LCSH: Functionalism (Linguistics) | Systemic grammar. | Language
   and languages--Style.
Classification: LCC P147 .M55 2021 (print) | LCC P147 (ebook) | DDC
   410.1/833--dc23
LC record available at https://lccn.loc.gov/2021011879
LC ebook record available at https://lccn.loc.gov/2021011880

Typeset by S.J.I. Services, New Delhi, India

Contents

List of Tables

List of Figures

List of Appendices

List of Acronyms

CEFR	Common European Framework of Reference
CDA	Critical Discourse Analysis
CL	Corpus Linguistics
EAL	English as an Additional Language
EFL	English as a Foreign language
ESL	English as a Second language
FG	Functional Grammar
GP	Grammatical Parallelism
NNES	Non-Native English Speaker
PP	Pervasive Parallelism
RVAP	Reflection Verbal Art Pedagogy
SFG	Systemic Functional Grammar
SFL	Systemic Functional Linguistics
SF-MDA	Systemic Functional Multimodal Discourse Analysis
SFMS	Systemic Functional Multimodal Stylistics
SFTS	Systemic Functional Translation Studies
SSIs	Semi-Structured Interviews
SSS	Systemic Socio-Semantic Stylistics
SSS+	Systemic Socio-Semantic Stylistics plus PP
ST	Source Text
TS	Translation Studies
TT	Target Text

Acknowledgements

My thanks go to Equinox Publishing for permission to use much revised parts of my own 2007 paper: 'Construing the "primitive" primitively: grammatical parallelism as patterning and positioning strategy in D.H. Lawrence' (in Miller and Turci (eds) *Language and Verbal Art Revisited*) in Chapter 3. Gratitude also goes to Eleanor Whitman (née Whitworth) for permission to reproduce her recently deceased father's poem, 'Little', in Chapter 4, and to John Benjamins for permission to use, also in Chapter 4, certain reworked sections of Miller and Luporini, 'Guiding towards register awareness in an undergraduate EFL curriculum in Italy: the special case of verbal art' (2020). Moreover, I acknowledge that sundry fragments of my recent work on verbal art have inevitably made their (modified, and duly referenced) way into this volume, in particular parts of Miller (2016a, 2017b, 2019a). I also want to thank all colleagues who generously replied to my various mails to the *sysfling* list in search of verbal art practitioners of one kind or another. Among these is Christian Matthiessen, to whom I'm also grateful for granting me permission to cite from his outstanding unpublished draft paper (2013a). To be thanked as well is my colleague, Antonella Luporini, for her thoroughgoing scrutiny of the manuscript and of course those scrupulously assisting the production process: Valerie Hall and Sarah Lee at Equinox, and Freelance Editor, Cheryl Merritt. Last but not at all least, I am much indebted to the series editors for their perceptive and invaluable observations on the first draft, and especially to Gerard O'Grady, for his constant and patient support and helpful responses to my queries.

Preliminaries

Language, as Whorf said, is the best show man puts on. And perhaps the most amazing
performance in this repertory is verbal art... —Ruqaiya Hasan[1]

As its title clearly publicizes, this volume is dedicated to Systemic Functional Linguistics
(hereafter SFL) and verbal art, or to what I call throughout the book, systemic functional
stylistics. As I portray it, systemic functional stylistics encompasses two major strands:
one whose core is the theoretical and applied stylistic work of Halliday and another that
pivots around the theory and practice of Hasan on verbal art. Of course, the strands over-
lie each other to a great extent. Indeed, a section of Chapter 2 is entitled 'The Meeting
of Like Minds', with reference to the intense synergy between these two scholars' views
on language in literature. Moreover, the foundation of Hasan's framework of verbal art
is in every respect Hallidayan SFL. And yet, they need to be separated out for the reason,
also expounded in Chapter 2 and elsewhere, that Halliday's stylistics is almost invariably
taken into mainstream stylistics' toolkit, while Hasan's is unfailingly not. And since the
volume opts to place ample emphasis on Hasan's manifestly less valued work, as well
as on the relatively few scholars who openly express their regard for that work,[2] what
is presented is a two-fold systemic functional stylistics mirroring this disparity. Having
clarified the ethos of the volume, I turn to a thumbnail sketch of its structure.

None of this imbalance is considered in Chapter 1, however, which is meant to set
the scene. It provides a selective overview of the chiefly mainstream discipline of stylistics today and points up connections to and divergences from SFL's – and in particular Halliday and Hasan's – ways of thinking. Topics engaged with comprise stylistics'
ever-burgeoning toolkit, its diverse notions of style, the myriad sub-disciplines that
have emerged and the distinction between views on what it is that the discipline studies. The chapter also goes back in time with the aim of tracking down and describing
some of the most important historical roots of systemic functional stylistics, to the
Moscow and Prague Circles and the scholars that bequeathed a considerable, and crucial, part of the present-day DNA of both SFL and mainstream stylistics. Relevant later
twentieth-century developments in the field are also reviewed. Delineating the discipline's foundations is thus begun in Chapter 1, but also continues in Chapter 2, where
the seminal SFL positions on verbal art are addressed more directly, and the question
of how these may intertwine with the various strands of mainstream stylistics, or not,
continues to be attended to.

Chapter 2, as said, traces the intersection of Halliday and Hasan's evolving thoughts
on what Hasan called the language *in* literature. A key aim of the chapter is to show
how, thanks to both these scholars, verbal art has come to occupy a highly dignified
place within appliable SFL theory. Specifically dealt with are their reflections on the

'special' nature of literature, linked to the intricacy of the notion of context that this text type entails, and their views on the notion of deviation, markedly distinct from those of mainstream scholars, but also in part from those of their shared inspiration, Mukařovský. A lengthy section is dedicated to the presentation, scrutiny and evaluation of Hasan's 'double-articulation' model for the analysis of verbal art (1989 [1985]): the framework for what she says she practices: Systemic Socio-Semantic Stylistics (henceforth SSS).[3] This is composed of a semiotic system of language and a separate, higher order, semiotic system of verbal art, where foregrounded results of analysis at the lower level may be seen to articulate the text's deepest meanings, or theme. The final sections are then given over, firstly to a select review of the work of 'Hallidayan' (also including a small number of 'Hasanian') stylisticians, and then to subjective musings on what I call 'a politics of exclusion', with reference to the apparent ostracism of Hasan's stylistic work on the part of mainstream stylistics, but not only. In fact, even certain SFL stylisticians might be gently chided for giving Hasan's work short shrift. Select evidence of this neglect and thoughts on the reasons for it are also put forward.

Chapter 3 sets out my arguments, which some might already be familiar with, for 'slotting Jakobson into SSS' (e.g. Miller 2016a). This is a proposal that I never quite managed to convince Hasan of the need for, although I had made some headway before she left us. She had been at least somewhat intrigued by what had prompted my own thinking, hypotheses, experimentation and conclusions on the question, i.e. what Fowler (1986) dubbed 'The Mukařovský-Jakobson Theory', bringing together in an equation one theoretician, fundamental to Hasan's SSS, Mukařovský, and his contemporary, Jakobson, completely absent from it. Yet till the end she remained sceptical. Her various doubts/ issues are rebutted one by one and my case is rested with a bid for a fine-tuned SSS *plus* (SSS+), one that acknowledges the equivalence of Jakobson's theory of pervasive parallelism to Hasan's own means of foregrounding the artistic theme of what she calls the 'literature text'. The chapter continues with an illustration of SSS+ via the analysis of pervasive parallelism in one poem by D.H. Lawrence, 'Bei Hennef' (1913). Subsequently, seeking to illuminate and validate the findings emerging from the analysis of the poem, it probes its context of creation as Hasan defines it: a tri-dimensional entity consisting of the language, world view and artistic conventions of the socially-situated writer, all examined vis-à-vis those of the time/place of writing.

As is well-known, Hasan was a scholar for (nearly) all seasons. As is also widely known, she produced much valuable work on education and literacy in general, and on verbal art pedagogy and literacy in particular. Educational stylistics is the topic of Chapter 4, focusing on the teaching of the language in literature – with the tools of SFL/SSS+. An overarching concern of the chapter, however, is how to guide students to better reflect on meaning-making in English, thus also improving their overall language awareness, and, for learners, their language acquisition.

The chapter is divided into two distinct parts. Part I begins with briefly discussing teacher take-up of SFL concepts, metalanguage and pedagogy, whether applied to verbal art teaching or not. In speaking of the reasons for endorsing Hasan's SSS model in Chapter 2, the first to be mentioned is its being rooted in Hallidayan grammar and its study, grammatics. Here the educational significance of that grammatics emerges – as a meaning-focused metalanguage crucial to instructed language development. The chapter then moves into Hasan's ways of thinking about her own 'timeless journey' in the company of verbal art (2011a), her ideas concerning how one should engage with literature (1989 [1985], 2007), and her powerful theory of reflection literacy (2011b [1996c]). It then moves on to selectively surveying systemic functional educational stylistics studies. Again, the work referenced is largely based on Hallidayan stylistics but some is also specifically grounded in Hasan's SSS.

Part II presents a case study, a recount of the shared experience of guiding students toward 'special' register awareness in an undergraduate EFL curriculum in Bologna, Italy. The global pedagogical background is filled in before zooming in on the analytical activities of one 2017 and one 2018 verbal art workshop in the third year, in which students were guided to wield fine-tuned SSS+ in one poem in search of what gives us 'language that is artistic and art that is linguistic' (Hasan, personal communication, 15 April 2014). Recounted are our teaching practices and their rationale, but also our attempts at monitoring them, with the scrutinizing of empirical quantitative and qualitative evidence of students' perceptions of those practices, gathered through questionnaires. Also described is the action research that followed the emergence from these of perplexingly incongruous data, as well as the further steps consequently taken.

The chapter on the whole thus takes on the generalized criticism of what is often seen as a too heavy reliance on intuition in teaching stylistics (notably Hall 2014; Fogal 2015), by examining ways to defuse two significant sources of such peril: (1) an ingrained largely intuitive method of literature reading on the part of the students, and (2) a merely intuitive manner of assessing the effectiveness of one's own pedagogic practices.

Wanting to provide as wide-ranging a view of systemic functional stylistics studies as possible, Chapter 5 – entitled 'Systemic Functional Stylistics *and...*' – offers a synopsis of stylistics research wedded to multimodal/multisemiotic, corpus and translation approaches, also broaching certain of the many theoretical issues intrinsically implicated. Its nature is thus transdisciplinary. Nevertheless, fixed requirements for signalling studies were set up: 1) that they had to be at least clearly SFL-influenced, and 2) that they attended to literature as their object of study. The confines of 'literature', however, were necessarily widened to comprise research into any medium being exploited in the telling of fictive stories whose ways of meaning can be seen to 'relate to human social existence – its dilemmas and its delights', just as Hasan speaks of the mission of verbal art (Equinox online gloss to Hasan [to appear]). It emerges, however, that this Hasanian thematic aspect is explicitly addressed by these studies only at times. Indeed, the question of the 'art' of the text, of its registerial specialness, receives decidedly less manifest attention than it might do. In these cases, the 'and' constituent inclines to prominence and the artistic nature of the text tends to get lost sight of. Nonetheless, all of the stimulating research briefly described can be seen to systematically attend to contextualized meaning-making strategies in the texts examined. It also enriches our knowledge of work going on in (again mainly Hallidayan) systemic functional stylistics, as well as the theoretical issues involved, which is its essential aim.

Closing the volume is an 'Afterwords', which speaks to the future directions systemic functional stylistic studies might take. Here the field has been restricted to Hasan's SSS, to its future, since one can assuredly trust that Halliday's stylistic work will continue to receive due regard both within and outside the SFL community, while Hasan's stylistic legacy is indubitably less secure. Another choice made was to dialogue with Bowcher (2018), the closing chapter to a volume dedicated to Hasan and entitled 'Future Directions in the Study of Verbal Art'. Many are the suggestions for future research that she makes and it is these that are assessed and responded to in this final part of the volume.

In brief, from Bowcher's proposals there emerges a constant concern with the role of verbal art in society, with how this has evolved over time and with the importance of translation studies for investigating this aspect as well. Indeed, it is noteworthy, with reference to Chapter 5's transdisciplinary focus, that Bowcher puts forth various queries that she says would benefit from both corpus and translation approaches and calls for more interaction between Hasan's work and other approaches/ideas generally speaking. Relative to Chapter 4's spotlight on educational stylistics, she too stresses the need for verbal art pedagogy studies and intriguingly proposes 'a reflection verbal art pedagogy' (2018: 297), already referenced in that fourth chapter. Another leitmotif of Bowcher's is the art of verbal art, on which Hasan placed great emphasis, as we've seen, and the need for further study of just what makes verbal art special. Relatedly, she proposes further investigations into Hasanian foregrounding, aimed at better understanding the functions of language in various forms of verbal art. Moreover, she recalls that the findings of language research should also feed back into the general theory of the language and so would see more attention paid to the part that verbal art plays in the evolving nature of a language. My closing reflections interact with these and other topics she raises, in converging but also diverging ways.

What I will say, however, is that no clear blue-sky on the horizon is hailed at the end, essentially owing to the unhappy pall that the 'politics of exclusion' regarding this exceptional scholar cannot help but cast. But a suggestion for perhaps at least somewhat pushing back the clouds is, in closing, tendered.

Chapter 1

This Discipline Called Stylistics

1.1 Prelude

Stylistics is the study of the ways in which meaning is created through language in literature – but more and more in other text types as well – a point on which more will be said below. Here at the start I sketch a selective overview of the not unproblematically multifarious academic discipline of stylistics today: a very partial outline of mainstream stylistics as a nearly 100-year-old discipline that is still, I suggest, finding its way. That metaphor, however, presumes that there *is* one pathway that its practitioners collectively aim at discovering, and that is not at all the case. So, it would be best to qualify and call it a 100-year-old discipline only some experts of which would isolate a shared identity its practitioners can agree on. For the rest, the majority, multiple identities is not a particular problem.

At the same time, it is fitting to make a short journey back in time to attempt to trace the most important seeds, germinations and cross-fertilizations essential to contemporary stylistics and also to verbal art as it is theorized and analysed in SFL. Tracking down the roots of systemic functional stylistics is thus begun in this first chapter, though it continues even more substantially in the following one, where I zoom in more directly on seminal SFL positions on verbal art and also on how these may intertwine with the various strands of 'mainstream' stylistics, or not.

1.2 The Discipline, Sub-disciplines and Object of Study

So then, here at the start I would pose a double-edged question: what is stylistics? – or, for that matter, its root morpheme, style? Even just from the little said in the preceding section, it will come as no surprise that the answers to the query/ies will not be clear-cut. Until Hatzfeld brought out his stylistics bibliography in 1953, the word 'stylistics' had never even appeared in the title of any English book about style. Forty years later, Lecercle (1993: 14) asserted that nobody has ever really known what the term 'stylistics' means, and indeed sounded the death knell for what he saw as an ailing discipline. Yet, as Simpson (2014 [2004]: 2) rather triumphantly notes, Lecercle's black predictions on the imminent demise of the discipline were very much off the mark.

1.2.1 The Toolkit, or Stylistics' 'Boundless Appetite'

Indeed, the discipline has divided and multiplied, giving way to what numerous stylisticians praise as its ever-swelling 'toolkit'. A good example is the volume edited by

Nørgaard, Busse and Montoro (2010), which is decidedly peppered with positively evaluated mentions of the 'stylistic toolkit'. Wales dedicates her chapter in *The Cambridge Handbook of Stylistics* (2014: 32–45) to the concept – 'The stylistic tool-kit: methods and sub-disciplines' – emphasizing, from a mainstream position, that the toolkit metaphor is not a mere cliché, but actually symbolizes 'core attributes of the discipline (and its disciplines), notably its empirical and pedagogic nature and its "hands-on" approach, which also aims to be reader-friendly' (2014: 32).

Wales further decodes the meanings of the metaphor, in a manner perhaps more in keeping with an SFL approach. She notes, firstly, that it 'implies that stylistics is essentially functional, like a set of tools', then it 'also suggests that stylisticians as artisans can "unlock" the meaning or function of texts as verbal artefacts by using particular modes or models of analysis' (2014: 33). She also reads the metaphor as implying that stylistics exacts 'spade work', in terms of systematic analysis at all levels of text. As she rightly adds (Wales 2014: 33), such scrutiny presupposes 'a distinct correlation between the choices and textures and patterns of those elements or style markers in their particular generic contexts, and the "enactment of meaning"', after Carter (2010: 61).

In sum, she recalls her own observation (in Wales 2012: 10) that 'it is a characteristic of stylistics overall to be open to a variety of methodologies, "theory and practice interpenetrating, and at any one moment in time". This eclecticism or "boundless appetite" (Carter and Stockwell 2008: 209) is well known and documented' (2014: 35).

The rest of her chapter is dedicated to those 'methods and sub-disciplines' of its subtitle, among which 'Halliday's systemic grammar or systemic-functional model of language' (2014: 39) also figures. For now, however, let me just reaffirm that the toolkit is the metaphor now in vogue in mainstream stylistics, though of course it might also be viewed as the cliché Wales rebuts, or even as more of a grab bag of sundry contrasting and competing theories and practices that a 'boundless appetite' has spawned.

1.2.2 Concepts of Style

Presently I'll take a closer look at certain of these diverse stylistic schools that have emerged and those that took pre-eminence in stylistics though the years, leaving their marks. But first I'd offer a brief overview of an assortment of concepts of 'style'. In her entry on the notion, Wales (2001 [1990]: 370) rightly warns that its definition is hard to pinpoint.[1] One central reason for this is that, as Nørgaard, Busse and Montoro (2010: 155) observe, 'A definition of style is also further complicated by the different uses and the variety of senses that the notion of "style" has been credited with in the different branches of stylistics'. As illustration they note how, for socio-pragmatic stylistics, style may simply be a question of the level of a text's formality, and how the variationist-sociolinguist would tend to link it to socio-cultural variables such as gender, and anthropologists to the contextual domain. Illuminating Leech and Short's (2007 [1981]: 11) own definition: 'the way in which language is used in a given context, by a given person, for a given purpose', they comment: 'style is by no means restricted to the style of a particular author, but can be characteristic of a situation, a character, a particular text, a particular linguistic expression that is investigated over time and so on'.

This resonates with Wales (2001 [1990]: 371), where she affirms that style is 'distinctive: in essence, the set or sum of linguistic features that seem to be characteristic: whether of register, genre or period, etc.'. Thus the notion of style is rightly widened, well beyond the individual author's expression traits, to the vast array of motivating factors that will impact on how that author tends to make meanings. A correlated opinion that appears fairly undisputed in the literature and is also endorsed by Nørgaard, Busse and Montoro (2010: 156) is that style goes well beyond any notion of rhetorical 'ornamentation' of sense since it is, as Carter and Stockwell (2008: 295) put it, 'motivated by personal and socio-cultural factors at every level and is correspondingly evaluated along these ideological dimensions by readers and audiences'.

And systemic functional stylistics would not dispute the observation. But this interrelatedness of the factors motivating style had been argued long before these scholars made their more recent cases. Nowottny was a mid-twentieth-century literary critic who bravely followed in the tradition of British linguistics (including Halliday's mentor, Firth). She was firmly on the language side of English Studies in a time in which the language-literature divide was a formidable one, more intimidating to cross over than today. Understanding *how* literature works, how it means globally, was an objective that made her an early quasi-functionalist, aiming at understanding the significance of identifiable patterns of lexicogrammar but also questions of context. As she writes of the critic's task in her magnum opus, *The Language Poets Use*:

> the value of examining *objective* characteristics carefully ... is that this results, at least, in a recognition of the part played by the corporality of words, and by the structures which connect them, not only in determining lesser poetic effects but also in directing the larger mental and imaginative processes activated by the poem; it may well lead, further, to a recognition of the fact that *the various elements of poetic language interpenetrate one another with an intimacy which is of first importance in any consideration of how poetry 'works'.* (1962: 1–2, *my emphasis*)[2]

However, not all have attempted casting their style net so wide. The most enduring demarcated meaning of style – from the early twentieth-century work by the Russian Formalists, as we'll see, and down to contemporary stylistics theory – centres on the concept of deviation. Enkvist (1973: 15) maintains that, 'First, style can be seen as a DEPARTURE from a set of patterns which have been labelled as a NORM (*style comme écart*).' More recently, Jeffries and McIntyre (2010: 31) define deviation as 'the occurrence of unexpected irregularity in language and results in foregrounding on the basis that the irregularity is surprising to the reader', thus tying the phenomenon to reader response. Such definitions also easily link up to Shklovsky's notion of defamiliarization (1965 [1916]), which, together with foregrounding, I'll be coming back to below. The original concept of foregrounding is, indeed, the foundation of that of deviation.

Bloch (1953: 40) had argued the phenomenon of a text's formal distinctiveness or style in relatively ante litteram computational terms: 'The style of a discourse is the message carried by the frequency distributions and transitional probabilities of its linguistic features, especially as they differ from those of the same features in the language as a whole.' Interestingly, Halliday partially cites these same words of Bloch on the subject, concurring with reference to his own notion of prominence, as we'll see in Chapter 2.

This seems hardly surprising, given his theory of 'language as a stratified probabilistic system' (Halliday 1991a: 48). However, on the ultimate value of the view of style-as-deviance, both Halliday and Hasan beg to differ. I defer saying more about precisely *how* until Chapter 2, however, as the terms of their arguments are grounded in notions that still need to be adequately disambiguated. For now, I add only that the popularity of style-as-deviation is amply attested by Nørgaard, Busse and Montoro (2010: passim), where they report the essential concern with the notion in branches of stylistics such as historical stylistics, corpus stylistics and reader-response criticism. Even just from the little said above, that these sub-disciplines should be interested in deviation, would seem unremarkable. They further note its place in pragmatic stylistics and its also being an issue in cohesion/collocation studies and narratology.

Before passing to a closer look at these and other branches of stylistics, a least one other current meaning of 'style' needs to be mentioned, given my specific brief, and that is style-as-choice. Many scholars have acknowledged that style has to do with choice. Early on, Hough (1969: 8–9) contended that, 'whatever view we may take of its nature, it is clear that in talking about style we are talking about choice – choice between the varied lexical and syntactic resources of a particular language'. Turner (1973: 21) too argued that 'an element of choice seems to be basic to all conceptions of style' (echoed in de Beaugrande and Dressler 1981: 16). And Wales brings us into the domain of the SFL view of choice in portraying the process as one in which an 'author is seen to select features from the whole resources of the language at his or her disposal' (2001 [1990]: 54).

For SFL, speaker choice is indeed made from the entire system of our language, our total meaning potential: 'how can its [literature's, DRM] language be understood except as the selection by the individual writer from the total resources at his [sic] disposal?' (Halliday 2002 [1964]: 17). No other branch of stylistics puts this in quite the same way. As far back as her doctoral thesis (1964: 7), Hasan argued for circumscribing the scope of 'style' study to 'some specific parts of the stratum of linguistic execution alone. This part would consist of the selection and combination of the patterns of language from the levels of form and phonology, extending over the entire text.' Thus, she puts the accent on phonological and lexicogrammatical choice. A few years later (1971: 345, n. 19), she was already defining these stylistic patterns at a higher level, in terms of her evolving framework for the study of verbal art's metalanguage, to be fleshed out in the next chapter: 'The study of style is the study of the fit of the language of a literary text to its theme and theme-symbolizing events.' And just as early on, both Halliday and Hasan insisted on the importance of the power of the model to be chosen for description. As Halliday says, 'if a text is to be described at all, then it should be described properly; and this means by the theories and methods developed in linguistics, the subject whose task is precisely to show how language works' (2002 [1964]: 9).[3] And Hasan further specifies the model's requisite wide-ranging potential by insisting that the setting up of ad hoc categories for each individual text be eschewed in preference for a model capable of dealing with a large variety of texts 'using the same theories, methods and categories' (1964: 34–35).

Of course, their preferred model is what soon came to be called Hallidayan, as is that privileged by Birch and O'Toole (1988). They too speak of choice, determined, for them, in part by personal style preferences but also by socially appropriate norms that regulate the purposes the text is serving (1988: 1). This opinion, incidentally, also pre-dates the voices legitimating those myriad motivating factors impacting on an author's style cited above. The duality of this characterization is slippery, however, since, as Nørgaard, Busse and Montoro (2010: 156) correctly note, the task of inferring meaning needs 'to move between a continuum of seeing each choice as stylistic and meaningful and potentially innovative, on the one hand, and of embracing complex conventions and norms, on the other'.

SFL would concur with the complexity of the task, as well as the need to confront the complex set of conventions involving the socio-cultural contextual parameters motivating speaker choice. In any event, for SFL language use *always* needs to be contextualized, as Halliday's stylistics also demonstrates so well. And Hasan's own model of verbal art actually systematizes the means for investigating such motivations of choice, as we'll once again see.

1.2.3 Stylistic Sub-Disciplines

And now to move on to a better look at various competing stylistic sub-disciplines. Focusing on the latter decades of the twentieth century, Wales (2001 [1990]: 373) breaks these down roughly into: formalist Generative Grammar in the 1960s; the move to functionalist Discourse Analysis and Pragmatics in the 1970s and 1980s; and then the input of Critical Discourse Analysis (hereafter CDA) and Cognitive Linguistics in the 1990s. As she also points out (in 2001 [1990] and 2014), and as I'll discuss separately in Chapter 4, linguistic stylistics has also become a pedagogical stylistics.

Unhampered by the concise Dictionary format, in their *Key Terms*, Nørgaard, Busse and Montoro (2010: 7–48) deal with the numerous sub-disciplines of stylistics with greater breadth and in decidedly more depth:

- cognitive stylistics/poetics, locus of a staunch concern with reading and the reader;
- corpus stylistics, the application of the methods of modern corpus linguistics to (literary) texts;
- critical stylistics, largely inspired and informed by critical linguistics and CDA, which explores the social meanings manifested through language and, as Carter and Stockwell (2008: 293) observe, sees itself as exceptionally distinct and strongly associated with stylistic investigations of *non*-literary texts, more on which below;
- the emotion approach, about which we'll also say more shortly, and the empirical one, which adopts a rigorous observational and analytical perspective (which is hardly unique to this branch alone, of course);
- feminist stylistics, sharing many of the theories and practices of other branches but specifically focused on how gender impacts on text production and interpretation;
- film stylistics, which could with no trouble insert itself into a larger, and growing, repository of multimodal/semiotic stylistic studies – something I do in Chapter 5;
- formalist stylistics, ignited with the work of the Russian Formalists, to which we turn presently;
- functional stylistics, which will clearly receive most attention in this volume;

- historical stylistics, privileging longitudinal studies;
- narratology, a discipline in its own right, born of 1960s structuralist views, which still adds to the stylistician's toolkit, however;
- then the already-mentioned pedagogical stylistics, which can either deal with the potential of stylistics for teaching (the language of) literature or develop the supporting role of stylistics in the teaching of language through literature;
- pragmatic stylistics, which, much like functional stylistics, focuses on language in use and context, but also reader-response criticism, concerned, very much like cognitive stylistics, with the role of the reader in literary interpretation but also overlapping with the agendas of the emotion and empirical branches as well.

Clearly then, these sub-disciplines are not watertight compartments. Far from being mutually exclusive, among them correspondences abound and diverse degrees of overlap are typical, though rarely explicitly declared. Nørgaard, Busse and Montoro (2010) supply key sources and theorists for each of these branches, as well as identifying shared concerns among these.

One possible reason for this silence comes to mind: although the very notion of the toolkit has gone some way over the years toward assuaging the friction between factions that has always reigned within stylistics, conventionally fossilized boundaries between sub-disciplines have not come tumbling down and even the newer ones erected tend to jealously guard their dominions. In addition, there still remains the long ongoing conflict between the linguist as champion of a rigorous descriptiveness of literature, and the literary critic's censure of linguistic studies of literature as being simply mechanistic and ultimately reductive of its value (cf. the renowned acerbic, if also at times amusing, Fowler-Bateson debates; Fowler and Bateson 1967, 1968). And even linguists themselves have shunned stylistics as being located at the too-soft end of the spectrum of their own discipline (cf. Carter and Stockwell 2008: 293). Moreover, the very number of 'sides' – evidently far more than two – enlarges the jousting arena. In short, though the one, big happy family image is flaunted as the official line, whatever the sub-discipline, one's impression is that most of its adherents would fight their corner, so to speak, tending to stick firmly and guardedly, if more or less tactfully, to their separate positions. An associated impression is that they are less than satisfied with simply occupying a recognized place in the extensive stylistics landscape and its burgeoning toolkit; they would, as is only normal, prevail.

1.2.4 Which Object to Study

Another controversy regards the very object of stylistics study, glossed above but about which more needs to be said. This volume concentrates on what Halliday and Hasan, among others, insist is the proper concern of stylistics: the language of *literature*, only (e.g. Hasan 1971: 299–300); yet a long-standing and currently mounting inclination to the contrary must be recognized. The expansion of the field to non-literary texts is not wholly 'new' of course: in the 1960s and early '70s there was already a short-lived branch of stylistics that focused particularly on style in non-literary language, argued notably in the work of Crystal and Davy (1969), and Enkvist (1973). But, increasingly in this twenty-first century, the move in stylistics has been away from a focus on the literary and even at times from the linguistic, to the point that one finds contemporary definitions of the discipline such as the following: 'Stylistics is the study of the ways in which meaning is created through language in literature *as well as in other types of text*' (Nørgaard, Busse and Montoro 2010: 1, *my emphasis*). Moreover, and somewhat disturbingly to more 'mature' scholars such as myself, one also finds many young researchers in the field who appear cheerfully unaware of there being any opposing point of view, or at least of there being any need to acknowledge one.

Speaking as adherents to, and in fact promoters of, this beyond-literature stylistic faction, Jeffries and McIntyre remark that:

> One of the most significant developments in the field is probably the move from being concerned solely with literary texts to seeing all text as having the potential for stylistic (if not aesthetic) effect. Many stylisticians throughout the world are still motivated largely by wanting to explain how literary effects are achieved linguistically, but there is a large and growing number who do not have this motivation as their sole focus and whose interest has increasingly been on the process of reading, the interaction of text and reader to produce meaning, and the effects of this process, whatever they may be. (2010: iv)

And here we see that their position harmonizes with their attention to reader response, already seen vis-à-vis deviation. Jeffries (2010: 3) frankly admits she has 'never considered stylistics to be limited to literary style', while Simpson categorically affirms that 'to separate off literature from other uses of language ... is not a desired outcome in stylistic analysis' (2014 [2004]: 55). But the implications of assertions such as Jeffries and McIntyre's above need to be teased out and some attempt to rebut them made. Presupposed in their wording is that 'the process of reading, the interaction of text and reader to produce meaning, and the effects of this process, whatever they may be' are *not* among the interests of stylisticians who are concerned solely with literary texts. This volume sticks resolutely to stylistics as the linguistic study of literature, as said, but this does not mean that the reader is discounted or that socio-cultural context is undervalued or, indeed, that any of the valuable concerns of the various branches of stylistics to have emerged above are necessarily slighted. Actually, what I argue, and hope to ultimately illustrate, is that Hasan's Systemic Socio-Semantic Stylistics (SSS) is a rich framework, one with the potential to meet such (regrettably and perhaps unnecessarily) fragmented concerns and that it is a robust cornerstone upon which potent comprehensive research edifices have been, are being, and can again and again be constructed.

From my own SFL/SSS position, I would endorse the stance Carter and Stockwell adopt vis-à-vis the stylistic potpourri: 'we would like to argue that stylistics is in fact a single coherent discipline: in fact, that it is naturally the central discipline of literary study, against which all other current approaches are partial or interdisciplinary' (Carter and Stockwell 2008: 292). This last epithet may strike some as puzzling, since it is quasi axiomatic that, as Wales (2014: 35) puts it, 'Interdisciplinarity is at the heart of stylistics', its function being to bridge the fields of linguistics and literary criticism but also to account for the socio-cultural contexts of texts, as well as for how their readers interact with them.

And on the surface she seems to have a point. But my espousing their stance is not to put forth any preconceived prejudices against interdisciplinarity as such. On the contrary, in the proper context its practice can be highly productive, as Chapter 5 shows, and at times can even prove essential. The point of Carter and Stockwell that I underwrite here is a circumscribed one: simply the plausible oneness of stylistics as a discipline for the study of literature, and thus ideally also the lack of any requirement for arduous negotiation of (inter)disciplinary, or sub-disciplinary, hurdles in its theory and practice. And, as an advocate of SSS, I naturally see an all-inclusive oneness as an unrivalled plus point, as this volume will continue to argue, but as will only become clear with further argument.

But now to go back a bit in time.

1.3 Where Contemporary Stylistics Came From

A longitudinal perspective is of course essential to most reviews of a discipline, however limited in their scope. Likewise, a humble, and humbling, sense of what has preceded one's own work is fundamental to any serious scholarship, if one would avoid attempting to reinvent the wheel. As Hasan herself points out, her SSS is not 'new': 'it actually predates the 1960s' structural stylistics' (2007: 21). Indeed, the early work that she built into her framework for the study of verbal art (1989 [1985]), and that Halliday also harked back to, was that of the Russian Formalists and subsequently the Prague Circle scholars, especially Mukařovský's (1977, 1978) and his 1928 discussion of 'foregrounding' (in Garvin 1964). So here is where I start, limiting myself to simply signalling what is considered the earliest precursor of stylistics: the classical world's rhetoric and elocution skill: 'the selection of style for an appropriate effect' (Carter and Stockwell 2008: 292; cf. Burke 2014a: 1–2; his chapter on 'Rhetoric and Poetics' in the same volume (2014b: 11–30); and Nørgaard, Busse and Montoro 2010: 2).

1.3.1 The Moscow and Prague Circles

I begin tracing work in early twentieth-century stylistics where other scholars tend to (e.g. Busse and McIntyre 2010), namely, with the ground-breaking displacement of the tradition of essentially author-centred literary theory that was initially prompted with the work of the Moscow Linguistic Circle, and especially with that of the most famous of the so-called Russian Formalists, Roman Jakobson. Going back is especially mandatory, as the ideas percolating in those circles in those years have bequeathed a considerable, and crucial, part of the present-day DNA of both SFL and mainstream stylistics. While reams, of course, have been written on these movements and their influences (e.g. Erlich (1981 [1955]), this brief account is circumscribed to the sum and substance essential to my purposes.[4]

Jakobson co-founded the Moscow Linguistic Circle in 1915, and, the following year, along with Viktor Shklovsky and Boris Eichenbaum, set up another Russian Formalist circle, the Society for the Study of Poetic Language (OPOJAZ). From 1920, for political reasons, he chose to live in Prague. In 1926, he was also one of the founders of the prominent Prague Linguistic Circle, which became critically engaged with the works of Saussure, and which grew into the most advanced and influential linguistic school of thought in pre-World War II Europe. The Prague Circle was deeply influenced by Russian Formalism, though it went beyond aesthetic isolationism in working toward a more-inclusive framework for critical analysis (cf. Erlich 1981 [1955]: Chapter IX, on the intricacies of 'Formalism Redefined'). Its golden years went from 1929 up to the outbreak of World War II in 1939. Post-war, it had no other choice but to put its powers at the service of the official Marxist-Leninist creed, as post-revolution Russian Formalism had previously been made to do.

Jakobson's collaboration with the Prague structuralists, particularly with Mukařovský, led to the hypothesis of an intrinsic aesthetic motivation to literature, as well as to attempts at identifying the formal *and* functional linguistic mechanisms articulating this impetus. Coining what would be an enduring notion in especially mainstream stylistics, Jakobson (1985 [1921]) argues that what literary scholarship needs to address is what makes a verbal message a work of art: its 'literariness'. These scholars were making a radical move toward a scientifically grounded literary criticism and in doing this were theorizing what would become other seminal and long-lasting stylistic concepts responsible for distinguishing 'poetic' language from 'standard' language, such as foregrounding by means of parallelism and, pace both Halliday and Hasan's subsequent censure of the notion, by way of deviation. But these vital concepts and their theorists dynamically intertwined with Shklovsky's equally long-lived and influential concept of defamiliarization, mentioned above. As Mambrol puts it:

> It [ostranenie, i.e. estrangement or making strange, or defamiliarization, DRM] is that aspect which differentiates between ordinary usage and poetic usage of language, and imparts a uniqueness to a literary work. While Roman Jakobson described the object of study in literary science as the 'literariness' of a work, Jan Mukařovský emphasized that literariness consists in foregrounding of the linguistic medium. The primary aim of literature, in thus foregrounding its linguistic medium, as Viktor Shklovsky described, is to estrange or defamiliarize. By disrupting the modes of ordinary linguistic discourse, literature 'makes strange' the world of everyday perception, and renews the readers' lost capacity for fresh sensation.[5]

Mukařovský was not alone in linking literariness to a foregrounding of the linguistic medium. Griffin notes how 'Jakobson argued that the distinctive feature of literary language was its self-reflexivity, its awareness of itself as a medium' (1999: 420). He saw literature as 'a special use of language characterized by a maximal, radical engagement of patterns of linguistic structure' (van de Ven 2010: 75). The means of such engagement are what Jakobson would later (1960) call grammatical parallelism (henceforth GP), the structural patterning in texts that he theorized as being the empirical linguistic evidence of his 'poetic function': namely, 'The set (Einstellung) toward the message as such, focus on the message *for its own sake*' (1960: 356 ff., *my emphasis*), which he'd begun to explore as early as in that same 1921 essay cited above. Literariness then, for Jakobson, is 'an unchangeable essence that is intrinsic to every literary phenomenon' (van de Ven 2010: 75), but it can, and does, transcend literature for other dominant textual functions. In short, literature texts have a primary poetic function but are not confined to it alone. This is something else I'll come back to in Chapter 3 in arguing Jakobson's rightful place in SSS via his theory of the poetic function.

This same opposition between literary and practical uses of language is the subject of Mukařovský's *Standard Language and Poetic Language* (2014 [1932]), which again takes on the questions of aesthetic norms and functions, emphasizing, in particular, the role of automatization versus de-automatization/foregrounding in delimiting the different functions of these two forms of language:

> This is the core of the foregrounding of the utterance. Foregrounding is the opposite of automatization, that is, the deautomatization of an act; the more an act is automatized, the less it is consciously executed; the more it is foregrounded, the more completely conscious does it become. Objectively speaking: automatization schematizes an event; foregrounding means the violation of the scheme. (2014 [1932]: 44)

So, in literature, the act of communication becomes subordinate to the act of expression which is itself placed in the foreground.

I suspect that Mukařovský's use of 'conscious' and 'consciously' above cannot easily be likened to Jakobson's 'self-reflexivity' of literature, a non-sentient entity, but am unable to offer further evidence. However, be that as it may, the two scholars are clearly of the same mind. The 'violation' defining foregrounding is plainly associated with deviation from existing norms, which Mukařovský deemed fundamental to the creation of the defamiliarizing effect he considered central to literary language, much in the same way as Jakobson held divergence (Differenzqualität) essential to literariness (cf. Erlich 1981 [1955]: 252).

Mukařovský's work on the role of foregrounding continued (cf. 1977, 1978), as did Jakobson's on GP and pervasive parallelism (hereafter PP) (1966: 423) and their theoretical intersection continued, despite the undoubtedly greater 'success' of foregrounding – not only in SSS, but in stylistics *tout court*. In addition to Halliday and Hasan's taking up the concept (more on which in Chapter 2), mainstream stylisticians in the last decades of the twentieth century, such as, for example, Leech and Short (2007 [1981]), were convincingly demonstrating the essential role of foregrounding (or in the Mukařovskýan terms preferred by Halliday (2002 [1982]: 131), the de-automatization of grammar) in literature. Despite widespread, if not undisputed, criticisms for their alleged emphasis on form over function and neglect of context, the mileage of these Formalists is indisputably striking.[6]

1.3.2 Moving On

With the Second World War, Jakobson's collaboration with the Prague structuralists came to an end. He settled in the USA in 1941 – where, in 1943, he co-founded the Linguistic Circle of New York. This move proved fundamental for the successive, and successful, spread of his ideas, not only in America but also in Europe, where work on style in literature was of course still being done, for instance in Austria by the philologist, Spitzer, who was experimenting 'objective' over 'impressionistic' research methods into the literature of the Romance languages (cf. Wales 2001 [1990]: 296–297), and also by French scholars like Auerbach, Bally and Guiraud, whose work would then impact on the development of the theory and practice of *analyse de texte*. Jakobson's move to the USA also had repercussions for the development, in America and Britain respectively, of the New Criticism and Practical Criticism movements, both of which employed techniques of 'close reading' of literature, a practice that was widespread for decades (1930s–1960s).[7] The first of these was mainly concerned with probing the aesthetic qualities of a literary text, while the latter, developed by I.A. Richards long before the 1960s' and 1970s' reader-response theory or the 1990s' cognitive stylistics, focused on the psychological aspects of how readers understand texts – what the first school called the 'affective fallacy' (Wimsatt and Beardsley 1949). As is well-known and highly cited, Fish (1980) argued against the devaluation of the reader, famously coining the label 'affective stylistics' and stating: 'I have argued the case for a method of analysis which focuses on the reader rather than on the artefact' (Fish 1980: 42). Fish also emphasizes the importance of including an account of the psychological processes involved in reading. But, as Nørgaard, Busse and Montoro (2010: 15) note, he never developed his suggested shift in research focus into a genuine theory of emotional responses to literature. Interest in such emotional aspects remained dormant pretty much until cognitive stylistics/poetics more recently revitalized attention to the role of affect and the reader's response. And here I recall Jeffries and McIntyre, and their assertions cited above on the growing interest that stylistics has for the process of reading and its effects, often in conjunction with diminished concern with literary texts. We will come back to Fish again in Chapter 4: to his general attack on the Hallidayan model, and then, in Chapter 5: to his charge of 'circularity' of interpretation and analysis in Halliday (2002 [1971]) and O'Halloran's corpus-assisted study (2007), explicitly designed in response.

Salameh (2010) offers a very neat synopsis of the distinctions between New Criticism and Practical Criticism, and other movements as well. When they first made their appearance, both were considered decidedly avant-garde. However, they have long been generally assessed by stylisticians as outmoded analytical paradigms of a purely descriptive nature, which was ultimately inaccurate and/or inadequate. Notwithstanding, Carter and Stockwell suggest that there was more to their presumed analytical focus on nothing but the words themselves, which was 'only dressed up in an apparent descriptive objectivity' (2010: 292). For them, their context-based interpretative decisions simply remained implicit. Unsurprisingly, Halliday (2002 [1982]: 128) sees their chief weakness as their failure to associate the text to the linguistic system, namely, to meaning potential. In essentially literary circles in the 1970s, their 'new' and, from certain perspectives, refreshing, critical focus on the text itself began to be sharply censured by Marxist critics as fostering the decontextualized and even dehumanized 'reification' of the text – as texts being treated as (sacramental-like) objects, divorced from history and the socio-cultural and ideological context of their creation.[8]

Yet in these years a more rigorous literary description was emerging in linguistics. Following Fowler (1981), Carter and Stockwell tell us that:

> Bloomfieldian structural linguistics evolving between the 1920s and 1950s offered a precise terminology and framework for detailed analyses of metrical structure in poetry. Chomsky's transformational-generative grammar from 1957 onwards provided a means of exploring poetic syntactic structure with far more sensitivity to detail than had ever been possible

in literary criticism. And Halliday's functionalism (Halliday 1973) added a socio-cultural dimension that began to explain how stylistic choices are meaningfully encoded in literary texts. (2008: 292)

Each of the above linguistics is represented as an improvement on the foregoing by Fowler (1981: 14 ff.). Fowler also remarks on the significance of Saussurean structuralism for literary studies in that

it provides three linked perspectives on texts: the text may be seen as a sequence of sentences each to be analysed linguistically; or as a single unified construction with its own particular internal structure in addition to the sentence patterns it draws from the rules of the language; third, a literary text may be seen as a unit within a literary system, within the context of a set of relevant other works (e.g. English Shakespearean sonnets, or Miltonic verse narrative) related to the semiotic structure of the whole culture. (Fowler 1981: 14)

He adds that all three perspectives were systematically probed in Jakobson's work, as well as in the later writings on narrative structure of Roland Barthes and Tzvetan Todorov. And, as Halliday tells us (2002 [1985]: 262), the work of Saussure was also one of the cardinal building blocks of his systemic grammar.

Before bringing this first chapter to a close, I would briefly revisit a point concerning the increasingly popular *non*-literary stylistics that had earlier appeared in the work of Crystal and Davy (1969) and Enkvist (1973), as noted above. Busse and McIntyre (2010) observe that work in non-literary stylistics was then basically dropped and only picked up again quite a bit later. Curiously, they speculate that this deferment may have been owing to the lack of linguistic frameworks able to engage with the novel propositions on the registerial context-text connection emerging, they maintain, precisely from Crystal and Davy's (1969) and Enkvist's (1973) work. As we know, however, in the late 1960s and 1970s, Halliday was working with a still-evolving but in part substantially fashioned functional linguistic framework within which an increasingly central role was played by context, both of situation and culture, and their connection with the realization of text and significance for register studies. In brief, although neither Halliday nor Hasan ever practised non-literary stylistics, the responsibility for the stalling of its theoretical development cannot be laid in these terms at their door, as an albeit still being modelled linguistic framework grounded in the context-text connection *was* coming to light. Indeed, Fowler (ed. 1966) is known not only for his laudable struggles to promote literature, pace the 'lit crits', as a legitimate object of linguistic study; he was also an early publicist for SFL's distinctive usefulness for stylistics and must be given credit, together with Leech and Short (2007 [1981]) and others, if it has enjoyed wide and frequent application in mainstream stylistics. We will have more to say about Fowler in subsequent chapters.

1.4 Coda

With the aim of laying the groundwork for the following chapters, this chapter has firstly offered an overview of the academic discipline and sub-disciplines of stylistics today: a brief but mandatory outline of mainstream stylistics as a nearly hundred-year-old discipline that only some of its practitioners would see as having a mutually shared identity – beyond a belief in its ever-increasing 'toolkit', which has been problematized. It has also made a short journey back in time to begin to trace the seeds, germinations and cross-fertilizations essential to the development of systemic functional stylistics. It will be the task of the next chapter, in particular, to say much more about Halliday's – but also and even primarily about Hasan's – account of rigorous literary text and context description. More will also be said about the qualities that distinguish systemic functional from mainstream stylistics, which at least Halliday's work has had no small influence on.

Chapter 2

Halliday and Hasan: The Development of their Language-in-Literature Theories and Practices

2.1 Prelude

Halliday's social semiotic model of language (1978, 1985, and subsequent editions) is the lens through which he and Hasan examine all text, verbal art included. In this chapter, I aim to show how, thanks to these two scholars, verbal art has come to occupy a highly dignified place within appliable SFL theory – one, however, which to my mind still leaves room for refinement and enhancement, a point I'll be speaking more to below.[1] The chapter sketches a by no means comprehensive map of the developing ideas on verbal art of both these scholars, focusing particularly on Hasan's SSS. We'll also be seeing further if – and if so, how – they 'fit' into certain of the other linguistic stylistic approaches to literature elaborated in the twentieth and twenty-first centuries. Other SFL practitioners are selectively brought into the discussion as well, also with reference to the issue of what I call, regarding Hasan's SSS, a 'politics of exclusion' (e.g. Miller 2010: 48).

2.2 The Meeting of Like Minds

In this section, it is obviously not my intent to establish who 'took' what from whom, but rather to show how the ideas of these two scholars on literature and its analysis evolved in largely, if not fully, parallel fashion, as the ideas of like minds in contact will. The influence of the Russian Formalists and Prague Linguists on Halliday and Hasan's stylistics is now taken as given. The key concept in both their views of the functions of the language in literature is Mukařovský's foregrounding, though Halliday prefers working with his analogous notion of de-automatization, more on which below. But, of course, the influences on their evolving thought were also other, more recent and closer to home.

As Lukin (2015: 350 ff.) rightly points out, there are various theorists who were essential to the development of Hallidayan linguistics in general (e.g. Saussure, Malinowski, Firth, Whorf and Hjelmslev) and have thus also had a hand in fashioning Halliday's stylistics 'by virtue of the fact that he [Halliday, DRM] draws on his general linguistic theory as the point of departure for the study and analysis of the literary text' (Lukin 2015: 350). And no less is true of Hasan's own stylistics, as Lukin also observes (2018). Significantly, both scholars cite Firth's seminal 1951 paper, 'Modes of Meaning' continuously in their stylistics work. Hasan does so as early as her PhD work, in arguing the need for an analysis of literature based on 'levels', 'strata', without which she sees a synthetic statement of the meaning of the literary text as hopelessly unfounded (1964: 7, et passim). This argument simply reinforces her early pinpointing of the scope of style as being 'the patterns of language from the levels of form and phonology', as noted in Chapter 1.

Both Halliday and Hasan see the analysis of literature as demanding the very same descriptive method as that of any other text; however, for neither of them is this the whole story. They both see the 'art' of verbal art as a defining principle of this special kind of text and investigate what this means for its description and analysis. In 1964 (i.e. the same year in which Hasan completed her PhD thesis) Halliday wrote: 'Literature is language *for its own sake*: the only use of language, perhaps, where *the aim is to use language*' (in Halliday, McIntosh, and Strevens, 1964: 245, *my emphasis*). This observation can be likened to Jakobson's definition of his 'poetic function', with its corresponding focus on the text itself, what he identifies as the factor of the 'message' itself, positing a 'focus on the message *for its own sake*' (1960: 356 ff.). In his study of Priestley's *An Inspector Calls* (2002 [1982]), Halliday drolly makes the point for the somehow 'different' nature of literature as text (already amply embarked upon in his paper on the language of Golding's *The Inheritors* (2002 [1971]), however) with the quip: 'the paradox of "poetic" language [is] that there is *no such thing* ... but we can all recognize it when we see it' (2002 [1982]: 134, *my emphasis*). In Halliday and Hasan (1989 [1985]: 42), in talking about texts and their registers, he elaborates more earnestly:

> Some texts are truly unique and indeed are highly valued for their uniqueness; it is this property we have in mind when we say that something belongs to the rather vaguely defined category of 'literature'. A literary text is a text that is valued in its own right, which must mean that it differs from all other texts.

From the start, Hasan asserts her conviction that 'in literature, art is language, language is art' (2002 [1971]: 300). Her insistence on this reciprocal relation leads her to affirm, not unlike Halliday, but in even more compelling terms, that:

> It is not that there is art [somewhere 'out there', so to speak, DRM], and the job of language is simply to express it; rather it is that, if there is art, it is because of how language functions in the text ... in verbal art the role of language is central. Here language is not as clothing to the body; it *is* the body. (1989 [1985]: 91, *original emphasis*)

But what does all this mean for the description and analysis of this special language of verbal art? In his study of Golding's *The Inheritors*, Halliday speaks of 'linguistic highlighting' in terms of motivated 'prominence' of grammatical features, 'whereby some feature of the language of a text stands out in some way' (2002 [1971]: 99). However, his primary concern there is not whether the highlighting should be called deviation from a norm or possibly even the establishing of some new norm, but rather with what he calls the 'criteria of relevance ... the problem of distinguishing between mere linguistic regularity, which in itself is of no interest to literary studies, and regularity which is significant for the poem or prose work in which we find it' (2002 [1971]: 88). I'll return to this point regarding deviation in section 3 below.

Halliday contends that 'a feature that is brought into prominence will be "foregrounded" only if it relates to the meaning of the text as a whole' (2002 [1971]: 98). In delineating better this 'as a whole', and explicitly following Hasan's own thinking (e.g.

1971), he proposes twin levels of meaning, both grammatically realized, but one 'underlying', and 'deeper' than, the first, 'immediate' level, also glossed as the 'subject matter'. Both these levels are the product of 'syntactic imagery'. They

> find expression in form, and through the same syntactic features. The immediate thesis and the underlying theme come together in the syntax; the choice of subject-matter is motivated by the deeper meaning, and the transitivity patterns realize both. This is the explanation of their powerful impact. (2002 [1971]: 106–107)

Taking the expression from Ohmann (1967: 237), who was, however, concerned with deviance rather than relevance, Halliday asserts that the deeper semantic meanings, crucially, 'serve *a vision of things* ... The vision provides the motivation for their prominence' (2002 [1971]: 104–105 ff., *my emphasis*). It will be primarily Hasan's task in the course of the 1970s and 1980s to more precisely theorize this motivating 'vision' and develop the double-articulation framework of its textual construal. But Halliday also continued to reflect on these dual levels.

As noted in Chapter 1, in Halliday (2002 [1982]), the term foregrounding is replaced by 'de-automatization', the Mukařovskýan term he preferred, in contrast to Hasan. In his 1982 analysis of Priestley's *An Inspector Calls*, he explains why and uses the notion to argue the dissimilar, if complementary, roles of these two distinct, if intrinsically interrelated, semantic levels.

> The term 'de-automatization', though cumbersome, is more apt than 'foregrounding', since what is in question is not simply prominence but rather the partial *freeing of the lower-level systems from the control of the semantics so that they become domains of choice in their own right*. In terms of systemic theory the de-automatization of the grammar means that grammatical choices are not simply determined from above: there is selection as well as pre-selection. Hence the wording becomes a *quasi-independent semiotic mode through which the meanings of the work can be projected*. (2002 [1982]: 131, *my emphasis*)

The meaning-making process in verbal art is unmistakably, and significantly, being characterized here as different, special. Absent from the modes of de-automatized literature meaning-making being hypothesized is any explicit mention of Mukařovský's key words: consciousness versus unconsciousness and deviation (2014 [1932]): 44; see Chapter 1). But we do find the notion of selection/pre-selection (i.e. the notion of 'grammatical choice') – never a fully 'conscious' activity in SFL, however, 'since we are concerned not with deliberate acts of choice but with symbolic behaviour' (Halliday 2002 [1970]: 174). These choices in literature are said to free themselves in part from semantic constraints, becoming quasi-autonomous (i.e. becoming instruments of meaning-making across the wordings of the text but also at another, deeper, level).

Significantly, what is being theorized here evokes the scaffolding of the doubly-articulated framework for the analysis of verbal art that Hasan began to model in 1971 and that is described more properly below. Moreover, Halliday's wording, 'that grammatical choices are not simply determined from above', also presages her own theorization of the 'special' language-context connection in verbal art, about which Halliday also reflects (cf. notably in 2002 [1977]: 58 ff., also reproduced in 1978: 145 ff.).

For the record, Martin (2012 [1985]: 61–63) disputes various points made by Halliday above and the SFL take on foregrounding generally speaking. Chiefly, he would modify certain of Halliday's terms and their function. Martin speaks of the literary text's 'connotative semiotics', previously equated with 'social context … a set of semiotic systems … which use another semiotic system (i.e. language) as their expression plane … termed register, genre and ideology' (2012 [1985]: 47). He argues that it is these connotative semiotics – rather than the semantics, as Halliday maintains – which are what de-automatization partially frees 'language' (rather than the grammar) from, in this way allowing foregrounded patterns of *semantic* choices.

Queried, Martin cordially replied (personal communication, 7–8 July 2020) that he very much still stands by the above assessment. The upshot of his comments on Halliday is hard, and fueled by his long-standing critique of what he sees as Halliday's blurring of the lexicogrammar/semantics border. Indeed, for Martin, Halliday's suggestion concerning 'the partial freeing of the lower-level systems from the control of the semantics so that they become domains of choice in their own right', and the rest of the paragraph, 'is confusing, reductive and inoperable … a grammarian's reductive view of deautomatization'.

I would beg to differ. As I would with another inexact critique of Martin's: his insistence that Hasan 'replaces' field, tenor and mode as a model of context with the 'superstructure' of symbolic articulation of theme (2012 [1985]: 61). However, as these notions will only be properly delineated below, I will come back to this once they have been.

Martin (2012 [1985]: 61–63) also offers various other, less confrontational ideas.[2]

But now, without abandoning the synergies of these like-minded scholars, Halliday and Hasan, I would briefly home in on their ideas concerning that special language-context connection in verbal art.

2.2.1 The Context(s) of Verbal Art

The extent to which Halliday theorized context of situation as both – and at the same time – a concrete material and a social phenomenon is well-known, as is SFL's dynamic, bi-directional connection between the contextual variables of field, tenor and mode and the semantic metafunctions and lexicogrammar of a text. An essential challenge for the analyst is to be able to identify the semantic options that are typically taken up in whatever the register in question, but also under which contextual pressures and why (cf. Lukin et al. 2011: 201). When the register is verbal art, however, that challenge multiplies.

To begin with, 'Whatever the role attempted or achieved by literature in society, as language it is self-sufficient and self-contextualizing' (Halliday, McIntosh and Strevens 1964: 246). Later he remarks that the context of situation's connection to fiction, to literature, is 'about as complex as it is possible for it to be' (2002 [1977]: 58). In describing the contextual variables of a Thurber story, he divides both field and tenor into two separate 'orders'. For field, these are a first extra-textual order, 'the social act of narration' (what Taylor Torsello [1992: 48–50] calls the *'reale'* [real] field and Matthiessen [2013a: 42 ff.] calls the 'Outer' one), and then a second, fictional order, 'the social acts that form the content of the narration' (for Taylor Torsello, that which is *'creato'* [created/fictional], and for Matthiessen, what is 'Inner').[3] Within the tenor of the Thurber text, Halliday operates a parallel division as well: the first being 'between the narrator and his readership, which is embodied in the narrative', and the second being located 'among the participants in the narrative, which is embodied in the dialogue' (2002 [1977]: 58). Mode – the enabling contextual parameter – remains one.[4]

Halliday also reflects on the vaster and multidimensional socio-cultural reaches of context in literature, noting that, because

> 'the context of situation' is seen as the essential link between the social system (the 'context of culture', to use another of Malinowski's terms) and the text, then it is more than an abstract representation of the relevant material environment; it is a constellation of social meanings, and in the case of a literary text these are likely to involve many orders of cultural values, both the value systems themselves and the many specific sub-systems that exist as metaphors for them. (Halliday, 2002 [1977]: 60, also cited in Lukin 2015: 357)[5]

In 2007, Hasan reiterates the differentness, the complexity, of the context-language connection in literature, and in terms much like Halliday's:

> In a non-literature variety, it is relatively easy to demonstrate the realizational connections from features of the social context in which an instance is embedded, right through to wordings: certain patterns of language – their meaning and grammar – can be shown to be activated by certain features of the variety's relevant social context (Halliday and Hasan, 1989 [1985]). In literature, turning to the context-language connection opens up yet another complex set of issues (Hasan, 1996a: 49–54). Thus attempts to model literature reveal fault lines of complexities in the exploration of both its semiotic and its social foundations. (2007: 23)

Hasan too theorizes distinct levels within the contextual parameters of verbal art (1996a: 49–56), elaborating a comprehensive discussion that expands on Halliday's first and second levels of field and tenor as hypothesized above (cf. Miller 1998: 282 ff.). However, she also – explicitly and significantly – links these up to her theorized 'context of creation' of verbal art, as well as to her descriptive/analytical framework of 'double-articulation' and in particular to the 'symbolic articulation' (Hasan 1971) of the work's theme. Moreover, she also links the contexts of verbal art to the notion of register. All of this is discussed in greater detail below.

As most will be aware, Hasan also appreciably contributed to theorizing the place of (*relevant*) context within SFL's progressive modelling of language in use, namely, register theory and practice (e.g. 2009). This long-standing research proved fundamental to her delineation of verbal art as being indisputably a kind of language use in a particular social context – so, by definition, a register – but *not* simply a register in the same way as any other. Thus, systemic functional stylistics can be said to occupy a unique place in the wider SFL architecture.

The essential premise of the SSS framework is that literature is '*created by languaging in a particular way*' (Hasan 2007: 16, *original emphasis*). In short, the ways of meaning of literature make it a 'special' register – a minority position among stylisticians today of course, as we'll see better below (cf. Miller 2017b, 2019a). At this point, we should be primed to accept as at least possibly true that such specialness is primarily due to the fact that the context-language connection in verbal art is fraught with complexities that other registers are simply not heir to (observed in, e.g. Hasan 1975: 54, 1996a: 49–54, 2007: 22–25). What she proposes is a 'multiple contextual framework', which is what cumulatively articulates the theme of verbal art (2011a: xxvi).

Called into play in this special register are: the 'real' context of the story-telling itself and the fictional context created by the text – as we've seen in Halliday above as well – and also the already-mentioned context of creation (1989 [1985]: 101–103), as Hasan dubs it, encompassing the language, world view and artistic conventions of the socially-situated writer, all seen vis-à-vis those of the time/place of writing, and, in addition, a context of reception, which impacts upon the meanings of the text for the equally socially-situated reader.

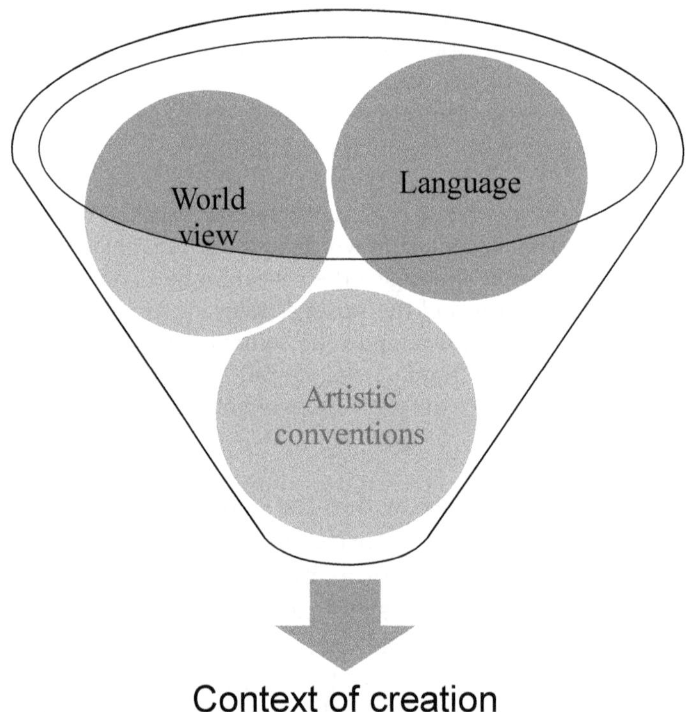

Figure 2.1 The context of creation of verbal art (Miller and Luporini 2018c)

Moreover, '[g]enerally speaking, the greater the distance between the context of creation and reception, the more inaccessible the meanings of the text become' (1989 [1985]: 102). And bridging that distance is often a challenging task:

When there is a disjunction between the contexts of creation and interpretation as with diachronic cultural distance, the question of readership for the literature text assumes even greater importance ... If it is true that texts place restraints upon what can be done with them interpretively, and if it is true that the author speaks from a particular social position at a particular cultural stage [as she argues, DRM], then listening to this voice across the cultural distances requires special expertise. (Hasan 1996a: 52–53)

Such expertise, however, is not innate; it needs attentive developing and, of course, implementing – a topic we'll come back to in Chapter 4. Of course, cultural distance does not always entail temporal distance. Very often, even just synchronically 'the habitual patterns of the conventional linguistic system are reworked to serve purposes at the limits (and beyond) of current collective understandings' (Halliday and Butt 2019: 622).[6]

All of these various contexts intersect and impact on the deepest meanings of the literature text and thus they all require the analyst's close attention (Hasan 1989 [1985]: 101–103, cf. Hasan 1996a: 50–54, 2007: 35 ff.), if, that is, he/she would objectively show 'how the meanings he/she claims to be "there" are actually made' (Hasan 1996a: 55). And objectivity is a crucial aspect of Hasan's stylistics: making 'a distinction between reading for private purposes and reading as a stage in the study of literature' (Hasan 1989 [1985]: 103). As she insists: 'the private must be made public; the internalised must be overtly externalisable – it should be possible to talk coherently about the bases of one's preference and evaluation' (Hasan 1989 [1985]: 27). We will also be reflecting on these ideas again in talking about SSS as an educational stylistics in Chapter 4.

2.2.2 Halliday and Hasan on Deviation

Before passing to an account of Hasan's SSS model, and in winding down my too-condensed considerations of Halliday and Hasan's ideas on verbal art, I will now say a bit more on the censorious stance Halliday and Hasan take toward 'deviation' from existing norms as a central stylistic concept, as promised in Chapter 1. They do not see it as an/the essential indicator of poetic language as do Mukařovský and, in a similar way, Jakobson, and, to some extent at least, a great many stylisticians up to the present day as well. It has, as already seen, enjoyed enduring acclaim.

In search of at least partial answers relevant to his main query concerning the criteria of relevance, Halliday dedicates a full section of his 1971 study of *The Inheritors* to 'Questions of prominence', intervening on some points raised at the 1958 'Style in Language' conference. The queries he poses are three: 1) whether prominence should be considered a departure from or the attainment of a norm; 2) to what degree prominence is a statistically measurable quantitative effect; and, 3) if it is possible to distinguish between prominence due to subject-matter and prominence having other causes (2002 [1971]: 98). I will say only a few words about his rich reflections on the first two of these queries.

Halliday cites the objection of Wellek (1960: 417–418) to a focus on deviation as giving us 'a science of discards' and his corresponding defence of the *undeviating*: 'But often the most commonplace, the most normal, linguistic elements are the constituents of literary structure.' He then elaborates on the two kinds of responses to Wellek's assessments there have been. The first identifies two different types of prominence, one negative, a departure from a norm, and one positive, the establishing of a norm. As illustration, also of the difficulty of distinguishing unmistakably between these, Halliday cites Leech (1965: 69) and Hymes (1967: 33–34) among other scholars. He concludes his reflections on this categorical note:

the norm that is established by a set of deviant forms excludes all texts but the one in which they occur. But for this very reason deviation is of very limited interest in stylistics. It is rarely found; and when it is found, it is often not relevant. (2002 [1971]: 100)

In short, a single text's establishing of new norms has little if anything significant to offer in terms of a characterization of style.

The second kind of answer to Wellek observes that departure may simply be from an anticipated frequency pattern (i.e. of a statistical nature). Halliday then cites Bloch, as anticipated in Chapter 1, remarking on the 'very reasonable proposition that prominence may be of a probabilistic kind, defined by Bloch as "frequency distributions and transitional probabilities [which] differ from those ... in the language as a whole"' (2002 [1971]: 100).

This reasoning leads Halliday – far in advance of the widespread corpus linguistics fervour, nota bene – into a consideration of the potential of quantitative/statistical inquiry and of the positive virtues of counting (i.e. its usefulness toward circumscribing the scope of analysis though not in and of itself methodologically sufficient). Further discussion on the role of the corpus in verbal art analysis is deferred to Chapter 5.

Hasan also expressly reflects on deviation with reference to how literature is different. In pondering what this difference consists in, however, she excludes 'deviance'. In her PhD thesis, Hasan began to scrutinize the notion vis-à-vis that of style (1964: 9–13), distinguishing between 'general' norms and register-specific ones, in literature and non-literary texts. As she would later succinctly put it (1989 [1985]: 92): 'non-conformity to a "norm" is not a characteristic of literature alone; lexical and grammatical metaphor is to be found in any register, including spontaneous face-to-face communication'. Besides, she declares, 'Today's deviation is tomorrow's norm.' She also overtly links this remark to her inventive call for a *shift of focus*, one that will abandon what she sees as the misguided search for isolated patterns in the language *of* literature and focus instead on what gives the text artistic value: the patterning of the patterns in the language *in* literature, by which she means the artistic role its foregrounding plays *in* the text, its functions (i.e. a shift in focus to just what it is that makes the text literature, or verbal art; 1989 [1985]: 92). And she also suggests the way to distinguish between what is verbal art and what, most likely, is not:

If the patterning [foregrounding, DRM] of patterns is consistently utilised for a second-order semiosis ... then the text in question is a literature text. If, however, such a role is not played by the patternings, then we have a literary text. The recognition of this distinction is important, not least because the techniques for the study and evaluation of the two are not identical. (1989 [1985]: 101)

What Hasan calls 'second order' here fully corresponds to Halliday's 'underlying' or 'deeper' non-immediate level of meaning spoken of in the quotation cited above, and will presently be disambiguated in discussing her framework. But in pondering the quotation just above from Hasan on the distinction between verbal art and what she came to call 'verbal art manquée', again Jakobson's thought comes to mind: this time his notion of literariness (see Chapter 1) and especially how the poetic function is to be found even outside poetry proper (1960: 357). In brief, for Jakobson as well, not all texts demonstrating evidence of a poetic function are to be considered literature. In arguing the case for Jakobson's place in Hasan's SSS in the next chapter, these ideas will be further fleshed out.

I now focus on Hasan and her framework for the study of verbal art, though fitting mention of additional parallels in Halliday's work will, of course, continue to be made.

2.3 The SSS Framework for the Study of Verbal Art: Double-Articulation

What follows is a rundown of Hasan's descriptive-analytical framework for the study of verbal art: what she ends up calling Systemic Socio-Semantic Stylistics (SSS, cf. n. 3 to Preliminaries). At the origin of the framework are her reflections on verbal art's special, complex, context-language connection, which seems to her to call for an equally special methodological take. Fittingly, it was precisely to manage those 'fault lines of complexities' cited above that Hasan tells us she devised her model, one that focuses on what gives us 'language that is artistic and art that is linguistic' (Hasan, personal communication, 15 April 2014), an unswerving concern of hers, as we've already seen, and for over more than forty years. As she explains the architecture of her model in her last published paper on verbal art:

> To manage this complexity, I have suggested (Hasan, 1971; 1985) a tri-stratal model of verbal art analogous somewhat to the SFL stratal model of the inner structure of language, which too is a complex phenomenon ... The basis for suggesting a stratal organization of verbal art rests on the observation that, as a variety of social semiotic practice, both the production and reception of verbal art almost always represent a specific kind of meaning exchange ... The construal of meaning calls for the recognition of distinct orders of abstraction. The strata postulated in the modelling of verbal art allow us to show how the artist's message is 'orchestrated'. By the same token, it becomes easier to assign functional roles to both language *and* to society, both of which are crucially implicated in the production and reception of verbal art. (2007: 23)

Thus she highlights how her framework is concerned with identifying the functions of *both* language *and* society: inextricably linked to the context of the literature text's creation/production and that of its reception, described above. To account for what she perceives as two distinct levels of abstraction, the framework is two-tiered, composed of separate levels that, however, work together. First there is the stratal model of language that is identical to that for any text and where, again as for any text, analysis begins (Hasan 1989 [1985]: 92), coupled with a refining stratal model of verbal art, where the patternings emerging at the first level are to be evaluated, at a higher order, in terms of their deeper significance and artistic value.

We've already seen how isolated patterning in verbal art is not what Hasan is interested in; patterning must be significant, working at the higher, second level. The notion of significant patterning links up to Mukařovský's view of foregrounding as 'consistent' and 'motivated' contrast with an established grammatical tendency in the text (Mukařovský 2014 [1932]), more on which below. However, as Lukin (2018: 11) properly notes, although Mukařovský's concept of foregrounding is particularly influential in

Hasan's work, 'in its combination with Halliday's SFL, Hasan would produce an account with a "tighter syntax" than that of Mukařovský (Hasan, 1985)'.

Such consistent and motivated foregrounding is explored at Hasan's second order of meaning, where first order meanings are seen to be *repatterned* in the function of the *symbolic articulation* of the literature text's *theme* – all of which is carefully scrutinized below. But first, a visual representation of the framework is in order. What we have then is what she dubs a model of *double-articulation* (Hasan 2007: 33, 35), which looks like this:

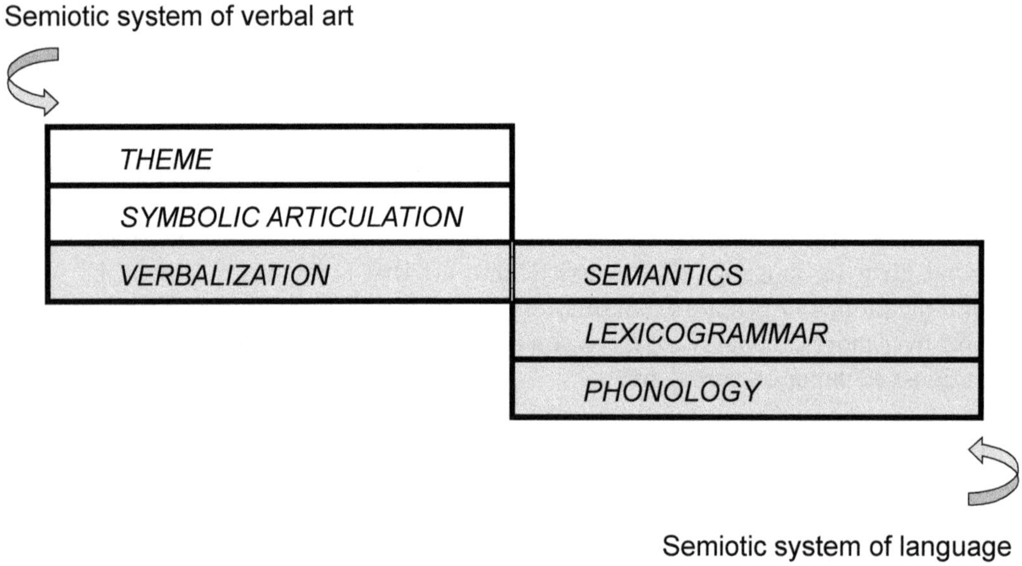

Semiotic system of verbal art

Figure 2.2 The overlapping semiotic systems in verbal art (based on Hasan 1989 [1985]: 99)

As can be seen, the semiotic system of language is the SFL multiple coding system made up of levels, or strata, each of which is realized (i.e. becomes *accessible* to us) through the one below it. In short, semantics, or meanings, are realized in lexicogrammar, or wordings, which become accessible to us in phonology, or soundings, or, in the case of a written text, in graphology, in written symbols (see also Figure 3.1 in Chapter 3). Above the system – at its source as it were, though not shown in the Figure – is the situation of context, which tends to activate the meanings that will most likely be chosen from the total meaning potential at the text maker's disposal, according to the features of the variables of this contextual configuration (i.e. its field, tenor and mode). As discussed above, for Halliday, Hasan, Taylor Torsello and Matthiessen, this context in verbal art is two-fold: its field, including the extra-textual 'social act of narration', as Halliday identifies it, as well as a fictional order, the 'social acts that form the content of the narration', while its tenor at one level addresses the relationship 'between the narrator and his readership, which is embodied in the narrative', and at the other involves the fictional 'participants in the narrative' (2002 [1977]: 58). Moreover, in relation to this intricate context of situation there is the global context of culture in which the social *languaging* activity takes place (cf. Halliday and Hasan 1989 [1985]: 46–47). At this level of the framework, there is no conflict with 'mainstream' stylistics, with the proviso that the toolkit is that of SFL.

As said, at the level of *language*, literature is to be analysed with the very same descriptive method, the identical tools and in exactly the same manner as any other text type. Elaborating on this point, Hasan tells us:

> the *starting point* for the description of literature is identical to that elsewhere ... these descriptive categories are applicable to all uses of language, irrespective of where they occur; the semantic values assigned to them in the clauses in which they occurred is also a constant. There can be no dispute that these patterns of language are not the prerogative of literature; wherever they occur, their *initial* analysis is the same. (1989 [1985]: 92, *my emphasis*)

But as also said, that is not the whole story. The words I've italicized in the segment quite clearly infer that there is *more* to the analysis of literature than there is to that of other registers. Indeed, as also said above, the results of analysis at this lower level then need to be re-explored. Note that the first level in the Figure is seamlessly contained within the lowest stratum of the semiotic system of verbal art: within 'verbalization', signalling its role as the basis of enquiry at the second level. Hence the broken line in the Figure. With verbalization alone, however, all one can do is paraphrase, summarize, say what the text is 'about', akin to what Halliday (2002 [1971]) glossed as the first, 'immediate' level of meaning, its 'subject matter'. This is achieved through an inventory of isolated language patterns, which, however, as already said, are insufficient for fully characterizing literature (Hasan 1989 [1985]: 93–94). What is needed to do this, she argues, is an emphasis on the *patterning of patterns* (1989 [1985]: 91, passim). Such patterning, or foregrounding, takes place in the middle stratum of the higher order, that of symbolic articulation, which is itself construed by verbalization. This is where it all happens, so to speak.

At the higher order of the semiotic system of verbal art, there is the very same relationship of realization/accessibility between strata that there is at the level of the semiotic system of language. But, although this higher order is by no means autonomous, for Hasan it is this second order of semiosis that is the critical criterion of the literature text. It is here that the special art of verbal art resides – in particular in its symbolic articulation, which is in a real sense the grammar of the text's deepest meanings – its theme. But it is a hidden grammar, located visibly only at the level of verbalization. As Butt (1988) puts it, 'symbolic articulation is the "implicate order" underlying verbal art' (Hasan 2007: 28).

To probe that implicate order is a question of laying bare that Mukařovskýan motivated consistency of foregrounded patterns spoken of above with respect to how it functions to turn the meanings at the first order of language into signs having a deeper meaning, having, i.e., a theme. As said above, the Mukařovskýan notion most basic to foregrounding is that of 'contrast'. But as also pointed up, for Hasan, the analyst is only concerned with contrast that is significant (i.e. significant enough to be called, because functioning as, foregrounding). Still, just what does 'significant' mean? And how can the analyst tell when it is significant? Although there is no simple map that unproblematically plots the road to certainty, there are certain modus operandi that can be applied.

'Significant foregrounding' is foregrounding that 'counts'. And what counts, for Hasan, is *not* occurrence or non-occurrence of linguistic mechanisms – at least *not in and of themselves.* What matters is 'consistency' and Mukařovskýan 'motivation'. If there is motivation, it means that the features are articulated in a way that is working toward the construction of some significantly deeper meaning, or theme. In short, it means they are symbolically articulating a theme. And, if foregrounding is noticeably meaningful, then such foregrounding will also prove to be 'consistent', and in two ways, both of which contribute to making foregrounding, or symbolic articulation, noticeable. Such motivated consistency of foregrounding then is a question of: the stability of its semantic direction, and the stability of its textual location.

For Hasan, stability of semantic direction means that 'the meanings which are being highlighted by the foregrounded patterns converge toward the same direction' (1989 [1985]: 95), and she immediately adds that 'Butt (1983) has coined the happy expression "semantic drift" to refer to much the same kind of phenomenon'. Often it is a semantic *tension* between fore- and background that is responsible for construing this kind of consistency. The second mode of consistency, the stability of textual location, does not mean that a stable textual location refers to predictable, regular, material locations in the text; rather it means that significant patterns of foregrounding tend to take place in textually significant places (1989 [1985]: 95).

But to say more about theme. Hasan glosses the theme as being tantamount to a generalization on some aspect of human existence.

> The subject matter of theme concerns some aspect of the human condition, a sense of what the flesh is heir to, what irks the spirit, what seems risible, what profound, what is subject to change, what immutable ... From this point of view, verbal art offers the best re-contextualization ... of the kind of knowledge that is based on the experience of everyday life as it is lived unselfconsciously by the members of some community. It is in this sense that verbal art is 'truer' than history: its truth is akin to hypotheses based in a deep understanding of the experience of being human. (2007: 25)

And such truths tend to be lasting, as a text's endurance as art will always rest on the value that is awarded it by successive generations of readers: 'The challenge for the creator of verbal art is that the symbolically articulated theme has to be capable of striking a chord in the reader over substantial distances in time and space' (Hasan 2007: 25). And, of course, the *analyst* of verbal art is also challenged: to painstakingly investigate the text's symbolic articulation of its theme. As Hasan describes this necessarily systematic process:

> To be taken seriously, claims about themes – indeed about any aspect of literature – need to be examined. But examined how? This is where a consideration of the level of symbolic articulation becomes crucial. If symbolic articulation is the grammar that construes the meaning configuration called theme, then any claims about theme have to be argued by analysing that grammar, i.e. by showing that the structuring of foregrounding indeed supports the reading of the postulated theme. It is neither the author's intention nor some authorized opinion that we need to seek or follow; what we need to establish is what Mukarovsky (1977) called the *artistic intention* of an instance of verbal art ... Theme is not what it pleases you or me to claim: theme is what the patterns of foregrounding support, just as the lexicogrammar of a clause supports its meaning construal. (Hasan 2007: 27)

As one would expect, Hasan's analyses of literature offer numerous illustrations of the symbolic articulation of theme. To take just one instance, Hasan (2007) examines the foregrounding/symbolic articulation of wordings that function to create the developing pattern of Celia and Rosalind's mutual relationship in Shakespeare's *As You Like It*. In particular, she focuses on patterns of the 'contrasting imbalance' of their use of *thou/you* and of the frequency of the questions they pose and the commands they issue to each other, displaying their semantic consistency as semiotic devices for engaging another in interaction. Hasan makes plain how this consistent foregrounding activates

> the second, higher level of 'reading', allowing, or more precisely, guiding, the inference of something which is more abstract in the sense that it is less specific, and by the same token, has a wider embrace, applying across a larger number of classes. In inferring this meaning, we are no longer at the level of paraphrase [verbalization, DRM]: Celia said this and Rosalind said that. *Rather, we are now at the level of symbolic articulation:* we infer something abstract: human relations are askew; all's not right with the world. In making such higher level inferences, the consistency of foregrounding plays a crucial and guiding role. (Hasan 2007: 33, *my emphasis*)

Subsequently, the analyst's task then becomes to research the context of creation of the text and, with these findings, to re-evaluate the validity of his/her provisional post-analysis formulated theme. Experience shows that validity is typically confirmed on the whole, though new and potentially significant fine points are also quite often unveiled.

Ultimately, the theme is the *sine qua non* of verbal art: in the absence of a reflection on the nature of human experience, and its symbolic articulation, there is simply, for Hasan, no verbal art (1989 [1985]: 100).[7] This is perhaps as good a description of what literature is as any other, but it is without question a vital feature of the 'specialness' principle, and in manifest contrast with what Fowler famously claimed back in 1981: 'No plausible essentialist or intrinsic definition of literature has been or is likely to be devised. For my purpose, no such theory is necessary' (1981: 81). Hasan would, I suggest, disagree. As she would disagree with Simpson's own monoglossically stated contention:

> To argue for the existence of a distinct literary register is effectively to argue for a kind of cliché, because it would involve reining stylistic expression into a set of formulaic prescriptions ... To claim that literary language is special, that it can somehow be bracketed off from the mundane or commonplace in discourse, is ultimately to wrest it away from the practice of stylistics. (2014 [2004]: 106–107)

Apparently being rejected here is the least hue of prescriptivism being permitted to colour the definition and interpretative tools of literature. Recalling Fowler's rousing dispute with Bateson over the 'lit-crit' academy's attempts to safeguard its domain from the intruding desecrations of the inept and irreverent linguist (Fowler and Bateson 1967, 1968), and Simpson's own project for debunking the age-old veneration of the 'lit-crit' for literature (2014 [2004]: 98 ff.), one wonders if these scholars didn't feel – consciously or not – that these in themselves admirable aims were somehow at cross-purposes with the specialness principle (i.e. that the liberation of literature had to mean a democratization that precluded its being exceptional in any way). Perhaps.[8]

But for Hasan literature is a text whose meanings articulate – symbolically, especially, successfully, and lastingly – a generalization on the nature of human social existence. As her online annotation to Hasan (to appear) puts it:

> Language, as Whorf said, is the best show man puts on. And perhaps the most amazing performance in this repertory is verbal art, which, thanks to the power of ordinary language, peoples the world with beings who, although they do not exist, *hold a many-angled mirror to human life*. They live, creating histories which possess deeper reality than our own real existence in society: through these histories is distilled *human experience*, made potent as an extended metaphor for *the essential human condition*. The deepest level of meaning, the themes in verbal art, relate to *human social existence* - its dilemmas and its delights, thus bearing witness to its socio-semiotic origins. All of this is achieved through a patterning of the patterns of language. (Equinox online gloss to Hasan [to appear], *my emphasis*)[9]

The art of verbal art, for Hasan, is a superlatively *human* art. And what Hasan has gifted us for its analysis is an intricate, organic, holistic model – and a challenging one. Indeed, it is not at all the 'easiest' analytic framework – and this most likely explains its admitted unpopularity. It is of course legitimate to ask if the deepest meaning(s) of verbal art can be revealed without doing the kind of meticulous analysis Hasan's model demands (cf. Bowcher 2018: 280). I would say not, but then also should say another word about why I champion the model.

I do so for many sound reasons, I believe. Firstly, her framework is entrenched in Hallidayan grammar and its study, grammatics (Halliday 2002 [1996]). Secondly, it associates text to choices in the linguistic system (i.e. to meaning potential) (e.g. Halliday 2002 [1982]: 128), and sees text as being both rooted in context(s) and socio-cultural paradigm(s) and as, at the same time, realizing these. Then, it also pays due attention to the socially-situated author and reader. In addition, SSS offers a 'socially accountable' framework (cf. Matthiessen 2012), one that is systematic, rigorous and explicit/visible, so also replicable, indeed 'a mode of analysis that is open to scrutiny, so that evidence for competing claims can be compared' (Hasan 2007: 34), that is, it ticks all three of the 3-Rs (rigorous, retrievable and replicable) that Simpson demanded for any worthwhile stylistics analysis (2014 [2004]: 4). What is more, it is 'an enabling framework, which is maximally applicable to the genre, irrespective of variations in time, sub-genre, and the critic's response' (Hasan 1989 [1985]: 91).[10] So, for undaunted practitioners, as well as for pedagogical purposes, as I'll argue in Chapter 4, it is, I submit, the unrivalled, if not at all the least problematic, choice. Indeed, one might even speak of rich rewards awaiting those willing to make the undoubtedly mandatory effort to become expert in its exacting practice. This, at least, is the opinion of one who believes she has frequently succeeded in reaping them.

Before closing this review of Hasan's model, I return, as promised, to Martin's claim that Hasan 'replaces register as a level with symbolic articulation in her model of the relation of theme to language' (2012 [1985]: 61). At this point I trust the untenable nature of the claim has been clarified. In my email exchanges with Martin (7–8 July 2020), in vain I argued the innately semantic rather than contextual nature of symbolic articulation.

To no avail I also stressed Hasan's totally distinct and quite elaborate development of the notion of context in verbal art, which is what 'replaces' a single configuration of field, tenor and mode, seen as a too-simplified model for this special register. Both these aspects of her framework have been elaborated on. But Martin remains unconvinced. I closed the exchanges by saying: 'I feel it's the "art" of verbal art that both Michael and Ruqaiya were trying to get at', a significant point that emerges time and again in this volume, and something that Martin's own (and Martin-inspired) genre-based literature text analyses fail to engage with, as also comes to light.

2.4 Hallidayan (and Hasanian) Stylisticians

Hasan's, like Halliday's, published analyses of literature texts are various.[11] But does the stylistic work of these two scholars receive the attention it deserves? Halliday's unquestionably does. Douthwaite (2000: 44) appreciatively writes, 'a major influence on British stylistics, as well as one of its "founders", is Halliday's systemic or [sic] functional grammar, itself a discrete descendant of Prague School linguistic theories'. Douthwaite's own research – primarily literary, though he does not ascribe to literature's special-ness – gives Halliday ample space in its eclectic toolkit. Indeed, tribute is ritually paid to Halliday in such terms outside the community. Lukin (2015: 352–353) also points up Halliday's stimulus to systemic stylistics, noting how a summary of some of this work can be found in Butler (2003: 445–446), but also in Lukin and Webster (2005), and Butt and Lukin (2009). As she notes, Butler observes that a number of Halliday-inspired main-stream monographs on stylistics have appeared (e.g. Leech and Short 1981 and Toolan 1988, 1990).

Butt and Lukin (2009) discuss and illustrate through analysis the complex richness of stylistic analysis in the Hasanian perspective. They also sketch developments in sys-temic functional stylistics. In what follows, I selectively engage in dialogue with their account, amplifying it with more recent work. The systemic stylisticians cited below are all followers of Halliday, but only a marginal minority of Hasan. Noteworthy links to her work are highlighted.

First mentioned by Butt and Lukin (2009) are North American systemicists who have worked in the field; among them the historical linguist of, in particular, Old English, Cummings, e.g. his 1983 introduction to the study of literature, co-authored with Simmons, as well as Gregory's studies of poetry and drama (e.g. 1974) and Fries (e.g. 2003). I would point out that Fries' paper, an analysis of how reality is construed in James and Hemingway, does reference Hasan (1989 [1985]), on patterning, the textual search for which he perceptively illustrates. Butt and Lukin then turn to eight dimensions according to which they elaborate their discussion (2009: 197–199).

- The first of these dimensions is in relation to 'core concepts, including the con-tact between the Halliday-Hasan methods and other traditions (Prague School and Russian Formalism)'. This interface has been amply, if hardly exhaustively, exam-ined in Chapter 1 but also here in Chapter 2 above.

- The second dimension is that of relations with other sub-disciplines of stylistics, also in part spoken of in Chapter 1, though without having mentioned the work of O'Toole (1982) and Thibault (1991) on narratology and Post Modernism, cited by Butt and Lukin. Both are far-reaching volumes that adroitly and innovatively blend critical perspectives both theoretically and methodologically.

- Butt and Lukin's dimension 3 involves individual literary genres, 4 encompasses authors and 5 takes in SFL anthologies, which the authors rightly note typically include work falling into categories 3 and 4 as well. Butt and Lukin also bring in SFL style analyses of non-literary culture, which allows them to note how Halliday's scientific argument in his investigation of Tennyson's 'In Memoriam' (2002 [1988]) accomplishes a significant grammatical overturning of the then-dominant literary criticism of the poem. Concerning dimension 3, I'd add that Taylor Torsello (2016) probes Woolf's *A Room of One's Own* in terms of genre, identifying three different ones – lecture, novel and essay – but showing that typical structural criteria make the match with each of these unsatisfactory. She suggests that the metaphor of hybridity fits the generic complexity of the text, and also that Woolf makes selective use of the conventional 'templates' available to her in what may be an attempt to free herself of the male-dominated literary code and inventively create a new genre with a feminine style. I'd suggest Lukin and Pagano (2016) fits in dimension 3 as well. In a solidly socio-semiotic, and SSS, perspective, the article examines Hasanian theme in Katherine Mansfield's short story, *Bliss*, via the textual interplay between the inner and outer worlds of the central character. They also probe representations of different characters' voices via Bernstein's coding orientations (e.g. 1974 [1971]), an application which Bowcher (2018: 301) applauds as signalling a rich vein of future research. They also briefly defend their approach against that of an increasingly popular cognitive narratology.

- Butt and Lukin's dimension 6 is that of 'the linguistic systems that are most crucial to the argument on textual organization and uniqueness (viz. those crucial to claims of a "dominant" in a work or suite of texts'). The authors correctly remark that, on one hand, 'it is the ensemble effect of patterns of choice from a number of systems which creates the "semantic drift" (Butt 1983)'. And I would suggest that Hasan's verbal art analyses illustrate this to perfection. On the other hand, however, they note that it is equally true that very often one or another of the metafunctions or systems can be seen to be dominant in the making of the text's deepest meanings – a thesis, as is well-known in SFL circles, which is famously argued by Gregory and Carroll (1978). Halliday's focus on textual resources in his work on *The Origin of Species* is the example Butt and Lukin put forth. To this I'd add Matthiessen (2018), which focuses on transitivity's role in the construal of the hierarchy of control that is part of the order of the world in a children's version of the Old Testament's story of Noah's Ark (Genesis 6–9). Probing clause by clause the flow of events as a configuration of process, participants and attendant circumstances, Matthiessen's expert analysis reveals who or what can act on whom or what. I would also mention two of the many mainstream stylistics transitivity studies of narrative fiction and characterization that could be cited – a choice dictated by personal familiarity and successful use with students. Analysis in

Kennedy (1982) reveals the linguistic construal of non-responsibility for murder in Conrad's *The Secret Agent*. In Ji and Shen (2004) the process of a character's mental transformation over time in Sheila Watson's *The Double Hook* is traced through a progressive change in transitivity patterns and linked to the development of the novella's theme of community – though Hasan is not explicitly cited. These two works are also pointed out in Lin (2016: 62). I'd also add another interesting study by a mainstream author who is, however, frequently SFL-inspired (cf. Chapter 5 below): Nørgaard's *Systemic functional linguistics and literary analysis: A Hallidayan approach to Joyce – A Joycean approach to Halliday* (2003). The volume systematically explores the grammar of both ideational and interpersonal meanings in Joyce's 'Two Gallants', three sections from Joyce's *Ulysses* and the first page of *Finnegans Wake*.

- Butt and Lukin's seventh dimension has to do with 'engagement with criticism and its domains of contestation'. To illustrate, they speak of Hasan's writings on ideology and semiotic distance and their bearing on interpretation, including that of the literature text. They also exemplify the importance of these notions for World English Literature with the working rapport between Singaporean poet, Edwin Thumboo, and the American linguist, Jonathan Webster, and in particular the latter's 'stylistic analyses which illuminate the subtleties of a poetry which draws on strong "local" connections as well as internationalist perspectives' (e.g. Webster 2001). I'd also signal that Webster's more recent volume (2015) dedicated to Thumboo and, exceptionally even among systemicists, strongly inspired by Hasan's (1989 [1985]) work. As he explicitly declares in the Preface: 'it was Ruqaiya Hasan's book, *Language, Linguistics and Verbal Art*, which prompted my subsequent interest in applying a systemic-functional approach to the analysis of poetry, in particular the poetry of Edwin Thumboo' (2015: v).

- Butt and Lukin's eighth and final dimension is that of stylistics in interaction with other modes of semiotic expression. Systemic functional multimodal discourse analysis (SF-MDA) applied to verbal art will be investigated in Chapter 5.

A ninth 'dimension' might be suggested. This is what Matthiessen (2009: 37) calls 'aesthetic linguistics', meaning 'a field of investigation dealing with ... the negotiation in a community of the value of works of art'. This sub-register of discourse *about* literature is subsequently addressed by Matthiessen himself (2013a and 2013b), where he investigates histories of literature, interviews with writers and with students for admission to literature programmes, and reviews.

There would be many others to add to this too-brief compendium of SFL-influenced stylistic work. In Chapters 4 and 5, selective attention is given to others who work on literature from specific transdisciplinary perspectives such as pedagogy, translation, corpus linguistics and multimodality, already mentioned above.[12]

But now to indulge, and divulge, a long-standing personal discontent.

2.5 A Politics of Exclusion?

Attention to Hasan's stylistic work suffers in comparison to that routinely granted Halliday's own. Regularly deprived of due regard, her rigorously argued theory derived from her questions about what it means to do stylistics and to teach literature, her verbal art framework, and her analyses, are almost invariably 'missing' from accounts of mainstream stylistics. Such conspicuous side-lining raises a question of what I have labelled a 'politics of exclusion' (for the first time in Miller 2010: 48), whose motives, however, still remain somewhat nebulous. I will now give way to some brief subjective (and declaredly biased) speculation as to why her colleagues in the stylistics discipline habitually fail to acknowledge her work.

It cannot be her contamination by the frequently slighted model of SFL that is at fault, as Halliday *is* widely cited, and surely he, as architect of that model, is even more 'tainted' in that sense than she is. Might the problem be her notion of literature as special, her theory of just what makes a text literature, or 'verbal' art? But, as we've seen, Halliday has analogous ideas on the subject. Can it be simply that he's better known and so harder to ignore? That he can (must?) be integrated into the mainstream toolkit (most often in terms of transitivity and/or modality), and that this is easier to do, as there's no need to take on a holistic analytical model such as Hasan's double-articulation? Is Halliday's prominence/de-automatization perhaps preferred, because less complicated than concepts such as 'symbolic articulation'? Indeed, can it be that Hasan's approach is just too 'different' from that of acknowledged mainstream stylisticians? And does 'different' mean too rigid, and/or too uncompromising, as discussed above? Is she perhaps perceived (imperceptibly of course) as not having paid her proper dues to the members of the 'club' themselves and/or their proclivities? Undoubtedly, she has always been unashamedly outspoken concerning her well-argued and sourced opinions, to the point of being what academic political correctness would most likely label 'judgemental'. Of this, and of often 'incur[ring] displeasure' (1996a: 55), she is aware. Perhaps even that 'fault' on its own is enough to account for her virtual absence from the mainstream stylistics scene.

But some evidence of this prejudice on the part of stylistics textbooks/handbooks by rights ought to be offered in support of my contention. The following is a briefly annotated selection of reputable contemporary stylistic texts that all pay proper, even extensive, tribute to Halliday's work, but not to Hasan's. Included are also a few exceptions to this rule.

- Toolan (ed., 1992) includes many contributions referencing Halliday, as is usual, but also one sole chapter marginally sourcing Hasan (1989 [1985]). Rather remarkably, the chapter does not examine verbal art but rather a non-literary medical text (Grice and Kramer-Dahl 1992). Medical discourse is of course a register that many systemicists currently work on, but in the volume's literary stylistics chapters – the majority – Hasan does not appear.
- Weber (ed., 1996) includes a section dedicated to 'Functional stylistics', within which is reproduced Halliday's paper on Golding's *The Inheritors* (2002 [1971]). The

sole mention of Hasan in the volume (1996: 69) occurs within that paper, where Halliday cites from her early work (1967: 109–110).

- Toolan (1998) – *Language in Literature* – leans heavily on SFL. Its title, however, is only an implied tribute to Hasan's recommended 'shift of focus' to the language *in* – rather than *of* – literature (1989 [1985]: 92). Toolan actually puts the 'in' in italics in his 'Preliminaries', in stating that: 'Stylistics is the study of the language *in* literature' (1998: viii), but fails to cite Hasan on this, though he is likely to have known the source. This emerges from what he does cite, besides the omnipresent Halliday and Hasan (1976) on cohesion in text: namely, her cline of dynamism, albeit without using the expression (1998: 89), in Hasan (1989 [1985]: 45–46).
- Goatly (2008) acknowledges, and in passing uses, Hasan's (1989 [1985]) work on the foregrounding of theme.
- Jeffries and McIntyre (2010) cite only Halliday and Hasan (1976).
- Wales (2001 [1990]), besides Halliday and Hasan (1976), also mentions Hasan (1978) on the notion of text in SFL.
- Nørgaard, Busse and Montoro (2010) mention only Halliday and Hasan (1976).
- Stockwell and Whiteley (eds, 2014): The only citations of Hasan in the *Cambridge Handbook of Stylistics* are by Lin in his chapter on 'Stylistics in translation', where he argues for 'a functional stylistics model' and even more especially for the application of Hasan's framework for the analysis of verbal art to translation studies (2014a: 576 ff.).
- Burke (ed., 2014a): the entire *Routledge Handbook of Stylistics* references Hasan solely vis-à-vis the customary Halliday and Hasan (1976). She is even omitted from the chapter dedicated to 'Functionalist Stylistics', featuring, besides Halliday and among others, also Fowler and Simpson.
- Simpson (2014 [2004]) cites Halliday amply, but not Hasan.
- Sotirova (ed., 2016b) stands out as a refreshing exception to the exclusion tendency. Indeed, my enthusiastic praise goes to the editor of the *Bloomsbury Companion to Stylistics* – and, of course, once more to the scholar, Lin, this time for his chapter on 'Functional Stylistics' (2016: 57–77), an exceptionally balanced acknowledgement of both Halliday and Hasan's work but also of SFL practitioners who work with both their frameworks. He also includes mainstream SFL-friendly scholars, ones who selectively follow at least Halliday, though they deny the literature as special principle, as in the cases of Fowler and Simpson.
- Page, Busse and Nørgaard (eds, 2018): although many chapters in the volume analyse literature, there is no reference at all to either Halliday or Hasan's work on verbal art. As expected, Halliday is cited much more than Hasan; she quasi-invariably is mentioned only in conjunction with him (1976). The one exception is Don's reference to Hasan's (1996b), with reference to ontogenesis (Don 2018: 269).

Moreover, apart from Halliday's own engagement with her work (cf. Lukin 2015: 352), only a handful of even SFL scholars working in the field have given Hasan's stylistic work due consideration. Foremost among these over the years are Lukin (e.g. 2018), Butt (e.g. Butt and Lukin 2009; Butt 2016), Webster (e.g. Lukin and Webster 2005; Webster 2015), Miller (e.g. 2010, 2017b, 2019a), and Miller and Luporini (2018a, 2018b). These

SFL scholars, along with Matthiessen (e.g. 2013a, 2018), and Lin (2014a, but also in other studies, as will be seen) might to varying degrees be dubbed the custodians of the Hasanian stylistic tradition. Thus, even certain SFL stylisticians might be chided for giving Hasan's stylistic work short shrift – a thought that was in mind when, in opening this chapter, I remarked that verbal art studies undoubtedly occupied a dignified place within SFL, but that this place could be improved on.

To mention just some examples: in his genre-based literature text analyses, on which we'll have more to say in subsequent chapters, Martin (e.g. 2012 [1996]) acknowledges Hasan's work on theme only parenthetically. Banks uses Halliday's work in his own sizeable stylistic production (e.g. 2008), but not Hasan's – by reason of his earlier acquaintance with Halliday and then his personal preference (personal communication, 20 January 2020). A case in point is Huisman (2016) and her otherwise admirable recent paper on English literature as a discipline in the light of SFL register theory, where – despite her having written much of value on the topic – she cites Hasan only in a footnote (2019: 115) – and does so by design (personal communication, 22 January 2020).[13] And an object lesson in thinly-veiled public censure can be found in the SFL-inspired volume edited by Birch and O'Toole (1988), to which Hasan is a contributor. The editors cross-examine her chapter, in asserting, with respect to her defence of detailed lexicogrammatical analysis, that 'For many people this is the stuff of the old polemical debates among linguists and literary critics' (1988: 3). They declare her chapter

> invites debate because it makes a claim that one model of analysis is particularly powerful ... and this position will not be without its critics ... The model [SFL, DRM] is not static. It is not something that was determined a few years ago and enshrined by systemicists as an unchanging blueprint for analysis. It, like the stylistics it generates and the language it is interested in, is in a constant state of flux. (1988: 3)

Of course, one could counter that 'the old polemical debates among linguists and literary critics' have never completely died out or been happily resolved in either the discipline stylistics or academia and, further, that neither the stylistics generated by Hallidayan SFL nor 'the language it is interested in' can unqualifiedly be said to be 'in a constant state of flux'. In any case, I read their not-so-nimbly depersonalized argument as entailing a considerable censure of Hasan's 'position', as well as of what they apparently see as the 'static' quality of her model itself. That she incurs their displeasure is, I'd venture to say, fairly transparent. A decidedly more Hasan-friendly estimation of her chapter in Birch and O'Toole (1988) is tendered in Butt and Lukin (2009: 196):

> A demonstration of Hasan's approach, which is carefully scaffolded for those working their way into stylistics and its mode of argument, can be found in her analysis of Anne Sexton's poem 'Old' (Hasan, 1988). This study encompasses not only an investigation of the language of the poem 'in the round', it positions the poem against critical evaluations which show what is at risk when critics do not have to provide a linguistic warrant for their appraisals.

If 'this is the stuff of the old polemical debates among linguists and literary critics', I (polemically) submit, they have reason to carry boldly on.

2.6 Coda

This chapter has outlined the developing ideas on verbal art of both Halliday and Hasan, focusing in particular on the latter. It has also reflected on where they 'fit', or not, into certain of the stylistic approaches to literature elaborated in the last and current century. The work of other select SFL practitioners has been briefly commented and the issue of what I call, regarding Hasan's SSS, a 'politics of exclusion', expounded.

I now turn to Chapter 3, dedicated to arguing that the relevance of Jakobson's work for Hasan's SSS is a vital further direction that systemic functional stylistics needs to take. The premise is provided by Fowler's keen (if censorious) perception of the unmistakable analogies between Jakobson's insights and those of Mukařovský (1986: 73). The thesis is that the application of Jakobson's concept of parallelism must be likened, just as Mukařovský's foregrounding is, to Hasan's symbolic articulation of theme in verbal art. In short, it too must be seen as capable of revealing what literature's 'art' resides in (e.g. Miller 2010, 2013a, 2016a). To espouse Jakobson's work, even in this postmodern era, is not to advocate an obsessively 'structural' approach to language: he continually expounded the inseparability of form and meaning. Rather than a stringent, die-hard structuralist, he was foremost a linguist, attentive to meaning and context as well as to form (cf. note 6 to Chapter 1). But much more on all this below.

Chapter 3

The Case for Slotting Jakobson into SSS

3.1 Prelude

As stated in the closing lines of Chapter 2, this chapter is dedicated to arguing that Jakobson's grammatical parallelism (GP, recall) must be brought into, just as foregrounding is, Hasan's theory of the symbolic articulation of verbal art. As also said, the proposal – extensively tested and argued repeatedly over the last years – is that the relevance of Jakobson's work for SSS is an essential further direction that SFL verbal art studies need to take. Thus (as in, for example, Miller 2010, 2013a, most thoroughly in 2016a, and also, if less extensively, in 2017b, 2019a), the correspondences between his poetic function and Mukařovský's foregrounding, this last a cornerstone of Hasan's model, are delineated. In short, Mukařovský is an intrinsic component of Hasan's SSS, and Jakobson is not. What are set out here are the results of research into *why not*. Also set forth are Hasan's reservations concerning the proposal and counterarguments to these.

The chapter also offers illustration of how GP, or actually PP, 'pervasive parallelism' (Jakobson 1966: 423) functions: just as Hasan maintains that patterning in verbal art must – as a 'consistent' and 'motivated' foregrounding device that symbolically articulates the 'theme' of a literature text. This is done with thorough analysis of one poem by D.H. Lawrence, with the tools of what is now being proposed as a fine-tuned SSS *plus* (SSS+, recall). In the attempt at formulating the poem's theme or deepest meanings, the study also includes scrutiny of the specific context of creation of the poem, as described in the previous chapter. Some authors' texts are more challenging in their ways of meaning than others; Lawrence can require considerable disambiguating efforts. Though the poem chosen for analysis here is among his most effortlessly intelligible, contextual background still illuminates its ways of saying/meaning.

3.2 The Mukařovský-Jakobson Theory

The heading to this section is the cornerstone of the proposal argued here. It was coined by Fowler (1986: 73), in rightly, indeed astutely, noting the theoretical intersection of Mukařovský's foregrounding and Jakobson's parallelism, which was concisely traced in Chapter 1: 'For both of these writers, literary language draws the reader's attention to its own artifices of construction.'

Fowler, however, explicitly and energetically, distances himself from their 'aesthetic' positions, setting up the dispute:

they claim that foregrounding and parallelism are special qualities of 'poetic language' which distinguish it from 'ordinary language': I maintain that 'poetic language' is not an objective, distinct entity, but an imaginary concept produced by the business of letters by way of publishing, reviewing, criticizing, theorizing and teaching. (1986: 72)

But surely poetic language is more than the mere brainchild of 'businessified' academia. As I intimated in Chapter 2, perhaps Fowler's aversion can perhaps be best understood against the backdrop of his non-essentialist definition of literature, formulated five years previously in his *Literature as Social Discourse* (1981), and characterized as being antithetical to Hasan's (but also Halliday's) belief in literature as 'special'. A more extended quotation from that definition now follows:

No plausible essentialist or intrinsic definition of literature has been or is likely to be devised. For my purpose, no such theory is necessary. What literature is can be stated empirically, within the realm of socio-linguistic fact. It is: an open set of texts, of great formal diversity, recognized by a culture as possessing certain institutional values and performing certain functions. (Fowler 1981: 81)

The never publicly debated Fowler-Hasan dispute needs to be further evaluated, however. We've seen that Hasan's definition of literature could be labelled eminently 'essentialist'. Nevertheless, there are also correspondences between her and Fowler's positions. Firstly, she would not disagree with the institutional values of literature; SFL speaks regularly about literature as belonging to the class of highly valued texts (e.g. Halliday in Halliday and Hasan 1989 [1985]: 42, as cited in Chapter 2; Hasan 2007: 16, where she delineates the complexity of the concept). Moreover, she would obviously not find fault with the general assertion of the fact of its 'performing certain functions'. And surely their respective views regarding the importance of culture and the social cannot be said to merely clash. Indeed, Hasan says that 'the literature text ... embodies precisely the kind of "truths" that most communities are deeply concerned with' (Hasan 1989 [1985]: 100). She also recognizes that the social impacts strongly on verbal art: indeed 'perhaps the most critical part it plays is in the shaping of the ideological orientations of those who write and those who read literature' (Hasan 2007: 25). And as we've seen, for Hasan, a text's endurance as art will depend on the value that its readers continue to grant it.

In spite of such harmonies, however, the sum and substance is a conflict in stances. Hasan does not invest the power for ultimately deciding what is or is not literature in the community, whether it be that of the time and place of the text's creation or at a further semiotic social distance (Hasan 2007: 34). Recall, as also stressed in Chapter 2, 'that texts place restraints upon what can be done with them interpretively' (Hasan 1996a: 52), and that, in the absence of a reflection on the nature of human experience (of, i.e. a theme, and its symbolic articulation), there is simply, for Hasan, no verbal art (1989 [1985]: 100).

And now to return to the Mukařovský-Jakobson theory.

3.2.1 Jakobson's Side of the Equation

In Chapter 1 we saw how Jakobson's thought on literary language emerges analogously to Mukařovský's. We also saw his assertion: 'The set (*Einstellung*) toward the message as such, focus on the message for its own sake, is the POETIC function of language' (1960: 356, *original emphasis*), made in the course of his pivotal modelling of the communicative factors and corresponding functions of language. Admittedly, Jakobson had no functional lexicogrammar with which to substantiate his claim, but simply provided examples based on traditional grammar and phonology. Admittedly too, nowhere does he explicitly speak of the role of foregrounding in articulating the aesthetically motivated theme of the work, but the analogies between his original and perceptive insights and those of Hasan are too many and essential to be ignored. Sketched out below are the ideas that are most relevant to this line of reasoning.

The poetic function – a point that many stylisticians seem to lose sight of, but one that is absolutely essential to Jakobson's hypothesis – has an 'empirical linguistic criterion', and that is GP, what he means by the much-quoted affirmation, deemed by Fowler to be 'only apparently cryptic' (1986: 74):

> What is the empirical linguistic criterion of the poetic function? In particular, what is the indispensable feature inherent in any piece of poetry? To answer this question we must recall the two basic modes of arrangement used in verbal behaviour, *selection* and *combination* ... The selection is produced on the basis of equivalence, similarity and dissimilarity, synonymy and antonymy, while the combination, the build up of the sequence, is based on contiguity. *The poetic function projects the principle of equivalence from the axis of selection into the axis of combination.* Equivalence is promoted to the constitutive device of the sequence (1960: 358). (1986: 74, *original emphasis*)

In SFL terms, this would mean shifting from a system to a structure perspective, from the paradigmatic to the syntagmatic. But just what GP is must be clarified better.

What GP consists of is the regular reiteration of equivalent units. 'By "equivalent" Jakobson simply means "substitutable in the same place in a syntagm"; *not* "identical" or "synonymous"' (Fowler 1986: 75). Lexicogrammatically, we are dealing with a noteworthy reiteration of elements, at all levels of the rank scale: in ascending order these include morphemes, words, groups (e.g. Deictic + Epithet + Thing...), phrases, and clauses (e.g. Actor + Material Process + Goal, or Finite + Subject, etc.). Parallelism of lexical units (i.e. of words) does occur; however, GP is not as a rule a lexical phenomenon, while it is always, and most importantly, structural. There are also other compositional hierarchies such reiteration takes place in: for example, in sound: phoneme – syllable – rhythm group – tone group; and in spoken verse/poetry: syllable – metric foot – line – stanza. And it is this marked reiteration at the syntagmatic level of phonological, metrical, morphological, syntactic and even lexical form that Jakobson sees as the empirical criterion of his poetic function. It is this, as pointed out in Chapter 1, that exhibits Jakobson's notion of 'literariness': that unchangeable essence that he sees as intrinsic to every literary phenomenon.

But where have SFL practitioners come across GP in Halliday's model of text creation? In SFL, GP is a structural cohesive device in the clause as message, realizing textual meanings, as in Figure 3.1 below.

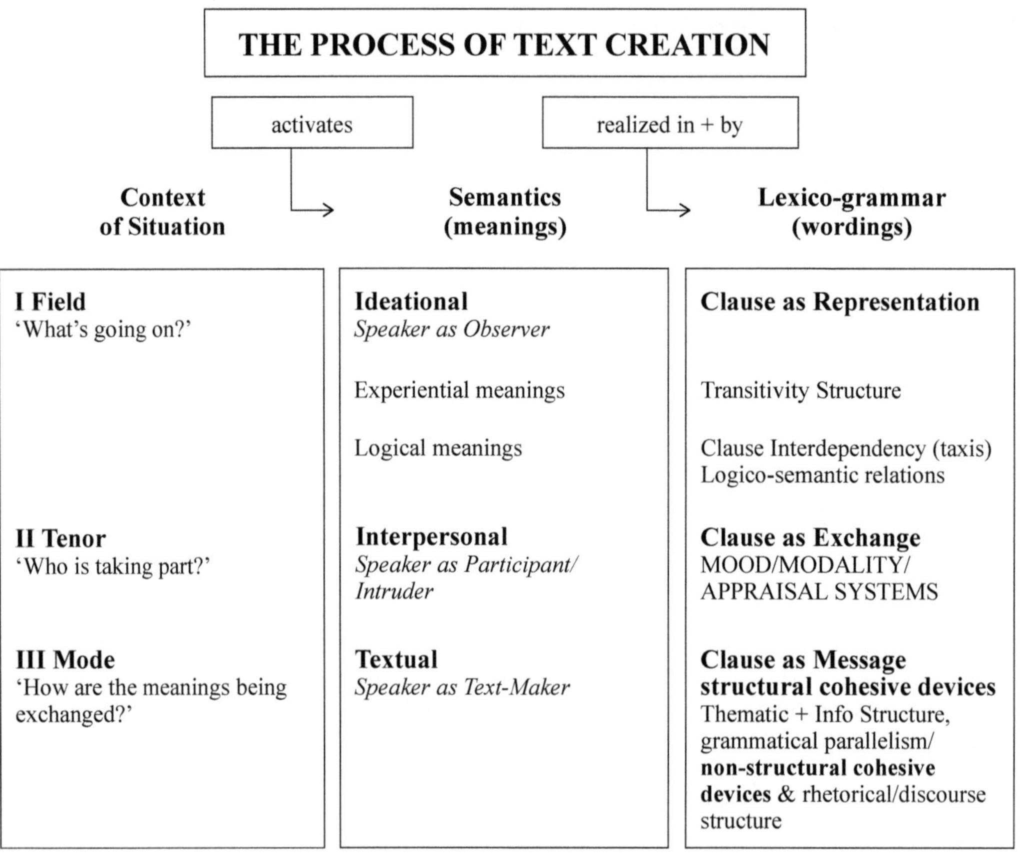

Figure 3.1 The process of text creation: based on D.R. Miller, 'English Linguistics' lecture notes: AY 2000–01

With reference to its role as a structural cohesive device, however, GP can often be seen to confer a notable surplus of cohesive harmony, or *more* than what is actually 'needed'. As Martin (1992: 386) puts it: '[g]rammatical parallelism ... is exploited rhetorically in contexts where strictly speaking it is not needed to realise the meaning at hand. The result is a "surfeit" of cohesive harmony.' In such a case, the phenomenon becomes textually superfluous; it effectively annuls its typical textual function. So, we can assume that cohesion is *not* the primary purpose of the marked (over)use of the mechanism.

But then, what can this rhetorical exploitation be seen to be unto? Because the assumption is that it is meant to serve some purpose, that such an excessive use of GP in text is presumably motivated (i.e. has been chosen for the purpose of instantiating some *other* kind of meaning). And, indeed, Jakobson's hypothesis is that the ultimate importance of GP lies in the fact that it is also – and at the same time – something else. The true significance of the notion of parallelism for Jakobson – following up on Gerard Manley Hopkins' 1865 insight (1960: 368–369) – is that GP is seen to call forth a corresponding recurrence of meaning, a recurrence of the 'sense' that the structures being reiterated realize. Accordingly, grammatical parallelism is, at one and the same time, semantic parallelism.[1]

Intriguingly, GP is closely linked to the mnemonic, incantatory powers of the oral tradition, or 'orality', which has always been theorized as involving a repetition of sense (Ong 1967, 1982). So, the question then becomes: what meaning(s) can such a markedly exploited excess of these 'gorgeous grammatical tropes and figures' (Jakobson 1960: 375), or 'syntactic imagery' (Halliday 2002 [1971]: 107) be said to construe/enact? Clearly this reiteration of sense does not function at the level of textual meanings. Therefore, what are being predominantly reiterated in the text are its ideational and interpersonal meanings. As Martin puts it, GP can be said to illustrate the (typically literary) process of 'de-automatization', one 'whereby a particular linguistic stratum makes meaning which is not predicted by its context' (Martin 1992: 386) – at least not in a typically straight-forward way. Apropos, here I recall Martin's related serviceable suggestion (personal communication, 7 July 2020, cf. note 2, Chapter 2) that 'whenever there is more pattern-ing in a lower strata than is required to realise a higher one, we have foregrounding' (i.e. what Halliday calls de-automatization and Hasan calls symbolic articulation). And we have already seen Halliday and Hasan's reflections on the multifaceted complexity of the notion of context with reference to verbal art.

Fowler, despite his reservations concerning The Mukařovský-Jakobson Theory, actu-ally dedicates many pages in his 1986 chapter, 'Extra Structure, Extra Meanings', to illus-trating Jakobson's 'poetic principle', the power of whose mechanisms to confer extra meanings to a text evidently absorbs him, and whose 'working is very simple':

> Two or more linguistic units, of whatever kind, are placed in the sequence of the text in such a way that this relationship is clearly perceptible in addition to whatever syntagmatic relationship the items may have. In this way an extra layer of structure is created over and above the structure of the text as 'sensible communication'. (Fowler 1986: 75–76)

My suggestion then is that 'the strikingness of these devices' (Jakobson 1968: 603) has an analogous function to that of Hasan's patterning of patterns, her Mukařovskian foregrounding that 'counts' – the motivated consistency of semantic direction for the symbolic articulation of theme in verbal art, what its art resides in.

But Hasan had reservations, which I attempted to allay with her, personally as well as in print, and I dare to think I *was* getting somewhere ... before she left us.

3.2.2 Hasan's Misgivings Addressed

As I've remarked elsewhere (in, especially, Miller 2013a and 2016a), some of Hasan's objections are easier to dispel than others. Firstly, she takes issue (1989 [1985]: 99) with what she feels is Jakobson's (and the Prague School linguists' generally) too restrictive notion of the aesthetic function of verbal art, seeing such functions as being wider. But Jakobson plainly and carefully stressed that, on one hand, 'the linguistic study of the poetic function must overstep the limits of poetry and, on the other hand, the linguistic scrutiny of poetry cannot limit itself to the poetic function' (1960: 357). In fact, none of his six communicative functions are ever seen as being mutually exclusive, though one typically dominates. Literature texts have a primary poetic function but are not confined to it alone. They also, adopting his categories, can be strongly linked to the emotive function (lyric poetry), the conative one (literature with a social message), a referential one (epic poetry), and so on. In any case, Jakobson hypothesized an *overlap* of functions in any one text as being the norm.

A more serious, if not unrelated, objection Hasan raises has to do with her critical distinction between verbal art versus verbal art *manquée*, mentioned in Chapter 2: she essentially mistrusts the degree to which Jakobson is equally firm on this division.

> Whenever the question arises which patternings of language are important in verbal art – imageries or metaphors or parallelism – my response has always been: depends on the work you are analyzing. If there is a work (purporting to be an instance of verbal art) where we do find a lot of linguistic patternings including parallelism, but most of it does *not* have the function of articulating some theme(s), the question arises (i) is the work to be seen as verbal art? or (ii) is it to be seen as verbal art manquée? I believe these considerations are important – there has to be some difference between pretty language as in belles lettres and verbal art. (Hasan, personal communication, 10 January 2011)

Yet, here again, Jakobson would fully agree with this distinction, and its significance. As already indicated in Chapter 1, for Jakobson the poetic function is not a property that is exclusive to poetry. He unmistakably held that the poetic function cannot 'be arbitrarily confined to the domain of poetry' (1960: 359), that it is to be found even *outside* poetry proper, where the poetic function is *not* primary (i.e. even in, to use Hasan's expression, 'verbal art manquée'). In these other varieties of text (among them, mnemonic texts, advertising, medieval law and Sanskrit theses!), he states that the poetic function does *not* have 'the coercing, the determining role it carries in poetry' (1960: 359). And yet, although Jakobson did *not* see the quality of literariness as being *exclusive* to literature, he unmistakably saw literariness as being *the* distinguishing feature of literary language, part and parcel of its self-reflexivity, its awareness of itself as a (special) medium. As such then, it is inseparable from the poetic function, and its empirical evidence: GP.

Most difficult to counter perhaps is the fact that Hasan does not acknowledge the central role of GP in her model, principally since she finds it hard to see it as *foregrounding in and of itself*. As is inferred in her personal communication above, she considers parallelism as merely one of any myriad variety of patterning mechanisms which may be there in a text, or not, a belief she then reiterates: 'If imagery, metaphor, repetition, parallelism – any patterning of patterns – is significant to the work then it will be there' (personal communication, 10 January 2011).

In an attempt to rebut this contention, Jakobson's notion of PP is now tapped, as it evinces even further the Mukařovskian/Hasanian emphasis on the foregrounding function of contrasting patterns. It also shows how Jakobson actually went a stage further than Mukařovský – if nowhere near the degree to which Hasan did – in specifying what is involved linguistically in the process. While any form of parallelism involves a choice of invariants and variables and works on the principle that the stricter the distribution of the former, the greater the discernibility and effectiveness of the latter, PP is wider-ranging. As Jakobson explains (1966: 423), it

> inevitably activates all the levels of language – the distinctive features, inherent and prosodic, the morphologic and syntactic categories and forms, the lexical units and their semantic classes in both their convergences and divergences acquire an autonomous

poetic value. This focusing upon phonological, grammatical, and semantic structures in their multiform interplay does not remain confined to the limits of parallel lines but expands throughout their distribution within the entire context; therefore, the grammar of parallelistic pieces becomes particularly significant.

Such parallelism then is 'pervasive' insomuch as it is distributed throughout the entire text at all levels of language. The point is that PP is not merely one among a myriad of patterning mechanisms at work foregrounding the theme(s) in verbal art; rather, it is that it can be likened to the process of foregrounding itself. In short, in conferring 'an autonomous poetic value', its particular significance is for the Hasanian symbolic articulation of theme. But now to see it at work.

3.3 PP as Symbolic Articulation of Theme: A Brief Illustration

It is commonplace, but compulsory, to note that only extensive evidence of the assertions made above could support their reliability in any adequate fashion. It is equally commonplace, but true, to say that there isn't space to produce such testimony here. In Miller's already cited work, however, liberal illustration of the pervasive tension between patterns of Jakobson's invariants and variables, proving to be co-textually consistent and also motivated, and so semantically fundamental to the articulation of theme, has been offered. This consists of analyses of nineteenth, twentieth and twenty-first century poetry texts, deliberately chosen to validate the hypothesis that the model is, as we've seen in Chapter 2 Hasan contends, 'maximally applicable to the genre [i.e. to literature, DRM], irrespective of variations in time, sub-genre, and the critic's response' (Hasan 1989 [1985]: 90). Among these texts figure: T.S. Eliot's 'Ash Wednesday' (Miller 2013a); various poems from different phases of D.H. Lawrence's oeuvre (Miller 2007 and 2019a); Blake's 'The Garden of Love' (Miller 2010, 2017b); Matthew Arnold's 'Dover Beach'; Siegfried Sassoon's 'Does it matter?' and John Whitworth's 'Little' (these last three in Miller 2016a).[2] Additional corpus-assisted studies are mentioned in Chapter 5. What I've chosen to offer here is an illustrative analysis of one early poem of D.H. Lawrence's, 'Bei Hennef' (from *Love Poems and Others*, 1913),[3] which I now turn to.

3.3.1 The Poem: 'Bei Hennef'[4]

//[1] The little river [[twittering in the twilight]],
....The wan, wondering look of the pale sky,
....This is almost bliss.

//[2] And everything shut up and gone to sleep,
//[3] All the troubles and anxieties and pain
....Gone under the twilight.

//[4] Only the twilight now, and the soft 'Sh!' of the river
....[[That will last for ever]].

//[5] And at last I know //[6] my love for you is here;
//[7] I can see it all, //[8] it is whole like the twilight,
//[9] It is large, so large, [[I could not see it before,
....Because of the little lights and flickers and interruptions,
....Troubles, anxieties and pains]].

//[10] You are the call //[11] and I am the answer,
//[12] You are the wish, //[13] and I the fulfilment,
//[14] You are the night, //[15] and I the day.
//[16] What else? //[17] It is perfect enough.
//[18] It is perfectly complete,

//[19] You and I,
......What more - ?

//[20] Strange, how we suffer in spite of this!

I've chosen to number the poem by ranking clauses, as is typical, despite those incomplete clause fragments in the first part of the poem especially. The presumably inferred process types are invariably relational or existential. Thus: 1) in what is labelled clause 2, before 'shut up', I posit 'is'; 2) in clause 3, before 'Gone', I hypothesize 'are'; 3) before 'Only' in clause 4, I deduce 'There is', or 'There are', and 4) at the end of both interrogative clauses, 16 and 19, I posit 'is there'.[5] Double square brackets conventionally enclose embedded clauses.

'Bei Hennef' is one of Lawrence's best known poems and among the first he wrote in free, unrhymed, and markedly parallel form. More will be said of the artistic conventions he had experimented with previously when dealing with the poem's context of creation below. Sound reiteration is the first level of GP that one tends to notice (cf. Ingram 1990: 145): stanza/clause 1's /tw/ of 'twittering ... twilight'; the /wa: / of 'wan, wandering', but also the dense /s/ and /z/ phonemes of 'This is almost bliss', where the pivotal Mood adjunct of degree, 'almost' sets up the pattern of not-quite-right feeling instantiated in the poem.[6] The first two lines, incomplete clauses, are also quasi-parallel in their experiential nominal group (henceforth NG) structure: Specific Deictic + Epithet + Thing + Qualifier (prepositional phrase: circumstantial element of Location: Place) in line 1, and Specific Deictic + Epithet + Epithet + Thing + prepositional phrase as Qualifier in line 2: two impressionistic NGs, made to wait to resolve themselves in anaphoric 'This' in the finally complete clause in line 3.

In the second stanza, more reiteration is at work, again experientially: in incomplete clause 2, the implied Attributes of 'everything': 'shut up and gone to sleep'; in incomplete clause 3's extended NGs (A *and* B *and* C: 'All the troubles and anxieties and pain'), and their implied Attribute: 'Gone under the twilight' – the second instance of both 'gone' and 'twilight' in the poem, this last implied as having debarred those 'troubles and anxieties and pain'. A dark, dormant and timeless (because tenseless) peace results, also because all this appears to be brought back, ambiguously, by the textual Theme 'And' to 'bliss', but again in incompleteness. There is no finite verb at all in this second stanza, a finding I'll come back to below. The grammar continues to tell us that completeness is elusive/illusive.

In the third stanza, again no finite appears to anchor clause 4's sole ('only'), two-fold, implied Existent: 'the twilight now, and the soft "Sh!" of the river', having another prepositional phrase as Qualifier. The circumstantial element of Location: Time 'now' fastens the 'twilight' to the immediate present, but the river, sh-ushing now, 'twittering' before, is defined by its embedded Qualifier as eternal. This series of timeless fragments seem to construe an eternal immediateness, as it were. They strike one as telling instances of what Hopkins – after the medieval Oxford theologian, Dun Scotus – called *haeccitas*: the thisness-and-not-thatness in all things, what renders each thing unique (cf. Bosco 2017: 107–108) and also of haeccitas as 'the phenomenon of the here-and-now, the flesh you can pinch and that feels pain, the base and raw material of life' (Warner 2005: 16). We'll also come back to this notion when considering the poem's context of creation below.

In the fourth stanza, there are four complete clauses. The end-focus of clause 6 is another circumstantial element of Location: Place, 'here', functioning as Attribute; and what is 'here' is recognized, and perceived, in clauses 7, 8 and 9, fully. Again, there is lexical repetition: 'last' for the second time, now nominal (vs clause 4's VG); 'twilight' for the third time; 'see' and 'large'. This word reiteration takes place within the parallel structures of perception featuring for the first time the poetic voice's 'I': //⁷ I can see it all, and //⁹ [[I could not see it before…]], with negative polarity, and also within those intertwining clauses of description of the poet's love: //⁸ it is whole like the twilight, with its circumstance of Manner: Comparison, and //⁹ It is large, so large. These work up to and culminate with the circumstance of Cause: Reason for the prior incapacity to 'see': 'Because of the little lights and flickers and interruptions,/Troubles, anxieties and pains', whose 'and'-extended NGs re-propose not only the triple NG structure of the second stanza's 'All the troubles and anxieties and pain', but its lexis as well. So then, we have convergences, though with divergences as well, also since the rhythms appear to function in opposite ways. Rather impressionistically, those in the second stanza might be said to lull, as it were, while these, at least in some measure due to their reiteration, seem rather to hammer home the poem's not-quite-right feeling.

The disquiet, of course, is primarily due to the prominent textual location of the repetition: as Ingram too notes (1990: 147). At the very moment of being able to perceive his complete and overwhelming love, the poet recalls what made him *incapable* of seeing it before. The foregrounded modality (because markedly scarce in the poem overall) of the 'can' of capacity in clause 7 is, in fact, promptly followed by, in clause 9's embedded comparative clause, a reminder of what, 'before', he 'could *not* see'.⁷ Thus these parallel clauses: 'I can see it all' and 'I could not see it before', diverging in polarity and temporality, construe another tension, now between ability/inability and/or possibility/impossibility, marking this relationship.

An essential structural, and semantic, change comes about in clauses 10 through 15 of the fifth stanza, with three almost-perfectly parallel, complete and coordinated relational clauses, one following the other, with identical subjects ('I'/'you') and explicit, or ellipted, verbs ('am'/'are') within each of these. The Values assigned to the Things being Identified are in each case typically strong antonymic collocates, the solemn identifying elements moving from the field of language ('call'/'answer'), to the domain of the sensual and/or spiritual ('desire'/'fulfilment'), to the once again natural and now cosmic rhythms of 'night' and 'day'.

> You are the call and I am the answer,
> You are the wish, and I the fulfilment,
> You are the night, and I the day.

But then the defining quasi-liturgical cycle stops, stopping short, and just short of incoherence, in clauses 16 through 19:

> What else? It is perfect enough.
> It is perfectly complete,
>
> You and I,
> What more - ?

The symmetrically located interrogatives are, significantly and foregroundedly, two. They are also parallel structures: Wh- + circumstantial adverbial group. In the first, in clause 16, the poetic voice seems to, ingenuously enough, demand information (from himself? From 'you'?) as to what else 'I' and 'you' can be said to be. But the following declarative's first instance of 'perfect' (clause 17), with post-modifier 'enough' – a veritable contradiction in terms[8] – betrays anxiety, and belies the second instance's positive intensifying function ('perfectly') of 'complete' in clause 18. In clause 19, with the reiterated, but now bonded, 'You and I', after the preceding expanded definitions of what they separately *are*, the poet's voice seems again to be searching for something further to define them, but the search winds up in another aborted clause: 'What more - ?' And any attempt to read these inarticulate lines as genuinely and confidently affirming the lovers' fulfilment is definitively thwarted by the last stanza's single, albeit complete and conversational, exclamative clause (#20), with its disturbed/-ing Thematic Comment Adjunct, significantly located as the concluding line of the poem, and thus also foregrounded, as well as its equally troubled/-ing explicit circumstantial element of Contingency: Concession – making the sixth circumstance of the poem:

> Strange, how we suffer in spite of this!

As Ingram (1990: 149) aptly comments: 'The source of the poet's potential happiness is also the source of his dissatisfaction.' And I believe we have seen how the grammar of the poem has enacted, perfectly, just this paradox.

The parallelisms in the poem are also, fittingly, those of *absence*. The incomplete clauses, devoid of finites, and thus Mood-less, have already been remarked. In this way, not only is time written out of the first part of the poem (cf. Butt on this aspect of the ending of Lawrence's *Sons and Lovers* [2007]), but the poem's interpersonal communicative function is continuously thwarted. And textually, many clauses, as we've seen, are incomplete, their Topical Themes being identifiable only if seen as being realized implicitly; that is, only if we see the key third line's 'This' as functioning, both anaphorically and cataphorically, as the node of a reference chain that is also an implicit, long, and complex Theme. Still, even if we do, the poem's initial method of development is decidedly erratic, as inconsistent as the poet's subsequent perception, and evaluation, of his love. I suggest that this method of development, together with the poem's inventive (in part explicitly paratactic, in part only implied, in part non-ranking) clause complexing can be said to demonstrate the power of what Butt calls 'latent patterning' in verbal art:

> The flow, the halting, the interpolating, the qualifying, and the varying of grammatical depths available to the impassioned speaker, along with the acoustic rhythms that enunciate the realizations of wording, are the most direct extension of unconscious bodily systems into the otherwise conventional architecture of natural language. (Butt 2016: 48, cf. 1988)

Table 3.1 below marshals the process types in 'Bei Hennef', letting us see more easily that the dominant type is relational: attributive (7 instances) – 2 of these, however, being only implicit, as are the 3 presumed existential types. The first 3 have 'natural' Carriers, while the others have the still non-human poetic voice's 'love'. Next in order numerically is the relational: identifying type: 6, all functioning to define 'You' and 'I'. To this pervasive relational process parallelism, there is also a circumstantial type to factor in: accounting for 14 of the total of 20 process types in ranking (or reconstructed as ranking) clauses. The remaining types are: those 3 supposed existentials and 3 mental process types, 1 of cognition and 1 of perception, with human 'I' functioning as Senser, and 1 of emotion, with human Senser 'we'. The other mental: perception type commented above is embedded in clause 9.

Table 3.1 Process types in 'Bei Hennef'

clause	-er role	Main verb	Process type	Tense
1	river ...look	is *almost bliss*	relational: att.	present
2	everything	[is] *shut up and gone to sleep*	relational: att.	present
3	all the troubles and anxieties and pain	[are] *gone under the twilight*	relational: att.	present
4	the twilight and the soft 'Sh!' of the river ....[[That will last for ever]]	[are]	existential	present
5	I	know	mental: cog.	present
6	my love for you	is *here*	relational: circ.	present
7	I	can see *it all*	mental: perc.	present
8	It	is *whole like the twilight*	relational: att.	present
9	It	is *large, so large* [[*I could not see ...because of...*]]	relational: att.	present
10	You	are *the call*	relational: id.	present
11	I	am *the answer*	relational: id.	present
12	You	are *the wish*	relational: id.	present
13	I	[am] *the fulfilment*	relational: id.	present
14	You	are *the night*	relational: id.	present
15	I	[am] *the day*	relational: id.	present
16	What else?	[is]	existential	present
17	It	is *perfect enough*	relational: att.	present
18	It	is *perfectly complete*	relational: att.	present
19	You and I, what more - ?	[is]	existential	present
20	we	suffer *in spite of this*	mental: emot.	present

The poem essentially describes/defines, against which background its poetic voice 'know's and 'see's and, with the loved one, 'suffer's. In terms of Hasan's cline of dynamism (1989 [1985]: 45–46), I/we's Do-er roles are to its passive end, their exclusively mental activities failing to impact on anyone or anything. The tense of the poem is invariably the simple present, although, as discussed above, the incomplete clauses, completed here for the purpose of identifying process types, construe a sense of timelessness – an eternal, natural, present, in recognition of which I have inserted a break after clause 4 in the Table.

With reference to evaluation in the poem, and without mapping the swing between the mostly evident variably +ve and -ve appreciation of that love enacted through its symbols (e.g. the 'twilight' and 'river' versus the 'little lights and flickers and interruptions,/Troubles, anxieties and pains'), I would reflect briefly on the engagement mechanisms at work in the poem (White 2003, Martin and White 2005). The Speaker's complete clauses are largely monoglossic: unarguable, bare assertions of what *is*. However, as we have seen, the confidence ostensibly communicated is vulnerable to an extreme. The foregrounded parallel interrogatives, 'What else? ... What more?' are presumably not instantiated with a view to actively Entertaining dialogic alternatives, or better, additions, to the bliss/completeness being thematically articulated. But, as we've seen, though they would act to conjure up perfection, the central tension of the poem is never happily dissolved/resolved and the asserted 'perfect enough' perfection is ultimately Countered: construed as not being enough. In short, paradoxically, 'strange'[ly], this 'perfect enough', 'despite' itself, gives way to 'suffer'[ing]: evaluated finally in a surge of invoked (afforded ideationally; Martin and White 2005: 62–68) -ve speaker affect: unhappiness/insecurity/dissatisfaction etc.

Provisionally then, on the basis of the PP analysis performed above, one might hypothesize the theme of the poem as being something like the very Truffaut-esque 'Love is both joy and torment'. The hypothesis is revisited at the close of section 3 below.

3.4 The Context of Creation of 'Bei Hennef'

As noted in Chapter 2, the context of creation of a literature text, for Hasan (1989 [1985]: 101–103), comprises the language, world view and artistic conventions of the socially-situated writer, each of these seen with reference to those of the time/place of writing. As also remarked, this needs to be investigated with a view to better identifying the literature text's theme.

It is always hard to tease out a writer's artistic conventions, language use and world view, since they are often very much intertwined; in the case of D.H. Lawrence, doing so is virtually inconceivable. Thus, what follows is necessarily undivided. 'Bei Hennef', as said above, is written in free, unrhymed and largely parallel form – as is Lawrence's poetry from this point in time on. Previously, he had experimented the technical strictures of the Georgian Poets but found Georgianism's embrace of traditional forms, especially their use of rhyme and metrical regularity, a way of writing increasingly at odds with his ever-more original way of thinking. The reasons for this emerge below, together with Lawrence's ideas on language use and of his very particular world view. But first, a caveat: it would be wrong to represent Lawrence's sayings and meanings cited below as a systematic, unwavering absolute; indeed, they partake of the same capriciousness and contradiction that imbued every aspect of his life and art. With this in mind, then, I proceed.

3.4.1 'The seething poetry of the incarnate Now'

The prevailing artistic and cultural movement of Lawrence's time was Modernism, and in particular, the German variant he came into contact with through his German wife, Frieda (i.e. Expressionism). How he 'fits' into the latter, in particular, is primarily in terms of his unwavering critical sense of the dislocation of the individual in the modern, industrial world. He saw wo(man) as being cut off from society, or better, he saw that society as no longer being fertile ground for the human, or capable of nurturing meaningful beliefs, values, roles (i.e. identities). He resolutely reacted against the rise of industrialism, which he perceived as causing the breakup of community and marked by new and ultimately sterile values of efficiency, productivity, profitability: by a utilitarian worship of the great bourgeois machine and the progress it promised. Yet here the fit ends.

Indeed, Lawrence has never been categorized as a 'Modernist' writer. As Ingram rightly observes, he is quite simply too *serious* about his art, and intrudes too much into it (1990: 16 ff.). He never 'plays' with technique, for the sake of technique alone, as many Modernists did. Language in Lawrence is manipulated, but never playfully, rather one might say, *prophetically*, spurred on, inspired, so to speak, by his impetus to get it right. Getting it right, however, meant writing and re-writing in terms of his Weltanschauung: what he dubbed his 'pseudo-philosophy' (1960 [1922]: 57), or 'two-fold way', about which there would be very much to say. In a word, this is what Lawrence posits as the intrinsically dual nature of both the individual and creation itself, call them the mental-spiritual and phallic consciousness, the Not-Self and Self, the mind and body, knowledge and feeling, light and dark, Lamb and Lion, etc.; his symbolic dyads are myriad (see appendix to Miller 2007). For Lawrence, both ways needed to be developed/perfected and neither was to be confused with the other. Ideally, each individual needed to be fulfilled in the opposite ways in him/herself, *before* searching out the 'other'. Otherwise, their coming together would be doomed to failure.

Lawrence construes the very act of writing as a key way of fulfilling himself: not just a way of saying/meaning, but a way of 'doing', of going forward, of giving utterance, of 'break[ing] through ... deliberately, *in knowledge*' (1960 [1920]: 178–179, *my emphasis*). But, as those who know his work well can testify, with time – as his fight against machine consciousness intensifies, along with his awareness of being defeated by it – he, slowly but irrevocably, abandons the move *forward* in knowledge, in mind, and the impetus toward transformation, toward attempting to put something of value in the place of the mechanistic modern order. This is replaced with the intensified urge for an elemental, 'natural' being, for an authentic ethos of life and living.

Lawrence ultimately comes down on the side of the past and the primitive: a primeval desire for an encounter with the cosmic, the symbolic, the ritualistic, the sacred: a yearning after *Mysterium tremendum et fascinans*, fear and awe in the face of the creative mystery (Otto 1958 [1917]: 53 ff.). Far from renouncing the urge to utterance, however, this move *backward* entails an uncanny shift toward straining to become the speaker of the unspeakable, as this primitive knowledge is a question of 'feeling, wordless, and utterly previous to words ... the primeval, honourable beasts of our being' (Lawrence 1974 [s.a.]: 759). And the rhetoric of celebration of such unutterable knowledge, in Lawrence, becomes more and more its imitation, or better, a kind of enactment, which is construed in very large part through parallelism.

Lawrence, in 'Hymns in a man's life' (1971 [1928]: 597), testifies to the powerful influence of 'the hymns which I learned as a child, and never forgot'. These hymns, or more precisely, their 'undimmed wonder' – a Lawrentian key word – stayed with him, he says, never ceasing to exert their deep and poignant sway.

> 'Sun of my soul, thou Saviour dear,/ It is not night if Thou be near.' ... it did not mean to me any Christian dogma or any salvation. Just the words, 'Sun of my soul, Thou Saviour dear' penetrated me with wonder and the mystery of twilight. (1971 [1928]: 599)

And note the enigmatic characterization of another key Lawrentian word, also a participant, indeed a non-human protagonist, in 'Bei Hennef': 'twilight'.

So it was his early religious training that first taught Lawrence to feel, in rhythms. And it was indeed his re-creation of such rhythms that caused the editor of his early Georgian poems, Edward Marsh, to react ambivalently. On one hand, he extolled Lawrence's 'imperfect' writing as having a 'great and rather strange power and beauty' (Hassall 1959: 193–194). At the same time, however, he strongly disapproved, along with most of Lawrence's Modernist contemporaries, of what he saw as his waywardness and scorn of technical formalities, judging the result different and strange, patently undisciplined, and therefore defective. Turning his back on his brief experience as Georgian poet and leaving Marsh behind, in 1913 Lawrence detailed for the latter his still embryonic ideas on his writing:

> I think I read my poetry more by length than by stress – [more] as a matter of movements in space than footsteps hitting the earth ... I think more of a bird with broad wings flying and lapsing through the air, than anything, when I think of metre ... It all depends on the *pause* – the natural pause, the natural *lingering* of the voice according to the feeling – it is the hidden *emotional* pattern that makes poetry, not the obvious form. (Lawrence in Zytaruk and Boulton 1981: 102–104, *original emphasis*)

Pace Lawrence, it is my contention that this emotional pattern is retrievable precisely *because* it has been made visible in the interweaving repetitive elements of grammatical patterning (i.e. precisely in the 'obvious form' of his poems). As Jakobson also had to say about the commensurable patterning of the poetic function, 'Only in poetry with its regular reiteration of equivalent units is the time of the speech flow experienced, as it is – to cite another semiotic pattern – with musical time' (1960: 358). In Lawrence's case, the fugue comes to mind.

In a typically Lawrentian two-fold manner, he developed a theory of two basic kinds of poetry. In his 'Poetry of the Present', he tells us that the first of these is traditional. This he calls 'The poetry of the beginning and the poetry of the end' (1994 [1919]:

181–186), explaining that it is not involved with enacting change, but only with looking calmly at what has been and what is to come. Such poetry for him is finished, whole, 'complete and consummate'. The second kind is the 'poetry of that which is at hand: the immediate present'. Such poetry is not meant to be perfect, consummate or finished: 'The strands are all flying, quivering, intermingling into the web.' And, though Lawrence appreciates the 'exquisite form: the perfect symmetry' (1994 [1919]: 182) of the former, by now it should be easy to identify which he thinks is best:

> The seething poetry of the incarnate Now is supreme, beyond even the everlasting gems of the before and after ... there must be the rapid momentaneous association of things which meet and pass, on the forever incalculable journey of creation: everything left with its own rapid, fluid relationship with the rest of things. (1994 [1919]: 183)

What Lawrence hypothesizes is a poetry that is as life and human beings, in his estimation, should be: nakedly alive, urgent and insurgent, unstable, unfixed, boldly shedding the old and donning the new, or vice-versa, as 'the logic of the soul' dictates (1961 [1915]: 36). All quite like what Hopkins called *haeccitas*, which was spoken of above. All a bit hazardous, and disquieting as well: the product of a 'demon' that Lawrence with time comes to know and respect and be less haunted by, or so he says (1994 [1928]: 849–852). But it was actually even earlier on, in 1915, that Lawrence had theorized the act of writing as a mysterious, almost metaphysical, process, something the writer, as the instrument of 'some greater inhuman will' (Clark 1969: 29), is neither completely in control of nor thoroughly apprehends. Moreover, 'It does not want to get anywhere. It just takes place' (1994 [1919]: 185). This kind of envisioned verse must clearly be 'free', bird-like. GP, I submit, is what gives it its wings.

And it is also a poetry with its roots firmly located in the mnemonic, incantatory powers of the oral tradition, as suggested above in speaking of GP. Indeed, the characteristics of oral-based thought, or the 'psychodynamics of orality', as outlined by Ong (1982: Chapter 2), read extraordinarily like a compendium of a psychodynamics of Lawrentian verse, generally speaking, but also of 'Bei Hennef'. Ong characterizes his 'psychodynamics of orality' as being:

- heavily rhythmic, with balanced patterns in repetitions or antitheses, alliterations and assonances etc.;
- additive, rather than subordinative (e.g. marked by an excessive use of biblical 'And');
- aggregative, rather than analytic (i.e. marked by crystallized clusters of often heavily modified, parallel terms, phrases and clauses, helping, according to Ong, to keep thought intact: 'As Lévi-Strauss has well put it ... "the savage [i.e. oral, DRM] mind totalizes"' [Ong, 1982: 39]);
- redundant, or 'copious'. Since the oral utterance vanishes as soon as it is uttered, repetition, exact or 'slightly modified', keeps speaker and hearer together, so that neither gets lost;
- conservative, or traditionalist, in the particular sense that much energy is invested in asserting, over and over again, the wisdom that has been learned only arduously, over time. Lawrence's own practice of reassertion is notorious;

- close to the human lifeworld: having no elaborate, written, analytical categories, oral culture must conceptualize and verbalize knowledge with close reference to the immediate and the familiar. For Lawrence, of course, this is a deliberate choice rather than a requirement;
- agonistically toned. As Ong puts it (1982: 44): '[Writing] separates the knower from the known ... orality situates knowledge within a context of struggle.' Lawrence says, 'It is the joy forever, the agony forever and above all, the fight forever' (1974 [1924]: 743);
- empathetic and participatory, rather than objectively distanced. Narrator, narrated and audience are made to fuse, and *communality* thus dominates, rather than either subjectivity or objectivity;
- situational rather than abstract. This quality links up to orality's closeness to the human lifeworld but also to Basil Bernstein's communalized role system (e.g. 1974 [1971]). His class-based 'restricted' and 'elaborated' coding orientations could indeed, Ong suggests (1982: 106) be relabelled, without undue distortion, 'oral-based' and 'text-based'.

So then, the proposal is that Lawrence's poetry can be seen to participate in these psychodynamics of orality, that a vital part of the foregrounding/de-automatization function in his poetry – but also, if less comprehensively/intensively, in his prose – is its painstaking process of authentication of the primacy of the oral, and that a strikingly oral-like GP/PP such as has been illustrated in the poem, 'Bei Hennef', is the foremost means of its making.

As seen in the case of Marsh above, Lawrence's style of writing is not to everyone's taste. That it tends to either bore or enthuse Lawrence's readers is certainly no secret and that it is, in fact, its hypnotic rhythmic quality that provokes such divergent reader subjectivities is equally well-known (cf. e.g. Balbert 1974). E.M. Forster very early on voiced a positive, minority, critical opinion, calling Lawrence 'the only living novelist in whom the song predominates, who has the rapt bardic quality' (1962 [1927]: 130). For the majority, however, that 'song' smacks strongly of self-indulgence. In his unpublished Foreword to *Women in Love*, Lawrence again explicitly describes his style, admitting its unpopularity and offering a justification of sorts for it, one that implicitly ties his 'form' to what might be seen as his artistic aim, in terms of content, or better, of representation:

> In point of style, fault is often found with the continual, slightly modified repetition. The only answer is that it is natural to the author; and that every natural crisis in emotion or passion or understanding comes from this pulsing, frictional to-and-fro, which works up to culmination. (1971 [1936]: 276)

As is presupposed in the above quote, it is this 'natural crisis', or 'culmination', that is Lawrence's concern, and perhaps only fully comprehensible in terms of Lawrence's two-fold way, which is fraught with combativeness, but also inconsistency. The means to this culmination, or as he often refers to it, 'consummation', is compulsive, propulsive, and at the same time also jarring, conflictual.

This brings us back to Hasan's observation that '[g]enerally speaking, the greater the distance between the context of creation and reception, the more inaccessible the meanings of the text become' (1989 [1985]: 102). And such distance need not be temporal. Culturally, the distance between many of Lawrence's readers, beginning with his contemporaries, and his *sui generis* world view, use of language and artistic conventions, made for a widespread lack of patience with his meanings and meaning-making practices and, ultimately, a lack of sympathy with them. Such reader responses are not, in the main, an issue with the pithy 'Bei Hennef', where the language, substantially of everyday speech, construes wordings/meanings most readers would find understandable and unobjectionable. The text at one level does not require those 'considerable disambiguating efforts' said at the start of this section to often be needed with Lawrence. And yet, the deepest meanings of 'Bei Hennef' are, I submit, illuminated by the considerations on context of creation offered above. These do not radically affect the theme provisionally formulated: 'Love is both joy and torment', but they do provide valuable context to the writer's idiosyncratic propensity for construing such a paradoxical message – 'It is the joy forever, the agony forever and above all, the fight forever' (1974 [1924]: 743) – as well as to its equally characteristic stylistic construal – by way of 'this pulsing, frictional to-and-fro'.

3.5 Coda

This chapter has further argued my case for the inclusion of GP in the systemic functional, and in particular Hasan's SSS, approach to verbal art, offering hopefully convincing substantiation for the proposition. I believe that analysis of PP in the poem above has credibly clarified which reiterated grammatical instantiations are operating, which patternings of meanings such choices are constructing and, ultimately, the higher order theme that these work together to articulate. All this has been illuminated, and validated, by inquiry into the context of creation of the text. Its context of reception has also been briefly commented, in terms of the divergent socially-located reader reactions that Lawrence's writing provokes. My hope is that this study might be usefully situated within the extensive long-term empirical research Matthiessen believes is needed before the special register of verbal art can be said to have been properly modelled (cf. Chapter 2, note 7).

In my research, I have repeatedly seen that, where there is consistent and motivated foregrounding, symbolically articulating a literature text's theme, GP/PP has an essential role in its construction. Hence, I propose its inclusion in Hasan's framework: as SSS+. My proposal, however, is actually no more than a modest one, since coupling Jakobson's insight with the tenets of SSS is, I contend, wholly unproblematic. SSS and GP/PP are not simply mutually illuminating perspectives on verbal art. Theoretically, and practically, GP/PP fits into the SSS framework; indeed, it is already there. After all, for Jakobson parallelism is the supreme empirical linguistic criterion of the poetic function (1960: 358) that, recall, focuses on the corresponding factor of the 'message' itself, the instantiated shape of its meanings. Between this proposition and Hasan's conviction that in verbal art 'language is not as clothing to the body; it is the body' (1989 [1985]: 91) there is indisputable affinity. Surely, it's time to recognize this.

The following chapter takes on the topic of pedagogical stylistics and does so from an SFL/SSS+ perspective. It also offers a case study of SSS+ education practices and attempts to monitor them.

Chapter 4

Educational Stylistics: SFL/SSS+ and Guiding to Language-in-Literature Literacy

4.1 Prelude

In Chapter 1, pedagogical stylistics was said to either deal with the potential of stylistics for teaching (the language of) literature or to develop the supporting role of stylistics in the teaching of language through literature. This branch of stylistics is characterized by a flourishing body of research (e.g. Burke et al. 2012; McIntyre 2011; Zyngier and Fialho 2016). The title to this chapter, however, uses the preferred SFL term for language in education: educational linguistics (as indicated in Matthiessen (2009: 38), who references Chapters 9–12 in Hasan et al. (2005) and Christie and Unsworth 2005, among others). Going back to the 1970s, Halliday (2003 [2001]: 274) pays tribute to how 'the work that was set in train by Michael Gregory at Glendon College in Toronto played a critical role in the evolution of an educational linguistics'. And to bring us fairly up to date, Mickan (2019: 537–560) provides a comprehensive overview of SFL research in education. Halliday and Hasan themselves published enough on the subject to have a full volume of their respective Collected Works dedicated to it: Halliday (2007), in which Part V is entitled 'Educational Linguistics', and Hasan (2011b).

This chapter focuses predominantly on the first of the aims indicated above – the teaching of the language in literature – with the tools of SFL/SSS+ and, regarding the practices recounted in the reported case study, with special reference to non-native English speakers (NNES). A more general focus in the chapter, however, is enabling students to better reflect on meaning-making in English, thus also improving their overall language awareness, and language acquisition. These purposes are not mutually exclusive (e.g. Byrnes 2009). The chapter is also concerned with monitoring and refining practices in teaching stylistics, as the case study also shows.

The term 'stylistics' continues to be used in what is considered its properly narrow sense: as the linguistic study of literary texts, or literary linguistics, and more especially systemic functional stylistics – the stylistics championed throughout this volume. It is also the stylistics that it has been my experience to teach over the years in the Department of Modern Languages, Literatures and Cultures (LILEC) of the University of Bologna, aiming to guide English as a Foreign Language (hereafter EFL) students to verbal art literacy in a Functional Grammar (henceforth FG)-based register perspective, specifically using Hasan's SSS framework, fine-tuned with Jakobson's GP/PP (SSS+).[1]

Throughout, the chapter has in mind the generalized criticism of what is seen as a too heavy reliance on intuition in teaching stylistics (notably Hall 2014; Fogal 2015). In particular, investigated are ways to defuse two significant sources of this peril: (1) an ingrained largely intuitive method of verbal art reading on the part of the students,[2] and (2) a merely intuitive manner of assessing the effectiveness of one's own pedagogic practices. The first failing is addressed immediately, and then continuously. What is known as pedagogical stylistics has been shown to improve students' linguistic sensitivity and awareness (e.g. Zyngier, Fialho and Rios 2007; cf. also Fogal 2015), and the role of SFL metalanguage in developing learners' critical capacities has been amply demonstrated, as Christie et al. (1991) observed and the discussion in Part I below amply reveals. In addition, a register perspective, highlighting the specialness of literature as a functional variety, has also been shown to facilitate the language-in-literature literacy process (cf. Miller and Luporini 2018b, 2020). Such a perspective steers the case study offered. The second intuitive shortcoming is addressed by the gathering and scrutinizing of empirical quantitative and qualitative evidence of students' perceptions of pedagogical practices (cf. Fogal 2015), also recounted in the case study.

The endeavour to guide EFL students to language-in-literature literacy beyond their current (commonly 'literary') competence involves many – some quite thorny – issues, the adequate treatment of which cannot be my mission. Thus, although certain of these problems emerge in the course of the chapter, not treated, except in passing, is the vital question, for instance, of teacher training and professional development, including language study for educators who need precise and relevant knowledge about how language works in their specific subject areas. Neither do the cardinal literacy theories of Bernstein and Vygotsky receive the attention they merit. However, explicit and 'visible' pedagogy (Bernstein 1990), as well as the teacher-student interactional learning space required to help the learner with what s/he cannot do alone – Vygotsky's 'zone of proximal development' (1978), are wholly, albeit tacitly, espoused. SFL has had much to say about their theories (see, e.g. various chapters in Christie 1999). Other gaps, for which I alone am responsible, will undoubtedly be observed.

In sum then, the chapter begins with Part I, where in section 4.2 briefly discussed are teacher take-up of SFL concepts, metalanguage and pedagogy, whether applied to the teaching of verbal art, or not. In Chapter 2, Hasan's SSS model was endorsed for various reasons, first among which was its being rooted in Hallidayan grammar and its study, grammatics; here those grammatics receive further attention. Subsequently, in 4.3, the chapter addresses Hasan's ways of thinking about her own 'timeless journey' in the company of verbal art (2011a), her ideas concerning engaging with literature (1989 [1985], 2007), and her theory of reflection literacy (2011c [1996]). It only then moves on, in section 4.4, to selectively surveying verbal art teaching in an SFL perspective. Most of the studies cited are based on Hallidayan stylistics; others are grounded more specifically in Hasan's SSS framework. This leads, in Part II's section 4.5, to a recount of the personal case study mentioned above, also involving the longitudinal monitoring of pedagogic practices and some lateral conjectures.

Part I

4.2 A 'Good Enough' Grammatics

In a chapter of *The Handbook of Educational Linguistics* (2008), Hudson, a UK linguist who worked under Halliday from 1964 to 1971 and who is perceived as forging ties between academic linguistics and the teaching of (and about) language in UK schools, notes that Halliday's SFL 'is strongly oriented towards education … enriched by important ideas such as textual coherence, genre and register variation, and social meaning' (2008: 63).

Of course Hudson doesn't teach systemicists anything new with his observation, but this circumscribed tribute to SFL from, in the main, an 'outsider' is indicative of a growing, if still often grudging, recognition of what SFL can gift the field of language education. Another instance, mainly reporting the adoption of Hallidayan theory by language teaching scholars, is Larsen-Freeman (2009). Still, most 'outsiders' are disinclined to acknowledge the effectiveness of Systemic Functional Grammar (hereafter SFG) as a powerful tool for understanding how language works to make meaning tout court, or to allow that SFG meaning-oriented metalanguage provides a rich and effective resource for both teachers and students for probing how grammar functions in texts.

The need for a metalanguage in teaching language awareness of both L1 and L2 has been debated for years (cf. Hawkins 1999), with metalanguage being downplayed as a legitimate component of pedagogical practices by those loath to underwrite the reasonable if-then statement: 'If teachers and students alike are to understand how language works to make meaning, then it follows that we need to develop a meta-language, a language for talking about language' (Dare 2010: 18).[3]

Indeed, the specific metalanguage of SFL has often been accused of unnecessarily muddying the waters. Gebhard et al. (2013: 108) note how 'critics argue that SFL metalanguage is jargon that is "too complex" to be "pedagogically relevant" (Bourke 2005: 93–94)'. They also remark on the unsurprising nature of the critique 'given the degree to which SFL is indeed a complex theory that places new demands on teachers and teacher educators'.

And they make a good point, one we've already had occasion to remark with reference to the perceived demands of Hasan's SSS. Moreover, as Munday (2016 [2001]: 159) observes, 'the basis of the Hallidayan model has been famously attacked by Stanley Fish (1981: 59–64) for being over-complicated in its categorization of grammar and for its apparently inflexible one-to-one matching of structure and meaning'. Munday also intriguingly infers that the ever-swelling mainstream stylistic toolkit has come about at least partly in response to such attitudes (cf. Chapter 1's reflections on the toolkit). But of course complex theories are typically required to characterize complex phenomena that serve complex purposes. On such purposes, it suffices to reflect on Halliday's famous assertion: 'The lexicogrammar of every natural language is (among other things) a theory of human experience, a resource whereby experience is transformed into meaning' (1998: 1). And reflection should extend to Christie's equally weighty reminder that to study language is to explore 'some of the most important and pervasive of the processes by which human beings build their world' (1989 [1985]: vii). In addition, 'demands' typically arise from concerns with not easily achievable systematicity and objectivity, which can only lead to better pedagogic practices. But demands are difficult, and difficulty is decidedly not stylish.

But the bond between language theory and language teaching, together with the rigorous qualities that a pedagogical language theory must have, were clearly defined nearly sixty years ago by Halliday et al. (1964), and without mentioning SFL, SFG or even the term 'metalanguage':

> Provided the theory is valid, comprehensive and consistently applied, *but not otherwise*, we can make statements about the grammar of a language which apply to vast numbers of different speech events, and are therefore of great value to the learner of the language. (1964: 31, *original emphasis*) ... This is the main contribution that the linguistic sciences can make to the teaching of languages: to provide good descriptions. Any description of a language implies linguistics; it implies, that is, a definite attitude to language, a definite stand on how language works and how it is to be accounted for ... The best suited linguistics is the body of accurate descriptive methods based on recent research into the form and substance of language. (1964: 166–167)

Endorsements of SFG metalanguage among systemicists in more recent times are myriad. In another chapter in the same *Handbook of Educational Linguistics* in which Hudson concedes SFL's 'important ideas', Macken-Horarik and Adoniou, as 'insiders', state that they 'aim to show how the metalanguage generated by genre and register theory can be applied to texts and linked to the ways of knowing (epistemologies) powerful in school English' (2008: 369). In the same year (2008), and then again together with her customary co-authors, Love and Unsworth in 2011, Macken-Horarik elaborates on the theme in papers that the title of this section pays tribute to: a 'good enough' grammatics. And although most readers will know what this 'grammatics' is, its link to the explicit teaching of language awareness should be plainly pointed up.

Macken-Horarick et al. (2015: 146) note that 'Halliday's separation of "grammatics" (as theory) from grammar (as practice) underscores the importance of intellectual inquiry into the study of grammar. From this perspective, grammatics provides "intellectual tools for reflecting systematically on language" (Williams 2004: 263)'. But it is worth citing the authors on this point at greater length:

> If grammar is the resource we use whenever we produce (or understand) the wordings of a language, grammatics is the theory we draw on as we reflect on this. In his seminal paper on grammatics, Halliday proposes 'the simple proportion grammatics: grammar :: linguistics: language' (Halliday 2002, p. 386 [in references, 2002 [1996], DRM]). He gives grammar a privileged role in the study of language, arguing that it is 'the part of language where the work is done. Language is powered by grammatical energy, so to speak' (Halliday, 2002, p. 387). The key point for us is that a grammatics is a grammatically informed metalanguage for reflecting on grammar. If it is a well-theorized metalanguage, we can use it to shed light not just on wordings, but on the texts in which these occur (Love, Sandiford, Macken-Horarik and Unsworth, 2014). In fact, if the metalanguage is oriented to meaning, we use it to shed light on visual and multimodal texts too (Macken-Horarik and Unsworth, 2014; Unsworth and Macken-Horarik, 2015). In our project, we stressed the intellectual potential of a functional grammatics in school subject English, arguing that it contributed

powerfully to creation of a 'dynamic and evolving body of knowledge about language' (Commonwealth of Australia, 2009, p.1). (Macken-Horarik et al. 2015: 146)

Thus a grammatically informed, 'well-theorized' metalanguage prompting systematic reflection on meaning-making, such as that of SFG, is seen as being fundamental for analysing texts, including visual and multimodal ones, and in 'school subject English' in general. But as Macken-Horarick et al. (2018: 277) note, Halliday (2002 [1996]: 416) also speaks of the broader and more powerful potential of his notion:

> I have found it useful to have 'grammatics' available as a term for a specific view of grammatical theory, whereby it is not just a theory about grammar but also a way of *using grammar to think with*. (*original emphasis*)

Nonetheless, as Schleppegrell (2013: 156) rightly observes, there is an appropriate way to 'use' metalanguage and a decidedly less appropriate way, citing Berry (2010) on the distinction between metalanguage conceived as *thing* (terminology) versus metalanguage seen as *process* (talk about language). Their own focus 'is not on teaching metalanguage terminology, but on using meaning-focused metalanguage to help students participate in grade level tasks and make effective discursive choices'. In short, simply making students memorize linguistic terminology in and of itself is not supportive of essential learning objectives. Schleppegrell adds that 'Learning to use new metalanguage is a skill in itself that needs to be taught', but stresses that, to be meaningful, such learning 'needs to be situated in instructional contexts where it resonates with and helps support content goals' (2013: 158). This brings us to the usefulness of a metalanguage in teaching specialized disciplinary literacy – or, 'linguistic systems relevant to the ways different school subjects foreground particular meanings through their discursive practices and favoured genres' (definition from Schleppegrell 2020 [2018]: 5, online version).

Dare ends his paper by asserting that his long experience has taught him 'that providing both teachers and their students in turn with a rich metalanguage is the most powerful way we have of building our students' capacities to make meanings *across an ever expanding range of contexts*' (2010: 24, *my emphasis*). Moreover, copious rigorous research demonstrates the benefits of FG-based metalanguage for guiding L2 English students' literacy development regarding various functional varieties of text. Pervading all register typologies dealt with in such work is a concern with a deeper understanding of specialized disciplinary knowledge but, even more significantly, with how it is that language creates such knowledge. Thus, Gebhard et al. (2013: 108) observe that SFL metalanguage has been shown to support L2 students' academic literacy development across content areas and, further, that the findings of the many studies they cite 'suggest that the use of SFL metalanguage in designing curriculum and instruction supports ESL teachers in developing a deeper understanding of both disciplinary knowledge and how language constructs this knowledge'. They observe that a review of these studies is beyond the scope of their paper.

A comprehensive review of their cited studies and of much additional research that could be referenced is also beyond the scope of this chapter. And yet, I would at least mention some relevant works that have come to my notice. Focusing on disciplinary literacy, Schulze (2016: 8) makes the important point that integrating SFL into pre-service teachers' training may enhance their knowledge of language but that on its own does not guarantee translating that knowledge into effectual enough instructional practice. Then, Harman (2017) is an excellent overview of a volume dedicated to the teaching of critical literacy in an SFL perspective. Further, a pioneering volume by Harman and Burke (2020) focuses on critical literacy and schooling in an SFL perspective but, inventively, concentrates attention on multilingual youth learning and civic engagement. Their research aim is to dynamically bring together students with teachers, but also with community activists, to foster extramural collaborative efforts supporting participatory multimodal agency and action.

Finally, one very recent study brings together the strands discussed above but also forcefully argues a 'whole school approach' to these issues. Forey (2020: 1–17) reports on the experience of such collective and collaborative action in one secondary school in the UK, a project in which SFL metalanguage is harnessed for explicitly teaching 'language for curriculum learning' (LCL) across disciplines. The findings from the year-long study are said to support the use of SFL metalanguage for both teachers' and students' understandings of disciplinary literacy. The paper maintains that disciplinary literacy poses challenges for all learners, whatever their sociolinguistic background.[4] But, precisely because of such challenges, the proposal is for all teachers in all disciplines to talk about language and meaning in their classrooms. Many are the scholars cited on this point, including Macken-Horarik et al. (2018) and Schleppegrell (2013, 2020 [2018]). However, it is noted how the importance, and know-how, of teaching disciplinary literacy is often sadly absent from teacher education programmes. Very much in line with many of the studies discussed above, data from the project suggests that the use of SFL metalanguage allows students 'to be more aware of the relationship between knowledge, language and how the choice of language makes meaning' (Forey 2020: 15).

Before zooming in on the teaching of language awareness in our 'special' discipline, verbal art, be it an approach based on Hallidayan stylistics or more specifically on Hasan's framework, it seems fitting to firstly discuss just what Hasan's own pedagogic tradition entails.

4.3 Hasan's Engagement with Verbal Art and Literacy

In this section, I enlist the work of Lukin (2018) and Williams (2016) to a great extent. And, as is only right and just, we all let Hasan speak a great deal for herself.

4.3.1 Hasan's 'Timeless Journey' Toward Language-in-Literature Literacy

Hasan once made a sweeping claim: first in 1975, then compellingly reiterated thirty-six years later:

> of all the applications of linguistics, *that to the study of literature is potentially the most challenging and most fruitful* (Hasan 1975): if truth be told, the real reason for my claim is that in my experience research on verbal art lays a foundation of respect for what is most central

to the humanities and the social sciences, i.e. for the far-reaching effects of language and culture on the formation of human history. (Hasan 2011a: xix, *my emphasis*)

Thus she declares and justifies her partiality for researching it, but also, elsewhere in the same essay, her appetite for teaching it. She recounts wrestling, from the early 1960s on, with the challenges of teaching English to NNES but especially with 'how to conceptualize the "teaching of literature" at the university level so as to enable the students to produce *their own reasoned analysis of a literary work*' (Hasan 2011a: xv, *my emphasis*).[5] Subsequently, this enabling and 'liberating' pedagogic aim is renewed and refined in her stimulating call for a *reflection literacy* (Hasan 2011b [1996c]): 199), more on which below. For Hasan, these questions were of the highest importance, 'socially, morally and pedagogically' (Hasan 2011a: xv, cf. Lukin 2018: 7).

And it was with these issues foremost in mind that she soon began to devise the framework of what she would call SSS – designed, that is, to be enabling. Indeed, it was here in her reflections on her career, that she began to speak of a 'social-semiotic stylistics'. More importantly, she reflects here on what the term means. As Lukin (2018: 14) observes:

> Hasan argues that verbal art relies on 'two indispensable matrices as its sources of energy ... the powerful semiotic system of language and the intricately woven fabric of the semiotically shaped culture' (Hasan, 2011a, p. xvii). These two 'engines of power' work together in the instantiation of a piece of verbal art; their interaction is not only defining of the essence of this form of artistic activity, but also 'throws light on both its production and its reception' (Hasan, 2011a, p. xvii). The socio-semiotically shaped culture provides the terrain for the germination of the 'poet's divine madness'. (Hasan 2011a: xvii)

As I've already noted, however, Hasan's 'social-semiotic stylistics' subsequently evolved into 'Systemic Socio-Semantic Stylistics' (see note 4, Chapter 1). Her rationale for the change (personal communication, 31 December 2014) was to elude the term 'semiotic', about which she was at that time feeling dissatisfied:

> I feel the word Semiotic and its derivatives have become a 'catch-all' term; anything that smells of meaning becomes semiotic ... But in so far as my research is concerned, I do not think that anything even remotely resembling the systemic nature of language can be found. Particularly when it comes to literature there is typically only the use of the linguistic system: I have been using the term semantics to refer to meanings made by the system of language. So you see why I would prefer to call the kind of 'stylistics' I do Social Semantic Stylistics. The semantic is a system functional one, not any other.

On 1 January 2015, she added the 'systemic' to the label for her stylistics.

Before saying more on Hasan's 'reflection literacy', her precepts on how best to engage with literature should be briefly elaborated on.

4.3.2 Engaging with Literature

So then, we've seen how Hasan's pedagogic aim is an enabling one. But more needs to be said, as 'to enable the students to produce their own reasoned analysis of a literary work' is a thorny task. Firstly, it means the students must get beyond the personal. As noted in Chapter 2, Hasan makes 'a distinction between reading for private purposes and reading as a stage in the study of literature' (1989 [1985]: 103) She insists that 'the private must be made public; the internalised must be overtly externalisable – it should be possible to talk coherently about the bases of one's preference and evaluation' (1989 [1985]: 27). In short, students must go beyond their subjective responses and engage with the linguistic mechanisms of the text (cf. Lukin 2008: 103).

Lukin dedicates a section of her chapter (2018: 21–22) to the thoughts on this subject that Hasan devoted much of her last published paper on verbal art to: her chapter in Miller and Turci (2007), which, as Lukin accurately points out, 'made this problem visible even in its title: "Private pleasure, public discourse: reflections on engaging with literature"'. But as Lukin also rightly emphasizes (2018: 21), 'Hasan was over and over drawn to comment on what it meant to give a public appraisal of a work of literature'. Indeed, she'd amply dealt with the question more or less explicitly for years before this, most particularly, and unequivocally, in 1989 [1985]. There she also uses the terms 'appreciation' versus 'appraisal' for the first time (1989 [1985]: 26–28) to denote this distinction between private and public engagement with literature, between, that is, 'a question of receiving with pleasure, of understanding and enjoying the meanings of the text' (appreciation) and 'a question of being able to state clearly the nature of one's response, and to examine explicitly the bases for it' (appraisal).

But is Hasan speaking of making explicit an 'individual' response to the literature text? Recall, as said above, that she felt 'students must go *beyond* their subjective responses'. And if 'subjective' is not synonymous with 'individual', what does it mean? What does Hasan mean by it? As also noted in Chapter 2, for Hasan, the individual reader is always to be seen as being socially-situated; thus even one's personal or private responses to literature are fundamentally learned social ones. As she puts it:

> although the actual act of experiencing is private, our judgments about those experiences and the significance we assign to them are, at their very source, socially nuanced. Our value systems are, thus, essentially social artifacts. The principles underlying the evaluation of literature, as of other text types/instances, could not be an exception to this generalization. (Hasan 2007: 18)

But then, if the 'individual' is but a social agent, what is it in Hasan's view that makes a response indefensibly subjective? 'What makes a response "subjective", she argues, is not its apparent individuality, but that it has no analytical framework' (Lukin 2018: 16). The relevant quotation from Hasan cited by Lukin is the following:

> What makes a judgement subjective is not that it is 'given' by nature, or that it is the manifestation of a mythical 'authentic self' not contaminated by the social: rather, the subjectivity of judgement lies in its not having been subjected to careful analysis – perhaps because there does not exist an argued theoretical framework, or because in certain non-specialist contexts we leave many things unanalysed, allowing their bases to remain unarticulated. (Hasan 2007: 18)

Hasan's ensuing line incisively underlines the point: 'Whatever the case, judgments will remain subjective so long as they remain unanalysed' (Hasan 2007: 18). And by 'unanalysed', she means not objectivized, not systematically probed with the tools of a theory-based linguistics: 'without linguistics, the study of literature must remain a series of personal preferences, no matter how much the posture of objectivity is adopted' (Hasan 1989 [1985]: 104). She would of course agree with Halliday on the prerequisites of the theory informing analysis: its validity, comprehensiveness and consistent application (1964: 166, cited above). As noted elsewhere, she too is legitimately demanding on this point.

Hasan also links this need for an explicit, public engagement with literature to pedagogy. If the academic discipline is to have any sense, and dignity, rather than being aimed at the imitation, or reproduction, of the teacher's, or the authoritative literature critic's, reactions to and extrinsic evaluations of literature, as it too commonly is, it should be about empowering the student to read literature as a phenomenon of '*languaging in a particular way*' (cf. 2007: 16, *original emphasis*). In her words:

> The author can only be read with the socio-semiotic capabilities the reader is able to bring to the task. The reader has to be able to 'speak the author's language' in more than one sense of the expression. Hence, my insistence that engaging with verbal art as an academic field ought to be about creating and enhancing this capability, not about inculcating the learners into the opinions of the acknowledged masters. (2007: 26)

For Hasan, 'The principle underlying such proselytizing is "doxic", not analytic' (2007: 19). And she further elaborates:

> Obviously such teaching is far from enabling; in fact, it is primarily reproductive. While pedagogy of any kind, official or local, continues to have a reproductive bias, and while reproduction appears to be an important and unavoidable part of any pedagogy, very little reflection is needed to realize that a *reproductive and doxic intuitive* approach is a recipe for fundamentalist fervour. (2007: 19–20, *original emphasis*, partially cited in Lukin 2018: 21)

But these potent evaluations bring us to Hasan's notion of 'reflection literacy', where they are elaborated on and further developed.

4.3.3 Reflection Literacy

To introduce this concept of Hasan's, I could do no better than to appropriate Bowcher's estimation of its special significance for verbal art literacy. Affirming the power of Hasan's analytical framework for demonstrating 'that language patterning and symbolic articulation underlie the artistry of verbal art', Bowcher stresses that 'it is in her work on *literacy* pedagogies that the key to teaching the artistry of verbal art may lie' (2018: 296, *original emphasis*). This is, indeed, the essential rationale for this section.

I also commandeer Lukin's sound synopsis of what reflection literacy for Hasan consists in:

> One of the many offshoots of this early thinking on the problem of teaching about literature was Hasan's work on education (Hasan, 2011b), and specifically literacy education. A

key paper, not widely read in educational linguistics as far as I am aware, describes various literacy pedagogies as 'recognition literacy' (concerned with letter sound correspondence [for instance, DRM])[6] or as 'action literacy' (developing pupils' discursive abilities in uncritically reproducing the registers of education). Hasan does not reject either of these forms of literacy pedagogy, though she is clear on their limitations. What she advocates in this paper is 'reflection literacy', because 'the endpoint of education has to be the production of new knowledge' (Hasan, 2011c: 193 [in references, 2011c [1996], DRM]). Only reflection literacy 'frees the reader from unquestioningly following the opinions of "authorities"' (Hasan, 2007: 34); when done successfully 'it should ideally produce in the pupils a disposition to distrust doxic knowledge. i.e. knowledge whose sole authority is the authority of someone in authority' (Hasan, 2011c: 198). (Lukin 2018: 12)

I now elaborate on her points. As Williams (2016) notes, within these three types of literacy there are also sub-types with distinctions among them and these need to be taken into account in evaluating the kind of pedagogic outcomes they ultimately lead to. As he observes (2016: 334), in Hasan's work, 'recognition', 'action' and 'reflection' literacy are arrayed in hierarchies. Firstly, one of value: reflection literacy has the topmost education qualities, but action literacy is decidedly preferable educationally to recognition literacy. The second hierarchy is of knowledge and skill, reflection literacy presupposing the outcomes of the knowledge and skills developed in action and recognition literacy curricula, but surpassing these.

Williams is also careful to point out that using SFL descriptions to merely teach students to pigeonhole constituents into, say, participants, processes and circumstances – akin to Berry (2010)'s metalanguage conceived of as *thing* rather than *process*, above – is merely to implement 'recognition' literacy (2016: 335). 'Action' literacy, much more focused on meaning, is seen as being practised by pedagogical sub-types, again with differences in their approaches. One of these is 'genre-based pedagogy', which, as Williams recounts (2016: 337), began in the 1980s with research carried out by Martin, Rothery, Christie and others. Their studies showed how the expectations for writing development in Australia's primary schools were such that only children from homes in which the privileged ways of meaning of the schools were accessible were likely to succeed – in line with Bernstein's own findings (1990), but in contrast, for instance, to Forey (2020)'s take on disciplinary literacy challenging all learners indistinctly, seen above. As a result, these researchers worked toward students being able to reproduce the text types that the schools privilege, and did this through explicit instruction in valued genres. The aim was/is from one point of view admirable, but it is nonetheless problematized by Hasan, Williams and others, notably Luke (1996), as essentially reproductive. The mainstay of Hasan's proposal is that education should aim to do more, and for all. The supreme outcome is, as Williams puts it, 'the linguistic ability to participate eventually in the production of knowledge through critical and imaginative reflection on language in use' (Williams 2016: 337–338).

In short then, reflection literacy would offer students the means to participate in the production of valued forms of knowledge, rather than just encourage their uncritical reproduction. 'Beyond' is a key word, as already amply seen. This ambitious goal clearly means going beyond inculcating students with prescriptive grammar rules (as recognition literacy would do), but even beyond enabling students to successfully produce and consume registers that are privileged in school evaluation (which is action literacy's – and genre-based pedagogy's – aim). It must be recognized that teaching the valued norms of privileged registers is to a large extent empowering, and also that it is, in itself, not an easy thing to do. But mightn't such an approach presume a perhaps overly complacent view of what truly successful school outcomes consist in? As Hasan puts it, 'The implied underlying message of this pedagogy is conformism, a respect for convention that is not required to be tempered by analytical reflection' (2011c [1996]: 193). Reflection literacy's message is that educators need to develop more aspiring goals for literacy education, ones that enable students to recognize and actively and systematically respond to texts that typically contribute to shaping society in ways that are, however, not typically unbiased or even-handed. And one way to do this is by furnishing students with tools for understanding how language use is not a minor or 'neutral' player in the social fields of daily life and also – why not? – encouraging them to investigate how such awareness can best be put to worthwhile social use.

But the 'project' is not an easily do-able one, as Hasan was well aware. Her blue-sky thinking is firmly rooted in grim reality:

> the brutal fact about the human social condition is that to live in a society is to collude to maintain at least some of the ways of being, doing and saying that are prevalent in that society; no one has yet shown us that to live in a society can mean anything else, and the natural line of literacy development is largely a process of reproduction. (Hasan 2011c [1996]: 192; also quoted in Williams 2016: 338)

So, on one hand, this 'doxic' quality of verbal art teaching is seen to homogenize the learner, and worse: it 'represents a negation of the heterogeneity of human culture' (Hasan 1996a: 41). But on the other hand, she says it would appear inevitable. So then, how to go beyond mere reproduction? Basically, by doggedly persevering in the attempt to guide learners to in-depth knowledge about language as well as to its relation to knowledge production. The barriers against putting into practice such guidance may be sizeable, even systemic, but even so, Hasan would cheer us on:

> For knowledge to evolve, what we need is someone – anyone – to perceive the problem(s), to develop the implications; this implies a search for explanations, raising how-questions and why-questions, using existing knowledge only as a point of departure, not as the end of intellectual journey. Vygotsky (1978) would add that these abilities develop within society, and to this extent knowledge depends on a society which allows such mental activities. (as cited in Williams 2016: 339)

And of course the question naturally arises as to whether our societies are or will ever be at a sufficient state of readiness to fully tolerate, let alone foster, 'such mental activities'. In most cases, the answer is not likely to be overwhelmingly or unalloyedly heartening. And neither, to this reader, is Williams' observation that reflection literacy pedagogy is still at the stage of being only a proposal of what is possible (2016: 339), with no practitioners. And yet, surely that's not *quite* right. For instance, Williams himself describes Hasan's own experience of teaching in this perspective (2016: 354, note 3) and presents his own case example of reflection literacy education in his chapter. Achugar and Schleppegrell (2016) recount the authors' experience of teaching history in keeping with the precepts of reflection literacy, and Miller and Luporini (2018b and 2020) describe similarly inspired pedagogic practices in teaching the language in literature. In brief, practitioners may not yet be perfect, and outcomes may still be very uneven, but efforts are being made. And, as Hasan notes with specific reference to her SSS project:

> It would be foolish to give the impression that such a research has actually been exhaustively and successfully accomplished: a project of this kind requires not just fifty years by one scholar but more than fifty scholars devoting their working life to it. (2011a: xxiii)[7]

I'll come back to this daunting consideration again. But it's now time to spotlight the pedagogy of language-in-literature awareness with reference to our 'special' discipline, verbal art.

4.4 Systemicists and Verbal Art Pedagogy

Below is a brief but representative sample of systemicists who offer evidence of their experience – both theoretical and practical – of teaching the language in literature. Invariably entailed in their studies is a grammatically informed metalanguage prompting systematic reflection on meaning-making. Most are approaches to teaching verbal art based on Hallidayan SFL; others are grounded more specifically in Hasan's framework. Likewise, some could be said to be substantially reproductive of existing valued knowledge in their (conscious or unconscious) objectives, while others would aim at going 'beyond'.

4.4.1 Genre-based Stylistic Work

A self-described educational linguist, deeply involved in teacher training, Rothery has worked since its beginning within the 'Sydney School's large-scale, long-standing and still ongoing research into literacy and learning in terms of genre-based pedagogy, already presented – and problematized – above. Her aim is to identify the range of genres expected in school subject English/Language Arts and to develop the language resources needed by students to successfully learn and reproduce those genres. Narrative is one of the key genres she deals with (e.g. Rothery 1996). Naturally, this is also true of other of her colleagues' work, in particular of the group's leading light, Jim Martin. Analogously to Rothery, Martin too emphasizes how learning the notions that confer advanced literacy means learning the language needed to talk and write about those notions. In a paper analysing an instance of Junior Secondary narrative, he explores the 'successful'/'valued' ways in that students are expected to demonstrate their understanding of narrative texts (and to identify Hasanian 'theme') in their public examinations (2012 [1996]). Discussion ultimately pivots around how 'non-mainstream' student subjectivities pose obstacles to successful critical responses. Martin argues the consequent need to make mainstream subjectivities available to these students, in spite of a certain resistance born of fears concerning the risk of devaluing those minority subjectivities.[8] Extensive coverage of the tenets and praxis of genre-based pedagogy and language-based literacy up to the time of its writing can be found in Schleppegrell (2004). A more recent article by Gebhard et al. (2013) is also a valuable overview of the same. An interesting genre-based literacy paper specifically addressing the teaching of narrative to children is Rose (2016). Still, as Bowcher (2018: 296) perceptively observes: 'While genre pedagogy has gone a long way in developing an understanding of the differences between, say, a "report" and a "narrative", it does not adequately deal with the nature of verbal "artistry".'

In other words, it does not engage with Hasan's insistence on verbal art being, as observed in Chapter 2, 'language that is artistic and art that is linguistic' (personal communication, 15 April 2014). I now pass to a look at systemic functional educational stylistics studies that focus more closely on that two-fold nature of verbal art.

4.4.2 Systemic Functional Educational Stylistics Studies

As seen in Chapter 2, SFL-inspired verbal art analysis has been practised by many and for many years. But published work on its *teaching* is apparently far less frequent. Perhaps this is because the experiences themselves are more infrequent – willingly or unwillingly. And if against one's will, then this may be due to the fact, decried by Hasan (2011a: xix), that within their academic institutions, verbal art 'scholars find their work too typically treated as optional extra', additional to '"proper" teaching in linguistics'. The exceptions to this lack of such teaching are chiefly among those I dubbed the 'custodians' of Hasan's verbal art legacy in Chapter 2: Lukin, Butt, Webster, Miller and Luporini, and Matthiessen, but not only. As said in note 1, my own teaching experience was mainly a question of luck, needing but substantial doses of resolve to keep up. Another systemicist who gives evidence of the freedom to teach the language of literature, albeit interdisciplinarily, with corpus stylistics methods, is Bednarek (see, e.g. 2008), who I come back to in Chapter 5.

But now to speak of a singular volume: DeCoursey (2012a), and in particular remark a number of unquestionably SFL-based chapters in Part I, dedicated to the use of English literature in the Language Arts classroom within Asian Contexts. Several of these are Hasan-inspired educational stylistics studies.

First, and foremost, is the paper by Butt (2012), 'On being a literature teacher: A language based perspective'. That perspective is SFL and, in particular, Hasanian. In stating the aim of the paper, Butt asserts that '[t]here are challenges and opportunities, that are peculiar to the teaching of literature. These challenges – and the academic rewards – are what I wish to illustrate and reflect upon'. As DeCoursey (2012a: 5) remarks: 'The strength of this paper lies in its problematization of the question – what is literature and how do we know.' Moreover, it lays bare 'the intricacy and complexity involved in articulating the literary qualities even of brief literary works'.

Butt ends the 2018 version of this paper with an apposite Hasanian premise: 'Being better informed about the craft of verbal art may also clarify for us all – students and teachers together – the role of our collective imagination in assigning value to human experience' (cf. Bowcher 2018: 298).

DeCoursey's own paper (2012b) probes the use of literature in the classroom with APPRAISAL SYSTEMS for the purpose of developing intercultural sensitivity. Wiratno

(2012) aims to integrate teaching both the linguistics and the literary aspects of literature in the EFL classroom. Among the linguistic mechanisms investigated in an SFL perspective are transitivity, collocation and cohesive repetition, reference and text organization. Veloso (2012) speaks to the use of multimodal comic books in the English Language Teaching (ELT) classroom.[9] Applying current SFL multimodal theory, he demonstrates the potential this text type has for exploring – and critiquing – social issues and identity construction. Veloso's work too will come into Chapter 5's treatment of SF-MDA of verbal art.

A final paper I'd point up in DeCoursey's volume is by Lin – the same seen in Chapter 2 as the author of an admirable chapter on Functional Stylistics (2016). In this paper, Lin (2012) returns to a topic he'd explored in a 2010 paper, applying SFL to the study of literature in schools, now firmly locating his study within World Englishes and problematizing the value – and methods – of teaching literature in the Asian context. Thus, he advocates the inclusion of new literatures in the curriculum and greater attention to the exploration of self and social identity. He argues once again for a stylistic analysis based on SFL but also for the need to explore the artistic patterning of Hasanian theme in the literature text.

Lukin has been frequently cited in this and previous chapters. She is not only an aficionada of systemic functional stylistics and well-versed in its roots and developments (e.g. 2015, 2018), she has shown her analytical competence as well (e.g. Lukin and Webster 2005; Butt and Lukin 2009). In addition, she has also argued and illustrated how one of the undeniable advantages of Hasan's approach is that it allows students to go beyond their personal, subjective responses and to engage hands-on with the linguistic mechanisms of the text (Lukin 2003, 2008). She is also mentioned by Matthiessen (2013a: 23) as being among the Australian educational linguists whose work has exposed the deficiencies of the teaching of English literature in Australian primary and secondary schools. For these reasons, she is brought up here.

Butt's work on the whole, one instance of which is referred to just above (Butt 2012), has had particular resonance, as the following quote from Lukin and Webster (2005) attests:

> Butt also delivers on one of the early difficulties for systemically oriented stylistics. Reflecting on the early work in this field, Halliday noted the problem of how to deal with the role of interacting choices in different systems in 'shap[ing] the personality of a text' (1988: 31). Perhaps as a function of his claim that consistency of foregrounding in [Wallace, DRM] Steven's work is typically both intersystemic and intrasystemic (1983), Butt's work provides the most elaborated exempla in systemic functional work for the integration of features across systems and functions, within ranks and between structural and non-structural properties of text. (Lukin and Webster 2005: 426)[10]

This is also true of the analyses provided in his papers on teaching stylistics. But as already seen, he also links up to larger socio-cultural issues, very much in the Hasanian tradition. In his 1996 paper, Butt states:

> My main argument is that verbal art is the central problem-solving activity in the culture, that its function is to address the culture's deep difficulties through experiments in textual

organization or semantic design. Far from being isolated, privileged and totally affective – as prejudice sometimes presents them – literary traditions, in fact, show a broad concern for the community's deepest problems, particularly those concerns that continue unresolved or that need to be negotiated with each generation. (1996: 86)

Although 'the Classroom' figures in the title of Butt (1996), only minor illustration of how his notion of semantic design is applied in classroom activities is provided. Interestingly, however, Bowcher (2018: 297) picks up on a segment of the above quote from Butt to ingeniously reflect on the educational stylistics issue, as follows:

> Perhaps we need a reflection verbal art pedagogy (RVAP) that would involve teaching children to produce novel 'experiments in textual organization or semantic design' (Butt 1996: 86), and new ways of artistically addressing a society's 'deep difficulties' (Butt 1996: 86, cf. Hasan 2011 [1996]: 198). Important to RVAP would be children's exposure to and engagement in different forms of verbal art suited to different levels of educational advancement. Along with this would be an appropriately pitched means of leading children through to an understanding of the place of verbal art in society, the employment of an empowering model of language, and of instruction in the ways in which 'society's difficulties', including their own, can be artistically-linguistically articulated.

Many of the ingredients of Bowcher's 'recipe' for RVAP are indeed spoken to in Butt (1996), as they also are in Butt (2016), in which he revisits 'many of the dimensions of the thought and linguistic technique of Ruqaiya Hasan' (2016: 24), especially those regarding the study and teaching of verbal art. Among the myriad aspects of Hasan's thought, he showcases the by now familiar dual artistic-linguistic nature of verbal art and Hasan's oft-reiterated contention that 'if we are to claim a teacher's role with respect to literature and verbal art, we need to address the central activity: namely, "wherein lies the artistry?"' (2016: 50). Moreover, as Bowcher (2018: 298) notes,

> Butt relates how Hasan encouraged her students and colleagues to dispense with teaching literature 'through the hegemonies of taste' and 'to be methodical about semiotic and semantic differences: examine the cultural parameters and grammatical systems through which a work is interpreted, as well as those in which it may have been constructed' (Butt 2016: 50).

These are, of course, among the fundamental aspects of Hasan's reiterated positions regarding verbal art – on its teaching and its context of creation and reception – with which we are by now well-acquainted, but which Butt dependably discloses and staunchly upholds, as custodians are ever wont to do.

To close this section, I cite a final example of systemic functional educational stylistics. Similarly upholding the Hasanian tradition, Miller and Luporini (2018b) argue a multiple-strand thesis: namely, that any objective and replicable analysis of literature needs a linguistic approach; that Hasan's SFL-based SSS is arguably the best analytical framework for the task; that its value extends beyond verbal art literacy to benefits for EFL students' increased language awareness and even competence, and that, in the final analysis, SSS can be seen to be a thoroughly rewarding appliable linguistics indeed. An example of SSS+ pedagogic practice at the university level is now offered as illustration.

Part II

4.5 A Case Study, or Guiding Toward 'Special' Register Awareness in an Undergraduate EFL Curriculum in Italy

What follows is an example of educational stylistics in practice, aiming to guide undergraduate EFL students to verbal art literacy. This was done in an explicit 'special' register perspective, using Hasan's SSS framework, fine-tuned with Jakobson's GP/PP – all of which has been amply described in Chapters 2 and 3. The experience expounded is a shared one: performed by Miller and Luporini (cf. 2020), and inspired by the conviction that probing a literature text's consistent and motivated linguistic patternings and multiple contexts is instrumental to teaching the language in literature, and at the same time to both enhancing our students' cultural awareness and improving their already appreciable language skills. Recounted are our practices, but also our attempts at monitoring them, with the gathering and scrutinizing of empirical quantitative and qualitative evidence of students' perceptions of these.

4.5.1 Setting the Scene

This case example took place at the LILEC Department of the University of Bologna in Italy. The experience is part of the 'linguistics' component of our third-year undergraduate course, which teaching staff is responsible for. The dual nature of our undergraduate courses is reflected in their official denomination: English Language *and* Linguistics. The linguistic component is divided into circa thirty hours of lectures and about sixteen hours of guided interactive workshops. The students' practical skills are nurtured separately, within the 'language' component, by mother tongue certified EFL instructors, aiming at the C1 (advanced) of the *Common European Framework of Reference* (CEFR) level at the end of this third year.

Our stakeholders are students who are enrolled in one of the two undergraduate degree programmes currently available at the Department: *Foreign Languages and Literatures* and *Asian Languages, Markets, and Cultures*. Very much in line with the general trend of both degree programmes, the students are mostly female, and aged between 19 and 24. They are also almost exclusively NNESs: the vast majority reside in Italy (between 97% and 100% depending on the degree programme and the academic year). Still, they demonstrate a substantial competence in use of English. Their level, tested upon admission to the three-year degree course, is at least B1 CEFR level, but in most cases (approximately 69%) it is higher: between B2 (fully independent user) and C2 (proficient user). This allows English to be our sole medium of instruction.

This advanced communicative competence, however, clashes with a generalized negligible level of explicit language awareness, which the English teaching staff, in the early noughties, opted to contend with by designing an SFG-based curriculum, and which we believe has helped. The discussion on SFL/SFG metalanguage and grammatics above has amply clarified their essential empowering nature. Indeed, just as many of the scholars cited at the start of this chapter, we too were and are still convinced that meaning-making is central to instructed language development, to refining students' language awareness and analytical skills. We also believed/believe that internalizing how a language 'means' is an essential precondition for learning how to 'mean' in that language. In addition, the aim is to give our students the tools to become active producers – rather than just passive consumers – of knowledge, meaning that we would work toward a reflection literacy, or better, an RVAP, with all of the admirable objectives, but also thorny strictures, discussed above.

4.5.2 More on the Three-Year Curriculum: Materials and Methods

Our three-year undergraduate syllabus progressively explores the analytical usefulness of the FG model with the students. Attention is constantly paid to the notion of speaker choice: to the meaning potential of lexicogrammatical options in contextualized text. In the first year, focus is on the textual metafunction, the grammar of which students are generally familiar with (e.g. thematic and information structure); thus, what is for them a new, 'function-centric' perspective is more readily acquired. The second year is centred on the ideational and interpersonal metafunctions. When working with the TRANSITIV-ITY SYSTEM, we also introduce Hasan's notion of the cline of dynamism (1989 [1985]: 45–47), distinguishing between more 'active'/'dynamic' and more 'passive' participant roles. We then apply it to text analysis in a set of oral class activities, through which the students, in groups, begin to work 'hands-on' with different text types. Verbal art is introduced in the second year through short texts or text segments that are relatively straightforward stylistically, and/or may attract early Generation Zs. For instance, the cline of dynamism is used to explore characterization in select passages from *Dubliners* and the *Harry Potter* series and interpersonal meanings are investigated in particular in patterns of evaluation in extracts from Rhys's *Wide Sargasso Sea* (cf. Luporini 2019).

Finally, in the third year, this prior knowledge is theoretically refined, built on and truly 'animated' (i.e. put into practice as a set of analytical tools that are systematically applied to investigate registers, the focus of the course in this year). Adopting as course book Miller (2017a), on register theory and practice, knowledge and know-how acquired in the first and second years is now visibly scaffolded in explicitly SFL-informed registerial terms. Hasan's verbal art framework is explicitly introduced and applied only in this year, where workshop methods are rooted in the notion of verbal art as 'special' register – a register like no other.

Our case study focuses on one 2017 and one 2018 verbal art workshop, in which we guide our students to wield SSS, which we 'fine-tune' with PP, as discussed in Chapter 3. But there is also a very practical pedagogic reason for opting to do so: students find SSS plus Jakobson's PP (SSS+) a helpfully concrete and straightforward way into the notions of foregrounding/symbolic articulation, which can pose challenges. Perhaps this is because they are guided to see GP rhetorically highlighting meanings in other registers as well.

The text is always, firstly, viewed as an instrument, a window onto the semiotic system of language itself, of which it is a concrete instantiation (following Halliday 2002 [1982]: 130–132). Workshop analysis is 'from below', moving from text to semantics and context along the cline of stratification. This we deal with, firstly, in the second year, with the semiotic system of language alone, while here, in the third year, we bring in the semiotic system of verbal art, where foregrounded patterns symbolically articulating the theme are probed through the helpful lens of PP.

The step from the semiotic system of language to that of verbal art is initially daunting for students, but ever-more readily negotiated through recurrent application. Texts in this year are chosen to foster work on a range of grammatical resources for meaning-making and patterning, but time constraints dictate that analyses are largely of short poems and selective as to the meanings/wordings probed. These, however, are in no way circumscribed to the primarily experiential analysis of the twenty-first century poem in the workshop presented below. Assorted instances of PP, which are essential to articulating theme, are explored. These include: patterns of appraisal (for example, those enacting a sui generis positive judgement of solitude in Lawrence's twentieth-century 'Lonely, Lonesome, Loney – O!'); patterns of Mood and cohesion (for example, in Rossetti's nineteenth-century 'Remember'), and patterns of meter/rhyme (as in Blake's eighteenth-century 'Garden of Love'). PP in prose is also explored, for example in Dickens's novels, a rich source of the phenomenon. Spanning various genres and centuries, the students can also concretely appreciate the 'maximally applicable' nature of the SSS framework (Hasan 1989 [1985]: 90).

The sample SSS+ class activities illustrated below were prompted by the stylistics seminar given by Hasan and Miller at the LinC Summer School and Workshop 2010 in Cardiff (cf. Miller 2016a). They were first introduced in 2017, and repeated the following academic years, so that student feedback could be examined comparatively. The two-hour workshop was centred on a contemporary elegy by British poet, John Whitworth (1945–2019), 'Little' (2010).

4.5.3 The Poem: 'Little'

//[1] When Archie died //[2] the year was dying too.	**a**
//[3] Late loitering leaves were drifting to the ground,	**b**
//[4] A time when dying has a lot to do,	**a**
And does it with a dry, susurrant sound.	**b**
//[5] Some say //[6] when Archie died //[7] it was not much –	**c**
A boy who did not walk or talk. //[8] But he	**d**
Did love to smile and laugh and look and touch.	**c**
//[9] He did do that. //[10] He did it constantly.	**d**
//[11] So small, so weak, so fragile, //[12] yet << //[13] when death,	**e**
That most ingenious and practiced thief,	**f**
Unlocked the house //[14] and stooped //[15] and stopped the breath,>>	**e**
He left a strong sufficiency of grief.	**f**
//[16] Now is a winter and a summer since,	**g**
//[17] And now the days of dying are come again –	**h**
A year since Archie died, our Little Prince,	**g**
A year of rain and sun, and sun and rain.	**h**

4.5.4 Workshop Activities

After reading the text aloud, the participants were divided into groups of 4/5 students with a spokesperson nominated for each. They were asked to work collaboratively on a small set of different tasks, designed to guide them in analysing the poem, moving from the semiotic system of language to that of verbal art. The groups were given 10/15 minutes for each task, and their answers were given and discussed before proceeding. The first two tasks are reproduced in Figures 4.1 and 4.2 below.

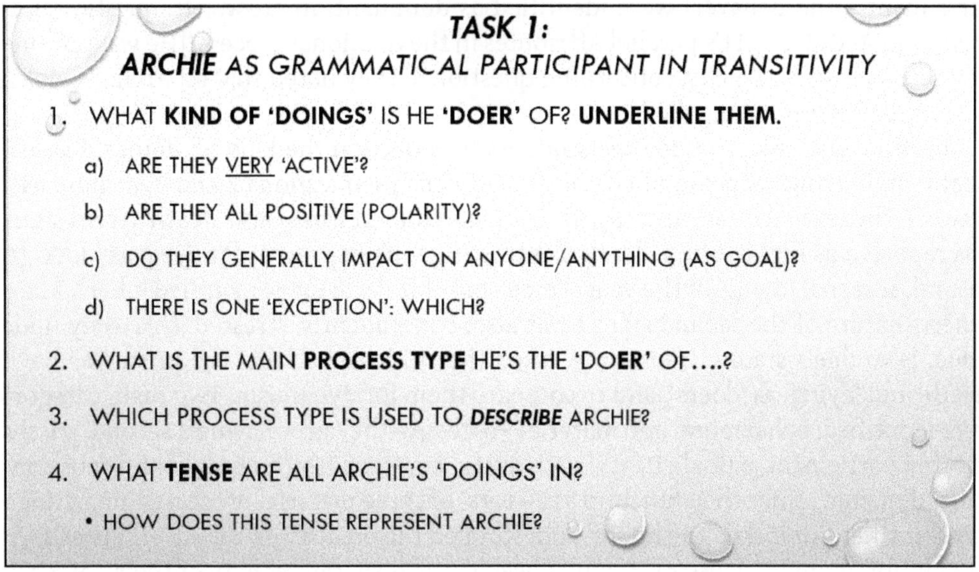

TASK 1:

ARCHIE AS GRAMMATICAL PARTICIPANT IN TRANSITIVITY

1. WHAT **KIND OF 'DOINGS'** IS HE **'DOER'** OF? **UNDERLINE THEM.**

   a) ARE THEY <u>VERY</u> 'ACTIVE'?

   b) ARE THEY ALL POSITIVE (POLARITY)?

   c) DO THEY GENERALLY IMPACT ON ANYONE/ANYTHING (AS GOAL)?

   d) THERE IS ONE 'EXCEPTION': WHICH?

2. WHAT IS THE MAIN **PROCESS TYPE** HE'S THE **'DOER'** OF….?

3. WHICH PROCESS TYPE IS USED TO *DESCRIBE* ARCHIE?

4. WHAT **TENSE** ARE ALL ARCHIE'S 'DOINGS' IN?

   • HOW DOES THIS TENSE REPRESENT ARCHIE?

Figure 4.1 SSS+ workshop: task 1

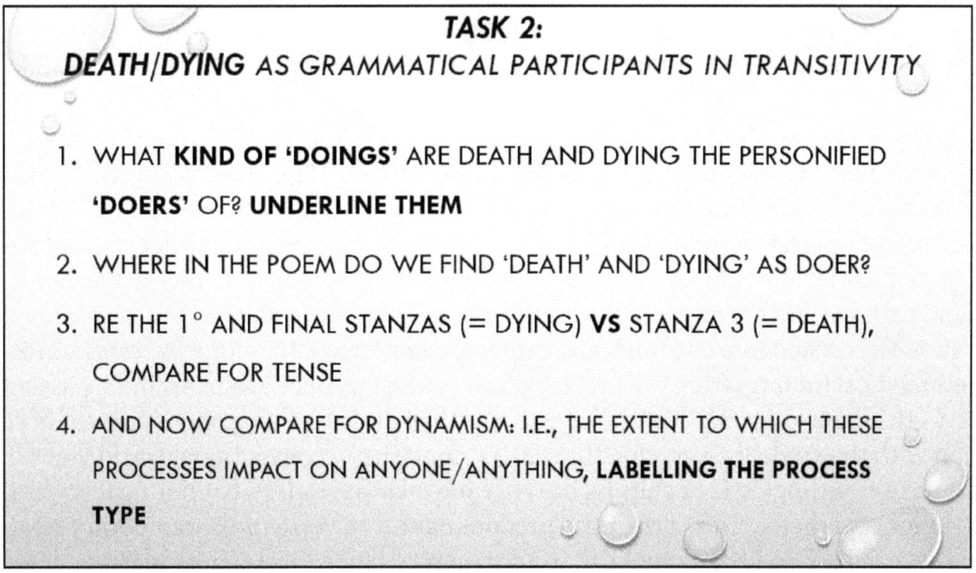

TASK 2:

DEATH/DYING AS GRAMMATICAL PARTICIPANTS IN TRANSITIVITY

1. WHAT **KIND OF 'DOINGS'** ARE DEATH AND DYING THE PERSONIFIED **'DOERS'** OF? **UNDERLINE THEM**

2. WHERE IN THE POEM DO WE FIND 'DEATH' AND 'DYING' AS DOER?

3. RE THE 1° AND FINAL STANZAS (= DYING) **VS** STANZA 3 (= DEATH), COMPARE FOR TENSE

4. AND NOW COMPARE FOR DYNAMISM: I.E., THE EXTENT TO WHICH THESE PROCESSES IMPACT ON ANYONE/ANYTHING, **LABELLING THE PROCESS TYPE**

Figure 4.2 SSS+ workshop: task 2

Regarding task 1's first question, in both years group spokespersons reported consensuses of opinion that: (a) overall, the transitivity patterns do not construe Archie as a very 'active' participant; (b) most, but not all, his 'doings' are positive, with the exception of 'did not walk or talk', clause 7, construing, it was suggested, either infirmity or, simply, infancy; (c) his 'doings' do not generally impact on anyone/anything – but, once again, (d) there is a notable exception: 'he left a strong sufficiency of grief' (clause 15), construing Archie's 'legacy'. As for question 2, behavioural processes (which we define as representing often involuntary forms of behaviour and also having a single participant – the Behaver) were identified as dominant. In answer to question 3, the groups quoted clause 11's parallel Attributes in the relational process '[He was] So small, so weak, so fragile'. Finally, concerning question 4, they noted that all Archie's 'doings' are in the past, his having died.

Question 1 in task 2 invited the students to reflect on the kind of 'doings' featuring 'death' and 'dying' as personified 'doers'. Concerning questions 2 and 3, a comparison between the textual location of 'dying' (first and final stanzas) and 'death' (third stanza) was reported as highlighting clearly contrasting tenses: present for *dying* as 'doer' (the natural, seasonal 'dying' of the year) versus past for *death* (as personified killer). The sui generis nature of the second stanza was also, consequently, stressed: this, they understood, is Archie's stanza. Question 4 asked the students to label the processes having 'death' and 'dying' as 'doers', and to compare them for dynamism. Two main categories were identified: behavioural and material Processes, the latter having a second, passive/affected participant, a Goal. 'Death' and 'dying' emerged from subsequent discussion as quite 'dynamic', since they function as 'Actors' of three material processes impacting on other entities ('unlocked the house' and 'stopped the breath' for 'death' – clauses 13/15; 'does it' for 'dying' – clause 4). Again, however, the disparate gravity of their doings was remarked. Subsequently, we talked over our full transitivity analysis with the students, having them summarize findings.

In the second part of the workshop, with tasks 3 and 4, we gradually steered the students toward identifying patterns functioning within the semiotic system of verbal art, focusing on instances of PP in the poem. These are reproduced in Figures 4.3 and 4.4 below.

Task 3 was dedicated to phoneme parallelism, in turn linked to sound symbolism – not at all an exact science, as the students were advised. That this task posed a certain amount of difficulty emerged from group reporting and discussion. Thus, we showed them select reiterated phonemes (/s/, /d/, and /l/) by text search, considering together their textual location and conceivable functions. In both years, it was suggested that sound patterns further stressed the 'death' permeating the poem.

Task 4 consisted in a conclusive, recapping comparison, this time in terms of PP, of the analytical findings from the first two tasks, stressing, once again, Archie's 'passivity' versus the more 'dynamic' 'death'/'dying'. We then discussed the poem's context of creation with the students, agreeing that 'Little' construes a conventional world view: one that creates no linguistic or cultural distance for them as readers, but noting it is written in rhyme and meter, rather than the predominant free verse of contemporary poetry. One actually offered the thought that its structure helped to keep its message understated. Finally, the students were asked to attempt a formulation of the poem's theme;

valid, text-based suggestions were then forthcoming: variations on 'grief brought about by a loved one's untimely death'. Several stressed the pathos of that loved one's being a child. In the main, student class work and exams show that PP analysis facilitates theme hypotheses, though frequently these are not adequately generalized.

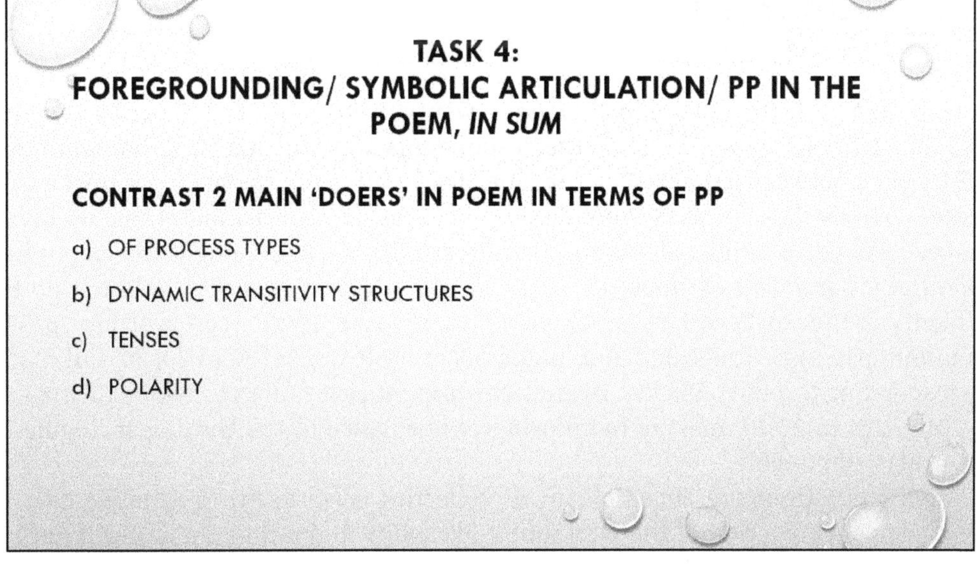

Figure 4.3 SSS+ workshop: task 3

Figure 4.4 SSS+ workshop: task 4

Now I pass to a summary of the steps taken to assess the effectiveness of our practices.

4.5.5 Monitoring Our Practices

At the end of each workshop, students were given questionnaires (with voluntary name disclosure), designed firstly to collect personal data, with what we thought were potentially significant particulars: second-year final *language* exam score; whether the respondent had regularly attended lectures and/or workshops; and whether s/he had prepared for this workshop (by, e.g., reviewing the relevant course book sections).

The following Table sketches a comparative portrait of students participating in the 2017 and 2018 verbal art workshops.

Table 4.1 Participants in Linguistics (verbal art) workshop 2017 and 2018: personal data collected through questionnaires

	2017	2018
Number of respondents	58	20
L1	All Italian	19 Italian
		1 Spanish
Age	98.3% between 21 and 25	90% between 21 and 25
Sex	89.7% female	85% female
	10.3% male	15% male
2nd year language component score	34.5% between 18/30 & 24/30	45% between 18/30 & 24/30
	65.5% between 25/30 & 30/30	55% between 25/30 & 30/30
[30/30 = full CEFR B2, grade A, aim of year 2; 18/30 = B2, grade C]		

All participants (fifty-eight in 2017; only twenty in 2018) filled in the questionnaire. As Table 1 above shows, in 2017, the respondents were all native Italian speakers, mostly aged between 21 and 25 and female, again reflecting the demographics of the degree courses. Data for 2018 is not dissimilar, except for the distinctly smaller divide between the two second-year language score groups. We had thought this might be a potentially significant datum to consider when evaluating students' opinions on the difficulty of the workshop tasks. The two groups were: 'lower' scorers (from 18/30 – minimum passing – to 24/30), and 'higher' scorers (from 25/30 to 30/30, full marks corresponding to a full CEFR B2). Overall, the respondents preferred anonymity (84.5% in 2017; 80% in 2018), making monitoring performance in the third year linguistics exam, alas, impossible.

But the questionnaire aimed chiefly at collecting quantitative/qualitative data on the students' perception of the workshop's likeability and utility, the difficulty of the tasks, and the validity of SSS+ as an analytical model. 'Scales' of data collected included the following types: Nominal (multiple choice/dichotomous – yes/no), Ordinal (rating scales) and word-based (open-ended) (see e.g. Cohen, Manion and Morrison 2007: 322). The questionnaires are reproduced in Appendices 1 and 2 to this chapter.

The following steps were performed by each researcher separately and then compared and discrepancies discussed until agreement was reached, thus ensuring inter-rater reliability. In each year, the questionnaires were numbered and further divided into two groups, according to the declared result in the second-year language exam. Then, for each of the two groups, the responses to each of the questions were taken note of and counted (i.e. we totalled the numbers of yes/no responses and choices made on the Likert-style scales). Replies to the open-ended questions were recorded separately and annotated with relevant data from responses to other questions on the same single questionnaires. For instance, responses on whether the model could be considered a valid one or not were cross-checked with responses concerning attendance and preparation for the workshop, the results taken note of and potential relationships between these data explored. All responses were then put into overall percentages for each group in each year and graphs (not produced here) created. Finally, the researchers discussed the global and local findings and took note of incongruous outcomes and their quantitative and potential qualitative import. The data is summarized below.

Likeability. Question: *Did you enjoy this workshop?* Answers were overwhelmingly positive (82.8% in 2017; 95% in 2018). In both years, most of the 'yes-es' (between 75% and 84.2%) also answered positively to the questions on utility and model validity. Negative answers in 2017 amounted to 12% (5.2% questionnaires provided no answer). Most of these respondents showed an across-the-board negative attitude, saying 'no' to utility and SSS+ model validity, and declaring that they had not prepared for the workshop. In 2018, the 5% negative response figure was skewed, corresponding to a single, wholly negative questionnaire.

Utility. The question in 2017 was *Do you feel you have learned new ways of saying through this workshop?* Positive answers were 70.7% of the total; most of these 'yes-es' also answered positively to likeability (90.2%) and model validity (78%). But what about those who said 'no' to utility? Rather than being negative overall, most of these students said they had enjoyed the workshop, and considered SSS+ a valid analytical model, making their negative responses to utility difficult to interpret. Partly for this reason, in 2018 we changed the question's wording to *Do you feel you have learned more about the language in literature through this workshop?* Positive answers increased to 80%. All these respondents also said 'yes' to likeability, and 81.2% were convinced of the model's validity. However, as in 2017, most of the 'no-s' were also positive about likeability and model validity. The change in the question did not make the answers 'easier' to read.

Difficulty. The students were asked to grade each task's difficulty, choosing a value on a Likert-style scale: *easy; slightly difficult; moderately difficult; very difficult.* They were also invited to leave comments. In examining the answers, we considered the second-year language exam score, explained above (cf. Table 4.1).

We had foreseen the lower second-year language score group having greater difficulty than the higher one, and in part this was the case. In 2017, most of the lower second-year language score group found all the tasks at least *slightly difficult*. None found tasks 1 and 2 *very difficult*, and a minority (5%) rated tasks 3 and 4 as being so. Of all tasks, number 4 showed the lowest percentage of those choosing *easy*, and the highest percentage of those choosing *moderately difficult*. Recalling that here students were asked to recap comparatively previous results, we may hypothesize that synthesis is more daunting, and requires more practice. In 2018, however, the 'lower' group chose *easy* more often, especially for tasks 2 and 3; there were no *very difficult*s at all, not even in task 4, where the other values (easy, slight and moderately difficult) were distributed uniformly. The discrepancy between the responses from these lower language score students in the two years was indeed puzzling.

As for the 'higher' second-year language group scorers, results in 2017 were surprising: most chose *slightly difficult* for the first three tasks (like the 'lower' group), and even *moderately difficult* for task 4. In 2018, by contrast, tasks 1 and 2 were perceived as overwhelmingly *easy*, values in task 3 were equally divided between *easy* and *slightly difficult*, and task 4 was mainly graded as *slightly difficult* – still worrying for some students, but not as much as in 2017.

In 2017, 37.9% respondents left a comment on the most problematic parts: of these, 68.2% spoke of process type identification, and only one mentioned PP. In 2018, a much higher percentage (70%) chose to leave a comment. Problems with transitivity emerged even more strongly (78.6%); 25% described theme formulation as problematic, not mentioned in 2017, and no one cited PP. Since transitivity is part of the second-year syllabus, performance in the SSS+ workshop would clearly benefit from a preliminary revision of previous years' curricula, were it possible.

Model validity. The question was: *Do you think SSS+ is a valid model for investigating the language in literature?* Another Likert-style scale was used: *yes, maybe yes, maybe not, not.* Answers were predominantly on the positive side (*yes + maybe yes*) – 74.1% in 2017, 80% in 2018 – and showed a strong correspondence to declared regular attendance of lectures/workshops. In 2017, negative answers amounted to 25.9%: 15.5% *maybe not*; 10.4% *no*. However, even most of the 'no-s' regularly attended at least the workshop, just as the 'yes-es' did. Results were more encouraging in 2018 (though the number of participants was lower): a higher percentage of unqualified 'yes-es', and no unqualified 'no-s' at all. But only 20% of the 'yes-es' declared attendance of lectures and workshops, and 40% declared attending nothing regularly. Moreover, 100% of the negative responders said they had attended both lectures and workshops regularly, making data, once again, hard to interpret.

Although correlation in itself does not prove causality, do we need to deduce that:

- attendance is simply not a significant parameter?
- and/or even that 'familiarity breeds contempt'?!
- and/or that the whole 'truth' is not being told?

Perhaps the answer lies in part with all of the above?

We had also invited comments on 'why'/'why not' valid. A full report on these is beyond the scope of this recount, but a representative taste follows:

Why '*definitely yes*'? e.g.:
'Because **it allows a complete understanding** of a text from several points of view, which makes it easier to understand the theme'

Why 'maybe yes'?
Of these, most *might* seem reasons for **why *'definitely yes'*** e.g.:
'**It helps understanding** the writer's choices in terms of language'

And note how the grammar – in bold – nicely construes SSS+ as the Causative Instrument of positive cognition.

Why *'definitely (or maybe) not'*? e.g. the often interconnected reasons:
'Because it is too abstract ...' and
'A poem is a poem. It should not be analyzed in a scientific way'

And yet, all who evaluated the model as too abstract also said the workshop taught them something about language – and that they enjoyed it: another contradiction that is baffling.

So then, concerned by such inconsistent data, research began in order to attempt to find some means of disambiguating it. The following section briefly summarizes the steps in this research, the subsequent action taken in 2019, and select results. Discussion then evaluates what we have done, and failed to do, and offers some final reflections on the study.

4.5.5.1 Post-incongruous data action research and discovery interviews

The illuminating, if tardy, research undertaken post-detection of the puzzling data led to discovery of the beneficial notion of *triangulation* (cf. Miller 2019b), but it also showed that our study was already somewhat 'triangulated'. To say how, we need to recall Denzin's (1978) four basic types of triangulation:

- *Data triangulation*: involving time, space, and persons;
- *Investigator triangulation*: involving multiple researchers in an investigation;
- *Theory triangulation*: using more than one theoretical scheme in the interpretation of the observed facts, and
- *Methodological triangulation*: using more than one method to gather data, such as interviews, observations, questionnaires, etc.

Concerning (1), we had collected two years of data, provided by two discrete populations of students; regarding (2), there were two of us doing the workshop, the questionnaire design and, separately and then jointly, the sifting of responses, so also providing, as said, inter-rater reliability. Then, regarding (3), that is, using more than one theoretical scheme to read data, even if instinctively, we'd had some idea of the hazards of 'the box', meaning we had tried not to confine data analysis to our own pre-defined agenda, despite having had in mind certain notions/values to be tested when designing the questionnaire of course. Also discovered were consolations regarding incongruous questionnaire results. As Cohen, Manion and Morrison (2007: 493) remark: 'discrepant, negative and disconfirming cases are important in assisting the categories and emergent (grounded) theory to fit all the data ... The process resonates with the methodological notion of triangulation.'

Lastly, concerning (4), we simply hadn't used more than one method to gather data, naively relying on 'face validity' (Bolarinwa 2015), trusting the information elicited through our painstakingly prepared questionnaires would, somehow, be sufficient. This meant, however, discounting, among other things, respondent characteristics, which are just as significant as question characteristics for response reliability (Borgers and Hox 2000). Information about these is said to be among the benefits of mixed data collection methods. Of these, the follow-up, one-to-one, semi-standardized, 'discovery' interview (cf. Bridges et al. 2008; Ryan, Coughlan and Cronin 2009) was brought into play.

The immediate problem was questionnaire anonymity – the students' right, and, as seen, overriding preference. Hence interviews were limited to the four respondents (of twenty) who had voluntarily disclosed their names in 2018, 2017 students being no longer accessible. They happily accepted to be interviewed about their responses. Interviews were carried out face-to-face, for the most part in English, lasted between 30–45 mins, and were recorded with the students' permission.

As emerged above, the contradictory data revealed by the questionnaires were various, showing puzzling conflicts between students' perceptions of the likeability and utility of the workshop, the difficulty of the tasks performed and the validity of the model itself. The four interviewees' questionnaires did not exhibit all the contradictions to be solved. Nevertheless, interviews did help to clarify, in particular, clashes between positive feedback on utility and less positive opinions of model validity. They also disambiguated the reasons for conflicting questionnaire responses with reference to task difficulties. General trends that emerged can be summarized as: (1) a perceived lack of sufficient expertise; (2) problems with memory and synthesis; (3) preference for more traditional approaches to literature; (4) insufficient preparation leading especially to uncertainty on model validity and task difficulties; and (5) the influence of respondents' personal characteristics and attitudes. These appear in square brackets below and have been deduced from each interviewee's overall responses, rather than solely from the illustrative quotes that follow.

Student 1: female, aged 21, in the upper group of second-year language results (27/30) and a regular attender of both lectures and workshops. She had also declared that she had:

- prepared for and enjoyed the workshop (likeability);
- learned more about the language in literature through it (utility);
- found all tasks *easy*, except for the summarizing task 4 (*slightly difficult*);
- and answered only 'maybe yes' regarding model validity, although she had construed SSS+ as an instrument of cognition: 'It helps understanding the writer's choices in terms of language' (see comments on why/why not valid above).

Here is an extract of the questions she was asked and her responses:

1) Q: 'Why didn't you answer "definitely yes" to validity then?'
A: 'Because I don't know enough about the model to be so definite! ...'
[Felt lack of sufficient expertise].

2) Q: You found most tasks *easy*, but task 4 was *slightly difficult* for you. Do you remember why?
A: (after seeing them again): 'Maybe more difficult because I had to remember the others and summarize?' …
[Difficulties probably having to do with memory and synthesis.]

Student 2: male, aged 24, at the top end of the lower second-year language results group (24/30), also a declared regular attender of lectures and workshops. He too ticked preparation for and enjoyment of the workshop, and answered positively to the question on utility. He also declared finding all tasks *easy* and answered *maybe yes* to validity – but his 'why' seemed to us to better explain a *definitely yes*: 'Because language is deeply connected to meaning: We can understand the true meaning of a text only by analyzing it with the specific methods, as we did today.' So he was asked:

Q: 'Why not *definitely yes* to validity then?'
A: 'Because maybe there are other systems to analyse literature I'm not aware of and maybe sometimes it should also be used together with traditional methods.'
[This much hedged response supports his original *maybe yes* choice. Again lack of expertise, but also attraction to more traditional literary approaches, emerge.]

Student 3: female, aged 32, in the lower second-year language results group (22/30), again a declared regular attender of lectures and workshops. She had ticked preparation for and enjoyment of the workshop and its utility. Primarily due to process type identification, she had found the first task *slightly difficult* and all others *moderately difficult*. She had answered *maybe yes* to validity, without leaving a comment to explain why.

Her reason emerged as: 'Well, I didn't prepare for the workshop very well. I couldn't say. I wasn't sure. Today [after the final exam] I say 'definitely yes'!' …
[*Insufficient workshop preparation – despite what she'd originally ticked – leading to her uncertainty regarding SSS+ validity, but also to increased task difficulties.*]

Student 4: female, aged 55, attending the degree course for professional purposes, her 2nd year language result was a minimum pass: 18/30. She too had described herself as a regular attender in the questionnaire. In addition, she:

- had not prepared for, though did enjoy, the workshop (likability);
- had declared she had learned more about the language in literature through it (utility);
- had found the first task *slightly difficult*, tasks 2 and 3 *easy*, and task 4 *moderately difficult*;
- had answered *maybe not* regarding model validity: 'Because I find it too abstract.'

In the interview, which she requested be in Italian, she was asked if she could clarify what she meant by 'abstract'.

A: 'Look, I prefer traditional literary criticism. Maybe I meant the theory – very hard. I liked 2nd year journalism register texts. But I didn't ... don't like FG, the waddayacallit? Metalanguage? I don't understand why we have to do it. But I study.' (*Miller's translation*)

She was pressed on this:
Q: 'But you did say you enjoyed the WS and learned from it.'
A: 'Well, I have to learn. Alone I can't do it. So I came and yes, it was ok, and I learned something anyway.' (*Miller's translation*)
[Likeability and utility seem to be a question of degree, and also of kind, but, once again, we are in the realm of our respondents' personal characteristics and attitudes.]

4.5.5.2 Discussion

The results of these interviews warranted a follow-up, though time allowed for merely tweaking the questionnaire for the 2019 workshop (see right-hand side of Appendix 4.2). We:

- offered degrees of workshop preparation: *scant, solid* or *truly in depth*;
- moderated the validity question into the much qualified: 'Despite not being an "expert", did the workshop leave you with the impression that SSS+ may be a valid model for investigating the language of literature?';
- highlighted the recapping nature of troublesome task 4; and
- in introducing the questionnaire, explained our research aims to the students in more detail, stressing our need for their collaboration in terms of name disclosure.

An overall picture of the data gleaned follows in Table 4.2, showing that our targeted interventions proved on the whole positive, if not resolutive.

Table 4.2 Improvements and residual problems post-2019 workshop

What's better	What problems remain
+ specifics re workshop preparation: 60% 'scant', rest 'solid'	Still conflict between likeability/ utility and validity
+ 'tentative' SSS+ validity question → more *definitely yes*-es; more reasons offered for all choices	Problems recalling 2nd year curriculum
Task 4 easier overall	PP – this time phonemic – as a comment on task difficulty
Nearly 60% name disclosure	Continuing 'resistance' to a linguistic analysis of verbal art

The discovery interviews reported above demonstrate that the probing of an interviewer is unquestionably crucial to getting more detailed answers than even valid questionnaires can provide (cf. de Leeuw 2005: 245). So, interviews were of course planned for the 2019 population as well. However, despite increased voluntary disclosure of identity, only a very few responded to contact and none of these had problematic questionnaires needing scrutiny. In future, mixed methods of data collection will continue, although we had evaluated replacing them with face-to-face Semi-Structured Interviews (SSIs), based on a pre-drafted questionnaire. Yet even these are said to offer at best mixed blessings. Firstly, SSIs do not satisfy the right to anonymity, obliging an unsatisfactory reliance on volunteers. Then, if on one hand they are 'superbly suited for a number of valuable tasks, particularly when more than a few of the open-ended questions require follow-up queries', on the other hand, the 'time and effort required to do all of it right is considerable' (Adams 2015: 493). And time is a commodity there is always less of, for us and our students.

Yet the need for more time as far as teaching is concerned has also emerged from our study: problems with recall of prior years' curricula would require some preliminary review, as said. Moreover, negative SSS+ validity data, though happily diminishing constantly over time, is still a thorny issue for us. We hypothesize a link to a lack of sufficient practice *doing* SSS+ – and so, consequently, also of an adequate achievement of the objectives we work toward. Thus, more time dedicated exclusively to SSS+ would be crucial, though institutionally not easy to arrange.

But what else might taking stock of discomforting research findings mean? We will of course continue to seek to bump up evidence of the benefits of our literature-as-special-register perspective and promote them better. But chances are we're never going to genuinely convince all our sceptical stakeholders, most likely because of die-hard preferences for traditional analytical models and/or even resistance to the two-fold course contents (i.e. English language *and linguistics*): as one student ticking *definitely not* to the model's validity commented, 'I only want to improve my English.'

I, particularly, have even made an effort to think outside the box and ask myself if we need to query the framework adopted in our stylistics teaching. Playing the devil's advocate, I provocatively debated: wouldn't students prefer to have their personal opinions count more than the analytical reasons for them, or simply regurgitate received lit-crit wisdom – as most have been trained to do? Undoubtedly, but recall that even a systemicist like Huisman faults Hasan's model for what she sees as its uncompromising insistence on the meaning of a literature text: 'a reductive structuralist move to one meaning, irrespective of the context of the individual reader' (cf. note 14, Chapter 2). Recall too Birch and O'Toole's critique of Hasan's paper in their 1988 edited volume: in particular, its 'claim that one model of analysis is particularly powerful' (cf. Chapter 2). In the face of such scholarly opinions, I wondered, can one fault students for thinking along similar lines, and disregard those thoughts, with impunity, refusing to be open to other approaches? Can one simply take refuge in a genuinely convinced adherence to Hasan's theory and practice of verbal art and her call for a reflection literacy, and in thinking one knows best? And mightn't one even need to ponder a potential conflict between reflection literacy's empowering justification and Hasan's holistic but admittedly relatively rigid framework? Does the correspondence between reflection literacy and the double-articulation framework give us a *good enough* fit? In short, could her model feasibly be seen as a form of straitjacketing indoctrination comparable to the kind of official doxic pedagogy that limits itself to reproducing 'received evaluation' (2007: 19)?

So then, such were my uncomfortable considerations, which, however, I have ulti-mately put aside – and for all of the reasons/arguments laid out in this as well as subse-quent chapters. In addition, however, another doubt came to mind. The queries above presume that the educator is doing things right, while perhaps that is not wholly and/or always the case. Recalling Hasan's acknowledgement of the unavoidably reproduc-tive nature of literacy education in our societies (2011c [1996]: 192), we too must admit to practising an impure reflection literacy, as it were, despite the aim always being to use knowledge about language to reflect on meaning-making in social context and encourage students to do the same. Presumably, one can only be vigilant and try harder, heartened by the predominance of positive student opinions, and intent on convincing the resisters with ever richer and more engaging methods. The still-fixed purpose is to become ever better practitioners of RVAP.

4.6 Coda

This lengthy chapter on educational stylistics is now at an end. In Part I the need for the use of the metalanguage of a 'good enough' grammatics was argued with the sourcing of many prominent SFL scholars. Subsequently, Hasan's engagement with verbal art and its teaching was discussed and her theory of reflection literacy briefly set forth. In addition, systemic functional educational stylistics studies were briefly and selectively illustrated. Part II presented a case study expounding a pedagogical experience of guid-ing students toward 'special' register awareness in an undergraduate EFL curriculum in Italy. The focus was on a workshop analysis of one poem selectively using the tools of SSS+, but the section was also concerned with monitoring and refining teaching prac-tices, and raising uncomfortable queries along the way.

In the next and final chapter, the perspective becomes transdisciplinary (or trans-sub-disciplinary) and examines select research into systemic functional stylistics associated with multimodal and/or corpus and/or translation approaches.

Verbal Art Workshop — April 26, 2017 — Data & feedback collection form

SECTION 1. PERSONAL INFORMATION

First of all, we would ask you to give us a few bits of information about yourself, so that we can put your other replies in greater context. This would help us monitor the effectiveness of activities such as the one we did today, which are part of a larger research project on SSS and English as a foreign language / culture teaching. Your responses will be treated with confidence, and at all times data will be presented in anonymous form.

PLEASE WRITE YOUR ANSWERS CLEARLY

Name and surname (*optional*):

Age:

Sex: Male / Female

Mother tongue:

Your score in the 2nd year language (Lingua-Esercitazioni) exam:

Do you hold an *official language certificate*? Yes / No

If 'yes', please indicate the type (e.g., *First Certificate*): and level (e.g., B2):

Are you a regular attender of the *Linguistics lezioni frontali*? Yes / No

Are you a regular attender of the *Workshop*? Yes / No

Please turn the page

Questionnaire #

SECTION 2. ABOUT THE WORKSHOP

The following questions are aimed at getting your impressions on the activity we did **today**.

Had you prepared for the workshop: reading the text analyses in Part II of your course book? Yes / No

Did you enjoy this Workshop? Yes / No

How did you find the tasks? *(Circle the degree of difficulty you had for each)*

Task 1	Task 2	Task 3	Task 4
Easy	Easy	Easy	Easy
Slightly difficult	Slightly difficult	Slightly difficult	Slightly difficult
Moderately difficult	Moderately difficult	Moderately difficult	Moderately difficult
Very difficult	Very difficult	Very difficult	Very difficult

Which was/were the most problematic part(s)? *(You can answer briefly below)*

Do you feel you have learned new *ways of saying* through this Workshop? Yes / No

Do you think SSS is a valid model for investigating the language of literature? *(Please tick one box only)*

Definitely yes / Maybe yes / Maybe not / Definitely not

Why? *(You can answer briefly below)*

Appendix 4.1 The 2017 questionnaire

Verbal Art Workshop — April 18, 2018 — Data & feedback collection form

SECTION 2. ABOUT THE WORKSHOP

The following questions are aimed at getting your impressions on the activity we did **today**.

Had you prepared for the workshop: reading the text analysis in Part II of your course book?

Yes / No

Did you enjoy this Workshop? Yes / No

How did you find the tasks? *(Circle the degree of difficulty you had for each)*

Task 1	Task 2	Task 3	Task 4
Easy	Easy	Easy	Easy
Slightly difficult	Slightly difficult	Slightly difficult	Slightly difficult
Moderately difficult	Moderately difficult	Moderately difficult	Moderately difficult
Very difficult	Very difficult	Very difficult	Very difficult

Which was/were the most problematic part(s)? *(Please answer briefly below)*

Do you feel you have learned more about the language in literature through this Workshop? Yes / No

Do you think SSS is a valid model for investigating the language of literature? *(Please tick one box only)*

Definitely yes / Maybe yes / Maybe not / Definitely not

Why? *(Please answer briefly below)*

Verbal Art Workshop — April 15, 2019 — Data & feedback collection form

SECTION 2. ABOUT THE WORKSHOP

If you prepared for the workshop, i.e. reading the text analyses in Part II of your course book, would you say your preparation was: scant, or solid, or truly in depth? Choose one and write below please.

The following questions are aimed at getting **your impressions** on the activity we did **today**.

Did you enjoy this Workshop? Yes / No

How did you find the tasks? *(Circle the degree of difficulty you had for each)*

Task 1	Task 2	Task 3	Task 4
Easy	Easy	Easy	Easy
Slightly difficult	Slightly difficult	Slightly difficult	Slightly difficult
Moderately difficult	Moderately difficult	Moderately difficult	Moderately difficult
Very difficult	Very difficult	Very difficult	Very difficult

Please indicate briefly below which you think was / were the most problematic part(s)? (e.g.: identifying transitivity or sound patterning, pervasive parallelism etc…and if possible why you feel they were).

Would you say you have learned something more about the language in literature through this workshop? Yes / No

Despite not being an 'expert', did the workshop leave you with the impression that SSS may be a valid model for investigating the language of literature? *(Please tick one box only)*

Definitely yes / Maybe yes / Maybe not / Definitely not

Below, please try to say briefly what it is that gives you this impression:

Appendix 4.2 The questionnaire (2nd page) in 2018 and 2019

Chapter 5

Systemic Functional Stylistics *and...*

5.1 Prelude

In order to provide a more extensive view of systemic functional stylistics studies, this chapter offers a select overview of research wedded to multimodal, corpus and translation approaches. Its nature is thus transdisciplinary. Nonetheless, fixed requirements for signalling studies here are: 1) that they be to some clear degree SFL-influenced, and 2) that they attend to literature as the object of study. The confines of 'literature', however, widen.

It is the multimodal – or multisemiotic – perspective that especially compels the relaxing of traditional categories of literature. Thus, by narrative fiction is meant simply 'story-telling', in the non-specialist sense. But it more markedly obliges seeing conventionally dubbed 'lowbrow' genres (such as comics) as literary mediums in their own right, ones whose ways of meaning can commonly be seen to 'relate to human social existence – its dilemmas and its delights', just as Hasan speaks of the mission of verbal art (Equinox online gloss to Hasan (to appear), cited in Chapter 2). This does not entail a change in my stance, as this volume has never shown bias on the side of the literary 'canon' (i.e. never been prejudiced against popular forms; cf. note 9 in Chapter 4). But ever-increasing transformations in contemporary art forms compel attention to studies of story-telling with associated images, even moving ones, including print literature that has been digitalized and even electronic literature that is digital born (as are the sensibilities and abilities of much of humanity's Generation Y and Z), as well as to studies that seek to create new tools for examining such meaning-making. That said, I have tried to target research that examines a minimum of narrative text definable as *verbal* art as well, and not solely from bias. As Toolan (2014: 457) properly notes, with reference to film, '[T]here are some indicators that point to the aural on occasion being more important than the visual.' But of course the oldest forms of literature (i.e. the performance art forms of primary oral cultures) were the first to teach us this (cf. Ong 1982: passim).

This may sound all very neat and tidy, but it isn't. The extent to which two or more of the 'and' (added) disciplinary categories overlap in studies proved somewhat surprising, as indeed was the productive nature of the synergies themselves. As is well-known, cross-disciplinary perspectives in theory and practice have been an increasing tendency for years. Yet, as is also well-known, transdisciplinary cooperation and collaboration in myriad fields have at times appeared to be more desirable than meaningful, given the nuanced differences among the frameworks, assumptions, and methods of the various domains of study involved. On the whole, however, such friction is not conspicuous. Can we see this as proof of a 'good enough' symbiosis? Perhaps. And yet, admittedly, the artistic question, and the specialness of the literature text, don't always receive the focal attention they might have in the studies cited below, be their methodologies those of multimodality, corpus linguistics (henceforth CL) or even, though less so, translation studies. The 'and' constituent too often inclines to prominence and the artistic element to being lost sight of. Noteworthy exceptions, of course, are pointed up.

The additional – but not mutually exclusive – disciplines are dealt with in the order in which they were put forward above (i.e. multimodality/multisemiosis), then CL, followed by translation studies. The overview is necessarily a selective one.[1]

5.2 Systemic Functional Stylistics and Multimodality

Ideally, a multimodal stylistic approach to 'literature' probes how the various modes of the work's composition interact with each other to produce artistic literary meaning. This approach to multimodality would then be seen as a sub-category of what is called systemic functional multimodal discourse analysis (hereafter SF-MDA), an ever-rapidly expanding field within SFL. A customized acronym is thus proposed: SFMS, systemic functional multimodal stylistics.

5.2.1 Toward an SFMS

SFL, for systemicists at least, has proven to be exceptionally fertile theoretical ground for SF-MDS to grow and mature in. As O'Halloran, Tan and Wignell put it:

> Michael Halliday's Systemic Functional Theory (SFT) most fully developed as Systemic Functional Linguistics (SFL) ... provides an unrivalled platform for modelling, analysing, and interpreting multimodal texts, interactions, and events involving language and other resources such as images, scientific symbolism, sound, embodied action, and so forth ... The resulting approach [is] systemic functional multimodal discourse analysis (SF-MDA). (2019: 433)

A more mainstream but no less enthusiastic scholarly opinion can be found in Nørgaard (2014), a stylistics scholar cited in previous chapters. She points up the fact that:

> the social semiotic take on multimodality builds on Halliday's functional linguistics and follows the multimodal credo that 'common semiotic principles operate in and across different modes' (Kress and van Leeuwen 2001, p. 2). In *Reading Images* ([2006 [1996] in references, DRM]) Kress and van Leeuwen thus explore the extent to which the fundamental ideas behind Halliday's approach to language are applicable to visual communication, and they develop a visual grammar that largely employs the same concepts and terminology as Halliday. Consequently, the addition of Kress and van Leeuwen's methodology to the stylistic toolkit will provide stylisticians with a consistent approach to – and terminology for – handling language *and* images. (2014: 471)

So we're given to understand that the SFL-multimodality connection as it developed was in a way a 'natural' one, bringing about a consistency of approach.

As Taylor reminds us, no matter what the approach to multimodal analysis, '[c]ertain tenets of SFL would seem to be omnipresent' (2017: 576). Besides the seminal and omnipresent *Reading Images*, an even earlier publication is often cited as being an equally central SF-MDA trailblazer. This is O'Toole's *The Language of Displayed Art* (1994). For Taylor, it 'can be said in many ways to have set the ball rolling' (2017: 575).

Even earlier, O'Halloran analogously, if more implicitly, pays tribute to O'Toole as a prime mover of this new field of SFL research in saying that 'Following O'Toole's (1994) *Language of Displayed Art* and Kress and van Leeuwen's (1996) *Reading Images: The Grammar of Visual Design*, interest in the use of SF theory for MDA has steadily increased' (2008: 444).[2]

O'Toole (2018), cited in Chapter 4, focuses on the process of interpretation in literature and the visual arts, appealingly highlighting the centrality of artistic texts to the study of multimodality. The semiotic systems discussed include literature, television, film, painting, sculpture and architecture. But, as with O'Toole (1994), the artistic quality of the mode is ever to the fore.

Many key scholars and their work are referenced in the publications by O'Halloran, Tan and Wignell, Nørgaard, and Taylor cited just above; these bibliographies are a rich source of indications for further reading, as of course are those in the works referenced below, several of which are sourced by these authors as well. O'Halloran, Tan and Wignell (2019) does *not* address multimodality in literature, but Nørgaard (2014) and Taylor (2017) do.

Nørgaard (2014) explicitly opts for the social semiotic approach to a multimodal stylistic investigation of the novel. She illustrates the Hallidayan linguistic and early Kress and van Leeuwen multisemiotic analytical frameworks with various twentieth- and twenty-first century works of fiction. Although she is not technically speaking a systemicist, much of her recent work is decidedly SFL-inspired, as noted in Chapter 2. Indeed, Gibbons actually says that Nørgaard 'has been *the* proponent of the social semiotic approach [to multimodality, DRM] within stylistics' (2015: 297, *my emphasis*). I cite in addition only her volume on much the same topics as her 2014 chapter, but evidently treated in much more depth and detail: *Multimodal Stylistics of the Novel: More than Words* (2018), an important contribution to SFMS, to the explicit stylistic study of multimodal meaning-making in the literature text.

Taylor (2017) is dealt with in the following section, focused on three eminent multimodal scholars.

5.2.2 Taylor, O'Halloran and Bateman

As his brief dictates, Taylor (2017) offers an excellent potted history of the 'reading images' field, bringing together his various fields of expertise: SFL, multimodality, corpus methods and also translation. The SFL constituents of discourse analysis receiving most attention feature textual organization and cohesion; in exemplifying the metafunctions, Taylor rightly notes, 'it is the enabling [i.e. textual, DRM] function that ties the text together' (2017: 585). He illustrates multimodal transcription and phase analysis (refined, e.g. by Baldry and Thibault 2006) of narrative texts, which include soap opera (Coronation Street) and film – 'the archetypal multimodal text' (2017: 588) – in particular *The Hours*, but he also reflects on audio-visual translation and audio description for the blind (ADLAB). Pointing out, as many do, that technological advances are vital to an optimum reading of images, he also looks briefly at corpus-assisted methods and eye-tracking techniques, considered especially useful for subtitling, another interest of his (cf. 2003 and 2004). Taylor's work on multimodality and translation – and on the benefits of a multimodal approach for translation – is copious and has also been influential across languages (cf., e.g. Chen 2019, on translating subtitles into Chinese).

Kay O'Halloran has explored multimodality in many different text types, among them advertisements and even mathematics, but has also analysed films and theatrical productions, thus practising what I've dubbed SFMS. One example is her own paper in her edited volume (2004), 'Visual Semiosis in Film', where, using then available video-editing software applications,[3] she also performs a detailed dynamic description and analysis of the meanings resulting from a combined use of semiotic choices, involving, e.g. proxemics, movement, gaze and gesture, together with semiotic choices in film production (e.g. lighting, music, clothing, props, as well as camera framing, angle, distance and movement). A more recent co-edited special issue of *Social Semiotics* (2016a) and a co-edited volume (2016b), both with Sindoni and Wildfeuer, indicate one of the expansions of direction O'Halloran's studies have taken.

The editors' abstract to the special issue on the languages of performing arts (2016a) clearly states that it aims at

> designing how the context of the latter can be illuminated by socio-semiotic and multimodal approaches to communication. In this Special Issue, performances and performing arts are described as multimodal semiotic acts that co-deploy a range of semiotic resources to produce and construct meanings across different cultures and ages. Seen as dynamic and interactive processes of meaning-making, their analysis calls for new and multidisciplinary frameworks which are collected in this Special Issue.

The issue includes studies on how the relationships between theatre, cinema and opera are, on one hand, interconnected, but also on their permeable boundaries. The papers respectively explore: stage directions; cinema borrowings from stage conventions, taken in their turn from theatre *mise-en-scène*; and opera as multimodal genre. They also compare children who listen to stories told by their parents and children who listen to the same stories told by a television presenter, and investigate how movement and interaction within the art installation can be seen to rewrite and thus transform, even dismantle, social paradigms. The paper by Tan, Wignell and O'Halloran (2016a) traces adaptations, from novel, to stage, to screen of the The *Woman in Black* by Susan Hill, showing how this Gothic horror genre develops due to socio-semiotic transformations and adaptations that affect viewership and so also contemporary socio-cultural events and practices.

In the co-edited volume (2016b), O'Halloran's own co-written paper, again with Tan and Wignell (2016b) – 'Multimodal Semiotics of Theatrical Performances' – explores the creation of particular effects in these by the interweaving of choices from multiple semiotic resources. Rossi and Sindoni (2016) does the same in opera as a multimodal performance event. The volume also includes interesting studies of dance, choreography and even social media – difficult, however, to classify as 'literature'.

Allegedly, John Bateman no longer considers himself a systemicist, although the report is a serious oversimplification of his complex position.[4] His work on multimodality is profuse and many-sided and simply cannot be adequately represented here. One explicitly SFL-grounded study is Bateman (2013), 'Hallidayan Systemic-functional Semiotics and the Analysis of the Moving Audio-visual Image'. But Bateman is a computational linguist (PhD in Artificial Intelligence, University of Edinburgh), as well as an admirable scholar of the theory and practice of multimodality. The combination of these areas of knowledge leads him to be persistently devising new empirically-based methodologies for pushing the state of the art further into a better future. One often-cited study (by, e.g., Taylor 2017 and Toolan 2014) is Bateman and Schmidt (2012), which offers an innovative approach to, and new tools for, the empirical analysis of film with the aim of concretely demonstrating just how filmic discourse means. Working with the syntagmatic and paradigmatic axes of organization, but also discourse semantics and innovatory 'layout structure', the authors devise a methodology by which the concrete details of film sequences can be seen to drive mechanisms for constructing filmic discourse structures.

Bateman, Wildfeuer and Hiippala (2017) is a ground-breaking overview of multimodality as a discipline, a textbook billed as 'the first foundational introduction to the practice of analysing multimodality' (abstract). Adopting 'a problem-oriented perspective', it provides the requisite theoretical bases and tools, but, innovatively, puts analytical purpose first. It also demonstrates Bateman's constant insistence on empirical validation of all concepts and assumptions. Discussed are multimodal artefacts and performances of all kinds. Bateman has been exploring and publishing on multimodality, genre and also corpus analytical methods for years. He also studies comics, as his work in collaboration with Veloso proves (e.g. 2013, on the semiotic resources of comics in movie adaptation).

5.2.3 Other (Mainly) 'Insider' Studies

I now allude primarily to other SFL 'insiders' who practise SFMS, but also to certain mainstream scholars, beginning, indeed, with one such study.

Toolan's chapter on 'Stylistics and Film' (2014), cursorily mentioned above, merits further comment. Toolan is a mainstream stylistics scholar, eclectic in his interests and prolific in his production. He is also selectively friendly to SFL, as already seen in Chapters 2 and 4. In this study, he problematizes many aspects of the stylistics and film liaison, reflecting on the challenges inherent in producing a stylistic representation of film. Interesting for us, given the unqualified praise for the SFL-*Reading Images* connection cited above, is his observation that Kress and van Leeuwen's 'principles and adaptations of systemic-linguistic ideas have been questioned, as forcing the fluidity of a two-dimensional image into a framework designed for the unidimensionality of language'. Critiqued is also the fact that they read '*fixed* images, not moving ones' (2014: 463, *original emphasis*).

Toolan does not reference that questioning. Others (e.g. Gibbons 2015: 295) do.[5] But the target of the critique is specifically Kress and van Leeuwen's work, rather than the interaction of SFL and multimodal analysis per se. Indeed, Toolan's 'Further Reading' section (2014: 469) features the above-mentioned Bateman and Schmidt (2012), which he praises for 'incorporating insights from multimodal analysis and systemic linguistics' (2014: 469). He also approves Bateman and Schmidt's (2012) accent on the empirical. And, as Bateman remarks (see note 4), he too has reservations regarding the SFL-*Reading Images* approach.

Another Further Reading signalled by Toolan (2014) is Piazza, Bednarek and Rossi (2011), for the wealth of perspectives it is said to bring to the study of film dialogue in general and particularly to the multimodal fashioning of characterization. The volume, in Benjamin's 'Pragmatics & Beyond' series, deals with the definition of characters in film and television fiction and focuses strongly on the relationship between represented and interactive participants. Theoretically, contributions can generally be seen as working in a social semiotics perspective, but the volume portrays itself as contributing to various fields, including pragmatics, CL, stylistics, narratology and even pedagogy. Toolan himself is a contributor (Chapter 9). I come back to Toolan's corpus work (2009) below.

Bednarek is indisputably a systemicist, but certainly not only. Her very often heterogeneous toolkit discloses another scholar with wide-ranging interests and knowledge of fields such as, in her case, pragmatics and media studies. She too regularly combines multimodality and corpus approaches. Her own contribution to Piazza, Bednarek and Rossi (2011: Chapter 10), however, is not a multimodal, but solely a corpus stylistic, study. It employs keyword and cluster analysis to evaluate the diachronic and intersubjective stability of the dialogue in the 'dramedy' *Gilmore Girls*. Bednarek is also a contributor to a volume purporting to work toward a 'new' discipline, multimodal critical discourse analysis: Djonov and Zhao (2014), in which the social semiotic approach to multimodality is well represented. Bednarek (2014) analyses the title sequence of the musical television comedy *Flight of the Conchords*, showing how visual choices link up to the social functions of television title sequences (e.g. attracting audiences, affording continuity, embodying the nature of a series and its genre, etc.). Bednarek (2015) is a corpus-assisted multimodal study that probes the interlacing of verbal and visual narration in a special corpus of scripts from the US serial *Nurse Jackie*. The multimodal analysis of a single scene from the series deftly reveals its complex semiotic meaning-making, but also how the visual can act to disambiguate the verbal text, whose analysis alone, it is argued, would result in a partial and even deficient picture of the medium.

We return to Bednarek again in speaking of systemic functional stylistics and the corpus. But to be signalled here is Bednarek and Zago's 'Bibliography of Linguistic Research on Fictional (Narrative, Scripted) Television Series and Films/Movies, version 4' (January 2021). It makes mention of the work of many of the scholars cited above, and below, and many others – not all working from an SFL perspective. Still, it is a treasure trove for those interested. Moreover, there is the less comprehensive but more selective 'A Bibliography of Multimodal Research: 1980s–2015', compiled by Hiippala (2015).

Television dialogue also receives prominent attention in Law (2020), a paper that would extend Carter's (2004) thesis on linguistic creativity to multimodal texts. Inspired by the concept of 'given' and 'new' in Halliday's work on information status, an original framework for creativity analysis is proposed and discussed using scenes from the TV drama *House M.D.*, the film *Casablanca* (1942), the sitcom *Blackadder the Third* (1987), as well as in videos, digital and fractal art, and so on. Law began his research into applying

'A Corpus Linguistic Systemic Functional Multimodal Discourse Analysis Approach' to creativity in his 2017 PhD thesis and has already published much on the topic.[6]

Besides Bednarek's chapter, Djonov and Zhao (2014) host various contributions from already cited authors, as well as a chapter by Unsworth, not yet mentioned. Unsworth (2014) performs critical interpretive analyses of evaluative stance in picture books and animated film adaptations. As seen in Chapter 4, pedagogical concerns for Unsworth are typically to the fore, a particularly salient topic being the role of both teacher and student in rapidly evolving contemporary learning contexts. Such concerns are also explicitly engaged with in Unsworth (2008), a volume whose chapters attend to the challenges of ever-increasing image-language interaction in schooling at all levels, and in particular those concerning the task of reconceptualizing literacy and literacy pedagogy. Many chapters deal with literature, especially narratives, including (almost ante litteram): 3D multimedia ones; digital multimedia authoring and online forums for discussion of prose fiction. Unsworth's own chapter in the volume is titled 'Comparing and Composing Digital Re-presentations of Literature: Multimedia Authoring and Meta-communicative Knowledge'. Illustrating his argument with canonical and popular narratives (Kafka's *Metamorphosis*, but also the *Harry Potter* phenomenon), Unsworth posits digital multimedia recontextualizations of literature as complementary to 'net-age' young readers' enthusiasm for fictional narrative, as well as affording possibilities for productive pedagogic tasks. An entry on *Multimodal Literacy* in the recent *Oxford Research Encyclopedia of Education* is co-authored with Mills (2017). That literature subjects can, and should, be taught in novel interactive ways in today's digital age is argued by an increasing number of scholars, as even the Book of Abstracts to the International Conference 'Approaches to Multimodal Digital Environments: from theories to practices', which took place in Rome in June of 2019, makes extremely plain.[7]

Martin's chapter in Unsworth (2008) does not explicitly take on the literacy issue but explores the enactment of evaluation in/by the words and images in the juvenile fiction book, *Photographs in the Mud* (Wolfer and Harrison-Lever 2005). Working from the perspective of his 'positive discourse analysis', involving the kind of discourse analysis that attempts to make the world a better place rather than merely deconstructing what is wrong with it, as CDA would, he examines intermodal complementarity in the book, and 'the importance of an underlying theme (in Hasan's 1985 sense)' (2012 [2008]: 325). He identifies that theme as reconciliation, part of an ongoing healing process rehabilitating post-World War II Japanese-Australian relations, concluding that the 'reconciliation message is what ultimately coordinates the verbal and visual meanings' (2012 [2008]: 325). Actually, Hasan would have put it the other way around: that it is the foregrounded meanings that are what articulates the theme, but it is in any case nice to see Hasanian theme spoken of, if only, as it were, by the way, as also noted in Chapters 2 and 4.

A volume by Painter, Martin and Unsworth (2013) tackles once again the popular topic of children's picture books. The authors work in a social semiotics MDA perspective based on Kress and van Leeuwen (2006 [1996]), but in several respects they also adapt, and even contest, certain of their concepts. They examine how the blending of visual and verbal resources in a variety of books for various age groups construct interpersonal and ideational meanings and also help to scaffold sensitization to literature, literacy and cultural paradigms in ways that are socially valued. Thus we are back to the genre theory perspective on literacy discussed, and problematized, in Chapter 4. A paper of the same title was published in *Functions of Language* (2014).

Maiorani (2015) is a representative study of how the multisemiotic resources deployed in films create engagement and interpretative patterns between the text and the audience. Contrasting the 'old' with the 'new', she applies SF-MDA to film as a form of social practice, examining the possibility of probing a pre-internet era film, Hitchcock's *Psycho* (1960), with a method successfully used to investigate films that make use of computer-generated technology. The experience is said to afford insights into filmic discourse analysis as well as audience reception, a dimension addressed by many studies signalled in this chapter.

Zurru (2010) too compares 'old' and 'new', in terms of stereotypical characterization of one of the best known icons of the fairy tale domain, Cinderella, in the animated *Shrek* saga, and intertextually. Her SFMS analysis reveals the saga's fundamentally successful, if imperfect, subversion of many of the typical ideological gender conventions as construed in the original fairy tale or in the famous 1950 Disney film.

Disney again comes into the discussion in Chen (2018), or rather, Disneyfication. The study probes the intralingual, interlingual and intersemiotic translations of the Chinese literary classic, *Mulan*, in picture books. Chen shows how verbal and visual materials collaborate to create/recreate different images of Mulan, from the Chinese folk heroine in the 'Song of Mulan' to the Americanized Chinese tomboy in Disney's version. The paper argues that what is needed is an interdisciplinary approach to study images via their multisemiotic meanings and the cultural paradigms they construct.

An SFMS and also translation study, Turci (2014) comparatively examines the way verbal and visual modes of representation interact in the English and Italian illustrated first editions of Kipling's *The Jungle Book*. Analysis of both Source and Target Texts (hereafter ST and TT) focuses on image composition, ideational meaning, and visual-verbal relationship. The chapter would challenge the still widespread logocentric tendency to marginalize the contribution of the visual in illustrated fiction. Turci, instead, argues its vital role in the construction of meanings that she then connects to context of culture. In particular, she probes the domestication of illustrations in the TT with reference to the historical and political context in Italy when the translated text was published.

O'Halloran (2008: 445), in speaking of the numerous challenges facing SF-MDA, points up the need for modelling grammars of semiotic resources other than language, including resources not mentioned till now: those of music and sound, and sourcing 'e.g. Steiner, 1988; van Leeuwen, 1999'. The first is an early study of how the systems of language and music interact in weaving the texture of an American Traditional folk ballad; the second is a seminal much-quoted social semiotic study of *Speech, Music, Sound*. A more recent and frankly intriguing study by Caldwell and Zappavigna (2011) uses a visualization technique for representing repeated patterns in text – arc diagrams – to study instances of graduation in the end-rhymes of a Kanye West rap song. They find that the song foregrounds the lyrical meaning potential of these consecutive rhymes – their sense, rather than their sound (2011: 240). Although nowhere is either Hasan or Jakobson mentioned, this study of foregrounded patterns of meaning unmistakably links up to the work of both in ways that merit serious explicit recognition – and pursuing.

An SFMS paper that explicitly, and perceptively, links up to both Mukařovský and Hasan (1989 [1985]) is Martinec (2000). This 'systemic-functional semiotics of action' study of a Michael Jackson video clip, *Jam*, identifies two substantial means of patterning: phases and foregrounding. The first of these is said to chart action development in the video, while the second, in Hasanian fashion, articulates identity-construing themes. Moreover, questions of audience reception are once again highlighted.

As seen above, many studies adroitly wield intersecting methods in their approach to 'literature'. Some others I opt to locate in section 2 or 3 below, depending on which approach seems ascendant. A final illustrative paper that brings together multimodal, corpus and translation methodologies is included here, as its multimodal aspect strikes me as dominant. Firmly rooted in SFL and social semiotic theory, Baumgarten (2008) competently explores the verbal-visual meaning relationship in corpora of 1960s' and 1990s' *James Bond* films, comparing the different conventions of making verbal reference to visual information in the English films and their German-dubbed versions. The two diachronically distant data sets are also interrogated with corpus tools. Significant distinctions in the choices made by the two languages in their handling of co-occurring visual information emerge in terms of explicitness/implicitness. Moreover, and as numerous other studies find as well, translation shifts are seen to involve variations in all three metafunctions, shifts that this study finds in turn affect narrative construction and cultural paradigms, such as gender relations.

5.3 Systemic Functional Stylistics and Corpus Linguistics

As is well-known, Halliday himself has always had an interest in quantitative method-ologies (cf., e.g. Halliday (2005 [1991b]). His interest began in the 1950s and 1960s with his manual analyses of Chinese and English grammar using very small samples, moved on to machine translation and then was extended to the possibilities for a probabilis-tic modelling of grammar, the determining of a 'probability profile of any grammatical system' (Halliday 2005 [1991b]: 67), both for the global language system and for different registers.

As is widely recognized, however, the SFL and CL relationship is not a clear-cut, trouble-free one. Often it is put in terms of divergence/convergence. For Thompson and Hunston (2006: 3–5), the two are strange, and mutually suspicious, bedfellows, which have, however, common concerns. Halliday (2006: 293) ostensibly suppresses the con-flict, speaking of 'a natural affinity ... a "symbiotic and synergistic relationship"' and seeing the large-scale corpus as vital to 'understanding and modelling the true com-plexity of a human language' (2006: 299). Thus he blesses the 'marriage', with, however, reservations that substantially regard research constraints on automated analysis, more on which below.

Of course, CL methodology has permeated most disciplines by this point in time and, indeed, neither are quantitative stylistic studies new. In searching for SFL (and SFL-friendly) practitioners publishing on the topic, one finds Bednarek (2008), cited in Chapter 4, which offers a brief introductory 'Language+Literature+CL Methods 101' in an SFL perspective, if not a Hasanian one, and Toolan (e.g. 2009) making the case for the analytic advantages of having corpus evidence to support qualitative findings. And we've already seen that many SFMS studies also make use of CL methods in their approach, as we'll also see is the case with some SFL-based translation studies. Indeed, corpus methods are to the fore in the ever-more hybrid methodologies being applied to register studies, including the 'special' register of verbal art.[8] But are these methods unfailingly easy to apply? And are the results they produce consistently positive? Some additional observations will be made.

5.3.1 Some Issues

One well-known practical limitation in using CL techniques for text analysis includes the time-consuming task of corpus construction, if, that is, the texts aren't readily available in electronic format. Then there are also related copyright issues, especially when one is aiming to create a retrievable and reusable resource, one that would also make the results of analysis replicable. But, as Matthiessen warns, '[t]he real constraint on automated analysis has to do with the "level" of analysis ... the upper bound is still located somewhere within the stratum of lexicogrammar' (2009: 53). Halliday and Matthiessen (2014: 70) spell out the dilemma this way: 'automatic analysis gets harder the higher up we move along the hierarchy of stratification' (i.e. it can handle orthographic word patterns and low-ranking lexicogrammatical patterns, but not full SFL clause or semantic analysis). So they conclude that 'we have a trade-off between volume of analysis and richness of analysis: low-level analysis can be automated to handle large volumes of text, but high-level analysis has to be carried out by hand for small samples of text'.

Whether the 'trade-off' between volume and richness is ever a judicious and/or advantageous one will depend on one's research questions and chosen level(s) of inquiry. If these are limited, lower (literally, with reference to stratification/rank hierarchy), then automated analyses won't be problematic. But if these aim higher (i.e. involve levels of semantics and context), then automated analyses alone won't enable desired/required findings. Appraisal analysis is a perfect example of such slipperiness, especially in the literature text, as discussed in, for example: Miller (2016b), which investigates evaluation of the noble* *Coriolanus*; Luporini (2019), which probes the evaluation of lemmata 'white/red' in Rhys's *Wide Sargasso Sea*, and Miller and Luporini (2018a, 2018b), which examine the appraisal of tru* in Coetzee's *Foe*, and the latter paper also investigates evaluation in Sassoon's 'Does it Matter?'. But the general issues raised by the attempt to 'marry' the methods and tools of CL to the SSS+ framework are in themselves thorny. I'd now briefly reflect specifically on these.

So then, just how do-able is an automated analysis of the literature text in the Hasanian perspective? As Hasan's analytical framework is 'dual', as well as being so painstaking in its precepts, categories, and in the very definition of its 'special' object of inquiry, the question of the extent to which automated techniques can be effectively deployed must be posed, as, for example, Miller (2016b) and Miller and Luporini (2015, 2018a, 2018b) do.

The essential query is whether foregrounding – at least at a preliminary investigative stage – is in fact quantifiable. These studies show that systematically tracing the symbolic articulation of theme in verbal art is a question of analysis at precisely those higher levels that Halliday and Matthiessen cautioned against using CL methods for.

Unsurprisingly then, the studies also show that contextualized meaning analysis always requires labour-intensive manual scrutiny, and close attention to the co-text, to logogenesis – that is to say, an attention to text 'in which the potential for creating meaning is continually modified *in the light of what has gone before*' (Halliday and Matthiessen 1999: 18, *my emphasis*). On this point Halliday (2006: 298) makes a fundamental distinction between logogenesis as the instantial construction of meaning in the form of a text – and that of a *corpus*. In the former case, the text is studied as object: it is valued as a discourse in its own right. In the latter, it is studied as instrument: its value is rather as a window onto the system. And as verbal art is clearly an illustration of the former (i.e. a discourse valued in its own right), the question as to whether CL can be effectively deployed in its study seems even more discomfiting.

For Halliday, foregrounding itself *cannot* be expressed statistically; nonetheless, he observes that '[a] rough indication of frequencies is often just what is needed' to evaluate what features deserve further investigation (2002 [1971]: 103). In short, if on one hand he warns that mere statistical frequency – the kind that CL calculates – is no guarantee of significance, of prominence as motivated foregrounding (2002 [1971]: 102–103), on the other hand, he does consider counting patterns a useful step toward determining which features may deserve further investigation. So, such counting is seen to be at least an important stage in contextualized meaning analysis. Indeed, as Miller and Luporini (2015, 2018a) suggest, the extent to which foregrounding is quantifiable would seem to be inscrutable without the assistance of corpus linguistic methods, especially when dealing with longer texts. But their findings show that it is not enough. It plays but a supporting role, guaranteeing data accuracy and statistical significance that cannot be manually achieved in longer texts, but by no means supplanting either the labour-intensive manual analysis of co-textual logogenesis that SSS+ requires or the need for purposefully 'shunting' (Halliday 2002 [1961]: 45) between different textual and extra-textual dimensions, using the corpus as a kind of 'echo chamber' (Thompson and Hunston 2006: 13).

And the use of the word 'assistance' above is not accidental: a distinction must be made between studies that are either corpus-*driven* or -*based* and those that are 'only' corpus-*assisted*, because purposefully mindful of the complexities of meaning-making and the language-context connection in verbal art – more than in any other text type. Miller and Luporini's own efforts have aimed at such vigilance, but a textbook example is Butt (2016), mentioned in the previous chapter and further commented below.

So, in sum, can/should corpus-assisted studies be part of the ongoing development of a rigorous SSS+? Has CL got a viable, and valuable, role in discovering the 'special' function of language in that special register, verbal art? The answer to such queries is a qualified 'yes'. Yes, if the role of CL is instrumental: a useful means for 'trawling' the corpus (Halliday 2005 [1992]: 64) to identify features of language that, in turn, must be further investigated manually, qualitatively, both at the semiotic system of language and at the higher order semiotic system of verbal art, in order to arrive at the text's deepest meanings, or theme.

And now, with this preliminary discussion in mind, diverse studies will be mentioned. Consistent with the principles pondered above, none of these see CL as the alpha and omega of stylistic analysis, but rather value the analyst's assessment of the usefulness and significance of the data CL provides. None of the mainstream scholars, regrettably, have anything to do explicitly with Hasan's SSS.

5.3.2 From Mainstream to Systemic Functional Stylistic Studies Using CL

There are, of course, several very well-known mainstream CL scholars who deserve mention as having also analysed literature, albeit not in a specifically SFL perspective. Mahlberg, Hoey, Stubbs and Teubert (2007), with an introduction by Sinclair, brings most of these figures together. Between these scholars and SFL there are explicit or implicit affinities and thus they are frequently referenced in systemic functional stylistics work as well. As Stubbs (2009: 116) notes, 'Sinclair's work draws on the British tradition of empirical text analysis developed by Firth, Halliday, and others'. And Krishnamurthy observes that 'Halliday, Sinclair, Stubbs, and Hoey have all extended Firth's ideas' on collocation (2006: 596).

Another scholar who has done the same is Bill Louw (e.g. 2014, with Milojkovic), who collaborated with Sinclair and whose knowledge of philosophy is remarkably profound. For years his work has focused on how prosodic patterns in word meaning extend outwards through collocation with other words, and within (Firthian but also Hallidayan) context of situation. Much like Hasan herself, Louw is candid and confident and thus has annoyed as well as impressed colleagues. One germane proclamation: 'I invented Corpus Stylistics in 1987 at A British Council Workshop chaired by Ron Carter at St Hilda's College Oxford' (https://billlouw.academia.edu/). A better-known and often-cited survey of some of the specific ways in which corpus analysis has been applied to the study of literature under the generic term 'corpus stylistics' is Biber (2011), which makes the case for intensifying qualitative engagement with corpus-derived findings. But Biber is not particularly SFL-friendly.

Neither is another renowned name in CL: Mahlberg. Yet, in numerous *non*-SFL-informed studies, Mahlberg perceptively applies CL to literature, noticeably Dickens. In their recent chapter on 'Literary Stylistics' in the *Routledge Handbook of English Language and Digital Humanities* (2020), Mahlberg and Wiegand endorse the 'corpus turn' in literary stylistics and argue the pressing need for dialogue between different research communities: e.g. corpus stylistics, stylometry and the digital humanities, as well as the need for corpus stylistics to contribute to developing visualization techniques. They show how corpus methods can contribute to better understanding patterns of meaning in nineteenth-century narrative fiction as well as to contextualizing literary examples within general language use. Especially interesting for me is their accent on meaning-making through repetition, though no reference to parallelism or Jakobson is made. The corpus of Dickens's novels, the 19th Century Children's Literature Corpus and the 19th Century Reference Corpus, retrieved via the CLiC web app, are all exploited.[9] Below I return to a co-authored study of Mahlberg's that does use SFL, to explore translation issues.

More SFL-friendly, as noted, is Toolan. Toolan (2009), mentioned above, uses keyword analysis generated from WordSmith Tools (Scott 1996–2020) to investigate eight parameters that he judges central to creating narrative progression and expectation in short stories. Typically, his theoretical and methodological toolkit is a richly varied one: interweaving strands from stylistics sub-disciples such as narratology and reader-response cognitive approaches with corpus work by Sinclair and Hoey, pragmatic approaches such as Gricean implicature, etc. His chapter on 'Collocation and corpus stylistics' has most to do with SFL, briefly describing the collocational theory of Firth, and its development by Halliday and Hasan in terms of cohesion, then illustrated. In Chapter 7 of her volume using CL to probe Jane Austen, Fischer-Starcke (2010) also investigates cohesion, in particular lexical cohesion in terms of reiteration, preferring, however, to follow Hasan (forthcoming [1984]) rather than Halliday and Hasan (1976). As will be seen, SFG-inspired cohesion analysis occurs in translation studies as well.

And now to turn to systemic functional stylistic studies using CL. As anticipated, we come back to Bednarek, this time regarding her more CL-informed studies. Bednarek (2010a), as in (2011) cursorily mentioned above, performs a corpus stylistic study of the 'dramedy' *Gilmore Girls* on monomodal corpora, adopting a three-pronged approach that moves from large-scale corpus analysis, through semi-automated small-scale analyses and then to case studies that are only manually analysed. The scales correspond to a hierarchy of research questions largely as described above: moving from concerns at the lowest (lexicogrammatical) level to those at the highest level (semantics and context). Working in an SFL corpus stylistics perspective, she investigates patterns revealing realization resources of interpersonal identity and bonding/affiliation among the characters. In her volume (2010b), she again focuses on *Gilmore Girls*, but bringing the CL approach together with a multimodal one. The construction of interpersonal identity and affiliation is again a central question, examined with appraisal tools. The volume also explores general issues regarding fictional television, its contextualization, its social position and its cultural function, including its effects on viewers. In Bednarek (2019) the spotlight is again on fictional dialogue, this time on swear/taboo words. The place they occupy in SFL is first of all examined and then their frequency and distribution in a small specialized corpus of dialogue transcribed from sixty-six contemporary TV series: the Sydney Corpus of Television Dialogue (SydTV), designed to be representative of the language variety of fictional US American TV dialogue. Results are said to show that swear/taboo words in the corpus are actually multifunctional. They can serve the purposes of characterization, of humour, can be a plot device or even a manager of evaluation/emotion.

We've already seen various studies by Taylor blending multimodal with CL/digital methods. Taylor (2008) pre-dates Bednarek's exploration of intersubjective stability in TV dialogue over time (2011). In a corpus-assisted study of predictability inherent in the repetitiveness and formulaic quality of the language choices and stock phrases in screen dialogue, Taylor explicitly relates such language choice likelihood to the equally recurrent situations of TV serials and film.

Now I turn to other SF corpus-assisted studies – of the written literature text. Miller (2016b), Luporini (2019), and Miller and Luporini (2015, 2018a, 2018b) have already been referenced above, albeit very succinctly. Butt (2016), also noted above – as a perfect illustration of corpus-assisted literature study – probes *Troilus and Cressida* as Hasanian verbal art. It initially exploits concordancing tools to investigate the dense lexical relations of certain key words in the text, building a picture of their logogenetic accumulation and illustrating their role in Shakespeare's artistry in the articulation of theme. He does much more, however, including reflecting on the theatrical performance of the text and, with his analyses of a small sample of Shakespearean sonnets, also demonstrating the 'latent patterning' (cf. Butt 1988, remarked in Chapter 3) of clause complexing, described as 'a profound, even visceral, dimension of the embodiment of language' (2016: 48). Semiotic distancing in adaptations of Shakespeare in different cultural contexts of reception is also discussed.

Taylor Torsello (2007) demonstrates how the frequency and the form of projections can function as an important discriminating factor across genres, across instances of the same variety by different authors, and even across diverse texts by the same author. The works of verbal art that are hand-tagged for types of projection and related phenomena, and analysed, using WordSmith Tools, include: *St. John's Gospel*, Woolf's *A Room of One's Own*, *Mrs. Dalloway* and *To the Lighthouse*, as well as Rowling's *Harry Potter and the Philosopher's Stone*. Taylor Torsello's findings offer evidence of the use of projection as an artistic strategy.

O'Halloran (2007) was cited in Chapter 1 apropos of the censure of Halliday by Fish (1980) for a perceived 'circularity' of interpretation and analysis in Halliday (2002 [1971]); one whereby interpretation preceded analysis, which was then used to corroborate that interpretation. Without underwriting the accusation, O'Halloran performs an SFL analysis of Joyce's 'Eveline' that is deliberately designed to avoid his own interpretation being open to any such charge, by producing more objective readings constrained by corpus data. He holds that, although arbitrariness in analysis and interpretation cannot be wholly removed, it can be reduced with CL methods and the practice of stylistics thus made more rigorous and systematic.

Goatly (2008) dedicates a chapter to a corpus-assisted critical SFG analysis of *Harry Potter and the Philosopher's Stone*. The world of the text that emerges from the concordance data is interpreted as being essentially sexist, authoritarian and obsessed with anxiety-provoking mechanisms of control – chancy values that 'may have a significant effect on the construction and reproduction of ideology in young minds' (2008: 58). Such findings are unexpected, given the 'inspiring life lessons' *Harry Potter* is frequently alleged to teach (cf., e.g. Bridges 2017).

Ideology and identity figure strongly in Dalamu (2019) as well. This is a curious work by an indubitable SFL enthusiast.[10] Putting SFG forward as a 'viable tool of digital humanities', Dalamu carries out a corpus-assisted analysis of a Nigerian poem, 'Area Boy', examining instantiations of TRANSITIVITY, MOOD and THEME SYSTEMS. One key finding is the dichotomy between past and present construed by the poem, which also works to construe the conflict between personal versus social responsibility for the boy's frustrations and failings.

Turci (2007) also exemplifies the use of WordSmith Tools as a preliminary step in verbal art analysis. The study manually probes the textual environments of the much-reiterated lemma dark* in Conrad's *Heart of Darkness* for experiential meanings. Ultimately, it shows that a corpus-assisted enquiry can provide a new angle from which to look at too long established and widely accepted critical paradigms, not unlike Halliday's dismantling of the dominant critical paradigm regarding Tennyson's 'In Memoriam', as remarked in

Chapter 2. Select findings of her study are cited in Mastropierro (2017: 230), to which I presently turn.

The following studies could well have been treated in the final section on systemic functional stylistics and translation but I opt to have them function as a boundary marker, and a sort of prelude.

Mastropierro and Mahlberg (2017) applies CL to an investigation of translated cohesion, using Halliday and Hasan (1976). Keywords are used as starting points for identifying cohesive networks and their meaning-making function in Lovecraft's *At the Mountains of Madness*. The complexity of these emerges from a comparison of Lovecraft's original novel and its translation into Italian. The study reveals how local alterations can have wider effects on text cohesion, in particular when the lexical item in question is thematically pertinent. The wider issue of applying CL models and methods to corpus stylistic analysis is also discussed.

Mastropierro and Mahlberg (2017) heralds the chapter on cohesion in Mastropierro's volume (2017). Through the analysis of Conrad's *Heart of Darkness* and four of its Italian translations, the volume investigates how stylistic features are significantly related to the major themes of the novel. SFL informs, in particular, Chapter 5, which analyses lexical cohesion. Qualitative analysis of the data gathered with WordSmith Tools shows how shifts in the original's stylistic features occurring in translation can also affect interpretation. 'Thus, discrepancies in the word relations result in discrepancies in the fictional representations ... In this respect, such alterations can be said to have manipulative effects' (2017: 203).

Both Pagano, Figueredo and Lukin (2015) and the further developed (2016) apply CL to translation. Solidly rooted in SFL, the studies aim at investigating ST-TT relations computed with statistical methods. In a corpus of retranslations, representative text patterns are manually annotated according to functional categories common to both source and target language systems. The corpus consists of ten translations of the story by Mansfield, 'Bliss' (seen regarding Lukin and Pagano 2016 in Chapter 2). The translations are into Spanish or Portuguese, all by different translators, and spanning six decades. Findings show similarities regarding the lexicogrammatical choices made by each author within the systems analysed. They also corroborate the results of researchers using other methodologies to test the 'retranslation hypothesis', i.e. the relative distance of a first translation from the ST, but also varied degrees of proximity to the ST of retranslations.

5.4 Systemic Functional Stylistics and Translation

In the summer of 2007, Matthiessen presented a paper at the ISFLC 2007 in Odense entitled 'Multilinguality: Translation – a "Feverish" Phase in SFL?'.[11] Since then, it's fair to say that the fever has only mounted. Matthiessen (2009: 41–42) provides a brief SFL overview of what he describes as 'one area within multilingual studies, viz. translation and interpreting studies'. In this section, however, the focus is solely on translation between languages and from a product-oriented rather than a process-oriented perspective (cf. Toury 1995: 10). Further, it deals with translation of the literature text only, which, as Steiner (2015a: 413) notes, Halliday early on described as 'the kind of translation in which ultimately the translation unit is the entire text in its context of culture, and nothing less (cf. already Halliday et al., 1964: 130)'. But before zooming in on select verbal art translation studies, some initial broader-spectrum comments are in order.

5.4.1 Systemic Functional Translation Studies (SFTS)

As Matthiessen (2009) points out, translation studies (henceforth TS) have been on the SFL agenda for a long time – at least since Halliday drew attention to the importance of the concept of choice for translation (2005 [1956]). The term coined for the SFL approach to translation is Systemic Functional Translation Studies (SFTS) (Matthiessen 2009: 25). Matthiessen himself defines the approach as 'the recreation of meaning in context through choice' (2014: 272) and ties the SFL notion of choice to degrees of intra- or inter-metafunctional translation shifts situated along a maintenance-shift cline (Matthiessen 2014). The SFL notion of choice has also been seen as useful in TS in general (Steiner 2015a: 413, citing Munday 2012). Matthiessen's work on translation is extensive, admirable, but cannot be adequately represented here. Still, as Steiner (2005: 488) puts it, Matthiessen (2001) could be regarded as 'the most comprehensive statement of an SFL-based view and, indeed, programme for theorising translation'.

But register is also a vital concept for SFTS. Steiner (2015a: 419) notes how Halliday's notion of register as a 'key organizing concept linking context and lexico-grammar ... proves attractive in a natural way to people working on texts, either as practising translators, or else as theoreticians of translation'. But the notion of context vis-à-vis register is, of course, complex, and no less so with reference to translation. Halliday (2001: 17) specifies that a translation's value can be identified with reference to various strata, ranks, metafunctions, contexts and even in connection with the perceived worth of the ST itself. In later writings as well, Halliday revisits the complexity of translation theory and practice and in particular the issues of modelling, but also evaluating, translation (e.g. 2013 [2009], 2013 [2012]). At the close of his paper, Steiner (2015a: 426) references Halliday (2001), linking its lessons up to his own conviction that in order to locate linguistics at the centre of textual studies, 'we need to carry our contextualizations beyond and outside the linguistic levels of description, through the interlevel of context of situation and into the cultural context'.

Steiner (2004) sees translated texts as being special text types, indeed cross-lingual functional varieties, or registers. Recalling the 'special' register of verbal art as discussed especially in Chapter 2, we might then see verbal art translation as having an additional layer of 'specialness' to take into account. Relatedly, in striking tribute to the special register of verbal art and specifically connecting up to Halliday's comments on de-automatization in literature entailing 'the partial freeing of the lower-level systems from the control of the semantics so that they become domains of choice in their own right' (cf. Chapter 2), Matthiessen (2001: 80) notes that 'there are contexts of translation where the translation has to be de-automatized ... This is most likely to happen in literary translation.'

Kunz and Teich (2017: 549 ff.) also examine the SFL notion of register as a basis for theorizing and modelling translation. In their view, of all the many conceptual categories that SFL offers for the modelling of language, the most productive one for TS has been, in fact, that of register, due to offering a framework for text analysis in cultural context. Moreover, they see it as having been instrumental in transcending the boundaries between theoretical, descriptive and applied TS, highlighting the importance of the last of these. Of the various approaches that they consider to be working to advance future integration of the register model into TS, they highlight quantitative corpus-based methods. These aim, in their opinion, at the identification of intralingual and interlingual variation, the latter leading especially to knowledge of how register patterns differ across languages. Such information, they feel, is vital to elaborating translation strategies that incorporate the factor of context-based choice. Ever-growing attention is in fact on the construction of multilingual corpora and their automated analysis.

And in this way they link up to Matthiessen (2009), not only concerning choice, but also to another observation he makes there: namely, that TS drawing on SFL have steadily gravitated toward automatic analysis of multilingual corpora. The intensely productive work of Steiner and the Saarland University team, among which Kunz and Teich prominently figure, offers the best examples of this trend in a registerial perspective. Kunz et al. (2017) is but one recent example of their empirically-based comparison of English-German translations of diverse registers in the GECCo-corpus, focusing on cohesion.

Steiner (2015b) – relevantly for systemic functional stylistics – points up how more significant quantitative distinctions in terms of cohesive devices are to be found in *fictional texts* than in all other registers in the overall GECCo-corpus, eight in all. Also revealed is a tolerance for local ambiguities in English fictional STs as opposed to their German translations (2015b: 360), including evidence of a weakening of demonstrative force and downgrading in terms of accessibility of referents in English TTs, in comparison to the German STs. But with these last observations, I have evidently slid into examples of studies dealing with verbal art translation in an SFL perspective, as anticipated above. There would of course be many more generally germane considerations to make, but at this point I turn to my specific brief.

5.4.2 SFTS and Verbal Art

As always, however, I'd first clarify that the studies commented below are the work of scholars who are not all strictly-speaking systemicists, but that, should this be the case, they have fruitful relations with SFL. Indeed, SFL has been harnessed even by translation scholars outside the community, as Manfredi (2008: 64–65), Kunz and Teich (2017: 549) and others point out. Among these are: Catford (1965), with which he established himself as the first translation theorist to base a linguistic model on aspects of Halliday's early work on Scale and Category Grammar; Hatim and Mason (1990), the earliest to have exploited the SFL concept of register (see also the more recent Hatim (2009); Newmark (1991), whose Chapter 5 is dedicated to 'The Use of Systemic Linguistics in Translation', beginning with the primary use of its notion of language as meaning potential; House (1997, 2001), also examining interlanguage register conventions and spotlighting function with reference to the contextual parameters of field, tenor and mode in her exploration of translation quality criteria, and Munday, who in 2008 harnesses CDA and SFL to explore ideology in translated texts and, in, for example, 2012 and 2015, builds on Martin and White's account of appraisal (2005) to show how STs and TTs may inscribe different types of evaluation.

Indeed, there are many other scholars working on the translation of literature in an SFL perspective whose toolkits privilege APPRAISAL SYSTEMS, as reported in Tajvidi and Arjani (2017). These include: 1) Pérez-González (2007), a study of the construal of 'naturalness' and interpersonal shifts in translated (dubbed) film dialogue; 2) Munday (2012: Chapter 5), which investigates (in)variability in appraisal resources in original Spanish fiction and its English translations; 3) Mouka, Saridakis and Fotopoulou (2015), a cross-linguistic and corpus-driven study that examines a subtitled corpus of racist-themed movies in two target languages (Spanish and Greek) for racist discursive shifts; 4) White (2016), which, in illustrating an original methodology for investigating attitudinal and registerial variation, compares the opening paragraph of Camus's *L'Etranger* with several English translations of it, finding that even minor shifts affect the TT profile; 5) Rodrigues-Júnior and Barbara (2013), which studies ten extracts from *The Picture of Dorian Gray* and their Brazilian translations for evaluative construal of characterization; and 6) Rosa (2013), which performs a quantitative investigation into the shift of power of the narrative voice in some 500 sentences from three novels in English and fourteen of their Portuguese translations. These last two studies focus on engagement mechanisms. Already mentioned in section 2 above are: Miller (2016b), which investigates the enactment of evaluation of the noble* *Coriolanus*; Luporini (2019), analysing the evaluation of lemmata 'white/red' in Rhys's *Wide Sargasso Sea*, and Miller and Luporini (2018a, 2018b), which traces the appraisal of tru* in Coetzee's *Foe*, and the latter, evaluation in Sassoon's 'Does it Matter?' as well.

The circumscribed review that follows proceeds somewhat geographically, and sometimes also culturally, from East, to South, and then West.

The Far East is indeed a rich repository of studies fusing systemic functional stylistics and translation. Huang (2014), for instance, investigates translations into English of Confucius's *Lun Yu* (The Analects), a text that, analogously to the Bible, can be seen as a sort of literary anthology – a collection of varied literary genres written by multiple authors over time. SFL studies of *Lun Yu* and its translations are various, as Huang observes, also by PhD candidates he supervises. His chapter focuses on the translation of the reporting clause instantiated in one dialogue and two of its translations, illustrating intricate issues related to the myriad interpretations of what are the only assumed meanings of a text written over 2,000 years ago.

As noted in Chapter 2, in his 'Stylistics in Translation' in the *Cambridge Handbook of Stylistics*, Lin advocates 'a functional stylistics model' and even more especially the application of Hasan's framework for the analysis of verbal art to TS (2014a: 576 ff.). He performs an illustrative analysis of an original Chinese Tang poem by Jia Dao, finding that its linguistic choices create the kind of consistent foregrounding at the semiotic system of verbal art that articulates a theme. In contrast, he finds the English translation falls short of a lexicogrammatical patterning sufficient to allow a second-level reading at all. Lin (2014b) reproposes the analysis in more detail and again resolutely calls for a greater extension of Hasan's work to the field of literary translation.

And here I cite once again Lukin and Pagano, the former in Australia at Macquarie, and the latter in Brazil – so both Southern hemisphere, if miles apart. Besides applying CL to translation, as seen above, Lukin and Pagano (2012) also analyses translation in terms of Hasan's model of double-articulation in verbal art. Starting from Catford's (1965) identification of equivalence with situational overlap, they examine how the contextual variables of field, tenor and mode function as the raw material in the symbolic articulation of theme. As in Lukin and Pagano (2016) (see Chapter 2), here too the authors make use of Bernstein's coding orientations to probe the complexity of social positioning – central to that theme – in the story. The text focused on is once more the oft-translated 'Bliss' by Mansfield and five of its translations into Spanish.

Once more, scholars having done their PhDs under Matthiessen's supervision prove to be fertile ground. Of course only a limited number of the many can be cited.

Probing translation shifts in particular vis-à-vis the parameter of tenor, resonating with interpersonal meanings, Yu and Wu (2016, 2017) focus on, respectively, the roles of MOOD and MODALITY SYSTEMS and those of personal pronouns in 'recreating the image of Chan master Huineng'. Both studies examine four temporally distanced English translations of the Chinese *Platform Sutra* and are corpus-assisted, using analytical tools created by Wu: in (2016) SysFan, and in (2017) SysConc. Both studies also argue that translators' choices and the images of Huineng recreated need to be understood in relation to the context of the translation.

Exploiting House's model for translation quality assessment, as well as SFL's notion of instantiation, Wang (2018) fashions a framework for a diachronic study that probes findings in the light of cultural context. Wang compares nine of Conan Doyle's detective short stories with two temporally distanced Chinese translations of these, pinpointing 'mismatches' but also correspondences between verbal process clauses. Investigation of these with reference to contextual parameters reveals the two TTs' quite distinct story situation types.

A volume co-authored by Wang and Ma (2020) provides an in-depth application of SFTS to the study of Chinese drama translation, investigating two English translations of the Chinese play script of *Teahouse* by Lao She. Working Bottom-Up, they first investigate shifts in instantiations of interpersonal, textual and logical meanings in choices of Mood (for dramatic dialogue), Theme (in monologue), and taxis and logico-semantic type (in stage directions), linking shifts in grammar to those in characterization. They then move to consider the contextual parameters, providing evidence for the lexicogrammatical choices. Among their findings are that: the fields of activity are recreated consistently; tenor relations are marked by differences in institutional, power and status roles; and textual choices are informed by rhyming patterns but also by interests of performability. There are two other noteworthy volumes by the co-authors. Ma and Wang (2020) addresses the Chinese translation of the English ST of *Stray Birds*, Rabindranath Tagore's collection of philosophical poems, and its four Chinese TTs. The authors propose an analytical framework for probing the graphological and phonological expression plane, the level of lexicogrammar and also that of context. Wang and Ma (2021) is the monograph in the Equinox Key Concepts Series dedicated to SFTS.

I now move back westwards. Sellami-Baklouti (2018), a Tunisian scholar, investigates the translation of dialectal varieties in Mark Twain's *The Adventures of Tom Sawyer* into

French and Arabic. She argues for the relevance of the notions of both register and choice for examining user-related linguistic variation in literature. She also makes use of Matthiessen's maintenance-shift cline (2014), referred to above, for evaluating translation quality. Among her findings is that the accurate rendering of ST variation in the TT means a better translation, even if it may also mean challenging target language ideology, a position comparable to that of House (2001), as seen above.

Another paper probing English-Arabic language pair translation is by the Jordan-based scholar, Othman. Othman (2017) investigates the different handling of explicitation mechanisms in three translations of Golding's *Lord of the Flies*. For Othman's research, the concepts of register and choice are essential ones too. He proposes an SFL-based model for both identifying and classifying translation shifts, which is also the topic of Othman (2020).

Marco (2000) also argues the crucial relevance of Hallidayan register analysis in literary translation, insisting, however, on the equal importance of the context of culture and also of intertextuality for translation analysis. He illustrates his approach with fragments of W.H. Auden's 'The Sea and the Mirror', in which the Shakespearean monster, Caliban, addresses the audience at the end of a performance of *The Tempest*. Register characterization of this complex speech is found to be vital, but the full cultural value of Caliban's rhetoric is seen as being established only intertextually. The ST is in part compared with Marco's own translation into Catalan, where maintenance of the complexity of the original is said to have been the aim.

And now to go back to Steiner and Yallop (2001), which, as we've seen, hosts Halliday (2001) as well as Matthiessen (2001), both cited above, but which also contains House (2001), also mentioned above. Two chapters, in particular, analyse verbal art in arguing their case. The first is in fact House, who takes up Halliday's question on how one knows when a translation is good. Reviewing in detail the various ways of approaching the question, and outlining her own mainly SFL-informed functional approach, she then illustrates and tests her method on a translation into German of an English children's story about a family of bears. She concludes that the translation is covert, the result of a process that denies the German child access to the original voice and in so doing underestimates, or ignores, children's learning and imaginative capacities.

The second chapter is Yallop (2001). Yallop was an expert on Australian Indigenous languages who, incidentally, co-authored a book on Lexicology with Halliday (Halliday and Yallop 2007). His chapter starts with a fascinating philosophical discussion on the notions of uniqueness and similarity that grounds the subsequent discussion of how it is that one can evaluate equivalence. Yallop then boldly undertakes an examination of a translation (of a kind) of Lewis Carroll's *Alice's Adventures in Wonderland* into the Australian Aboriginal language, Pitjantjatjara. Exploiting the back translation of the Pitjantjatjara provided in the book, he shows points of convergence between Carroll's original and the Pitjantjatjara version, but also points of extreme divergence. The published translation, *Alitji in the Dreamtime*, does indeed describe itself as having been 'adapted and translated' from the original. Yallop concludes, judiciously, that 'the question is, as always, what kind of similarity we are prepared to accept as equivalence in a particular context for a particular purpose' (2001: 242).

Taylor and Baldry (2001), in this same volume, is about SFL-informed computer-assisted analysis and translation, but deals only with advertisements. Of import, however, is their complaint of the lack of due attention to SFL in the translation field – a lack of that fever-ishness that a few years later Matthiessen presaged (2007), as seen above. During the 1990s, even before his 'multimodal turn' so to speak, Taylor's work was making intense and fruitful efforts to bring SFL and translation together. See, for instance, Taylor (1990, 1993, 1998), but also other publications in Italian that helped to spread the good word. From the noughties, his research into translation becomes over time more multimodal and computer-assisted, as seen. Both Baldry and Taylor being, in institutional terms, Italian, facilitates a slide into other work on the Italian scene.

Katan (2009 [2001]) demonstrates his anthropological application of the central SFL terms of context of situation and context of culture. This much-cited scholar views the translator as an intercultural mediator, applying a 'culture filter' to the foreign text and negotiating meanings for the TT reader. His examples are taken from various text types, including Calvino's *L'avventura di una moglie*/*The Adventure of a Wife*, the translation in English seen as foreignizing and creating negative stereotyping. Katan (2014 [2004]), an introductory volume for translators with numerous illustrative literary texts, once again displays a Hallidayan influence, albeit yet again with application that is cultural rather than grammar/text focused. Its third edition is forthcoming.

Manfredi (2008, 2012) echoes the call of Taylor Torsello for an SFG-based study of translation (1996: 88) and makes an important contribution to such study, including the translation of verbal art. Manfredi (2012) ponders teaching the translation of various text types, including the literature text, focusing on functional equivalence, in particular at the levels of stratification and metafunction. The study also reflects on how to narrow the gap between the theorist's descriptivism and the students' typical preference for prescriptivism. Manfredi (e.g. 2014), consistently shows how, on one hand, translation theory on its own is but an empty abstraction, and, conversely, that the practice of translation devoid of a valid theoretical grounding provides students with little more than pointlessly subjective tasks. Manfredi (2019) also makes connections between SFG and translator training, exemplifying with verbal art as well.

Johnson (2010) reports a qualitative but corpus-assisted study of point of view in two novels by the Sardinian writer, Grazia Deledda, and their translations into English. Working with a rich but balanced toolkit, including a robust SFL perspective, Johnson identifies the grammatical strategies used to translate markedly frequent clusters con-taining word forms of the lemmata 'parere/sembrare' (seem or appear). She then gauges the degree to which these approximate reader perception of point of view in the ST. The necessarily cautious conclusion is that there is a discernible shift away from the point of view of character in the ST to that of narrator in both novels' TTs.

Swain (2014) shows how Lemke's metafunctional-based theory of intertextuality (1995) provides a valuable framework for making generalizations about the complex meanings of metaphor. Further, she shows how the theory entails thinking in terms not of the 'transfer' of intertextuality, but rather of the contiguity between the ST and TT intertextual environments, thus expanding the range of parameters along which assessments of metaphor 'equivalence' are made. The paper probes how metaphors mean through intertextuality in D.H. Lawrence's and more recent English language renderings of two novels by Sicilian writer, Giovanni Verga: *Cavalleria Rusticana* and *Vita dei Campi.*

5.5 Coda

This chapter has offered a circumscribed overview of research into systemic functional stylistics wedded, respectively, to multimodal/multisemiotic, corpus and translation approaches. Theoretical issues have been raised and much stimulating research briefly described. The studies signalled have essentially been at least SFL-influenced and focused on literature. The definition of 'literature', however, has been stretched to comprise research into any digitalized or digital born medium that is exploited in the telling of fictive stories relating to some aspect(s) of human social existence. This Hasanian thematic aspect is explicitly addressed, however, only at times. Indeed, as was noted at the start, the question of the 'art' of the text, of its registerial specialness, receives decidedly less attention than it might do. In these cases, the 'and' constituent inclines to prominence and the artistic nature of the text tends to be lost sight of. Nonetheless, all research commented systematically attends to contextualized meaning-making strategies in the texts examined. It also enriches our knowledge of work going on in systemic functional stylistics, which obviously was my aim.

Knowing full well that there would be many other theoretical points to discuss and deserving studies to take note of, I close this chapter, and, fundamentally, this volume, here. There remains only for me to say something about how I see the future of systemic functional stylistic studies evolving: how I feel it might and how I would like it to – which are not the same things of course. This I do in the separate Afterwords, much too brief to call a chapter, which follows. There I draw back within the limits of Hasan's SSS once again.

Afterwords

To speak of the future directions systemic functional stylistic studies might take, I engage with Bowcher (2018), which has been referenced previously. 'Future directions in the study of verbal art' is the title of her closing chapter to a volume dedicated to Ruqaiya Hasan and many are the suggestions made 'against which future research might make sense' (2018: 280). It is these I will assess, and dialogue with here. Thus, I choose to narrow the field down once again to Hasan's SSS, having no doubt that Halliday's stylistic work will continue to receive due regard both within and outside the community. Hasan's stylistic legacy, on the basis of what has been amply observed, is much less secure.

First among Bowcher's proposals for future directions verbal art research might take, is to focus on the role it has in language development, but also on the how and why of its own development as a means of realizing certain functions, in particular with reference to society (2018: 282).

Posing such research questions would, I agree, undoubtedly be useful, if the studies were properly designed and formulated. But the nature of these questions seems to me to entail a need for large-scale diachronic studies on the part of collaborating study teams with the kind of corpus-assistance that Bowcher also approves. Indeed, elsewhere in her chapter, she puts forth related queries that might be investigated through corpus approaches: for example, on variation within an author's work and among authors in specific cultural domains and what these may tell us about the artist's/artists' take on their society. And here she makes specific reference to how large-scale studies of 'different instances of verbal art from different cultural and linguistic contexts could provide a means of better understanding how language is deployed across the social contexts of verbal art' (2018: 291). Society and the social are staples in Bowcher's reasoning on future directions.

As Bowcher says, the groundwork for such investigations has been laid, as a number of the corpus approaches to verbal and/or visual art pointed up in Chapter 5 have confirmed: for instance, Bednarek's (2019) use of the Sydney Corpus of Television Dialogue, albeit only US and only contemporary in nature. But Bowcher's point is a valid one. I'd also recall what Moore indicates as one current challenge to the Hallidayan tradition in general that still needs facing: its 'computational enhancement' (2017: 433, see Chapter 5, note 8). Notwithstanding, here too the kind of corpus research that Bowcher suggests requires, I believe, projects on which many scholars should, collectively and concertedly, collaborate. This is of course a tangible possibility, if such teams could be efficiently formed, and if their members were concerned with investigating the 'art' of verbal/visual/digital, whatever, art – a prerequisite, and one Bowcher too persistently stipulates, as emerges further below.

Beyond corpora, my research for this volume has repeatedly seen the future of stylistic analysis portrayed as being increasingly digital, by systemicists and non-systemicists alike. For example, Toolan (2014: 469), in speaking of film analysis in particular, represents the development as far more than a technological revolution, indeed as epochal: 'in the twenty-first century new digital media are central to the shaping and reflecting of new forms of sensibility, new "structures of feeling" (to use Raymond Williams' phrase)'. Mahlberg and Wiegand (2020: 322) are decidedly less rhetorical but also stress the significance of the digital humanities, for their interest: corpus stylistics. In Chapter 5 we have also seen how the digital turn inventively drives Unsworth's work on reconceptualizing literacy and literacy pedagogy for 'net-age' young readers. Of course his digital multimedia recontextualizations of literature pose challenges not only to teachers' IT skills but also to the very complexion of verbal art itself. One germane query that seems to me to arise – even more so than with multimodal stylistics research – is 'Whither goes the classic literary canon, and its Hasanian "appraisal"?'. The challenges for pedagogic practice in the increasingly digital world also receive attention in Mahlberg and Wiegand (2020).

And indeed, Bowcher then ties her promotion of large corpora to a topic also glimpsed in Chapter 5: text visualization (Caldwell and Zappavigna 2011, and again Mahlberg and Wiegand 2020), auguring its capacity for highlighting patterning in verbal art and the development of the technique to the point of allowing exploration of the meanings of verbal art in all their complexity. However, as I've intimated in Chapter 5, such a worthy goal would be greatly assisted if researchers into visualization techniques concerning what can be defined as literature would explicitly investigate and acknowledge the connections that there might be between their own approach and findings and Hasan's framework, and indeed also with Jakobson's work on parallelism. Otherwise, precious acquired knowledge is lost to a preoccupation with innovation. In short, I believe new hypotheses and applications need to humbly take account of the old, acknowledging correspondences where they exist. Research has to know where it's come from and the problems and solutions that went before, so it won't erroneously assume to be reinventing the wheel.

But a vital proposal Bowcher makes concerns the crux of Hasan's framework: foregrounding. She counsels further investigations into the phenomenon aiming at 'understanding the way in which language is put to use in different forms of verbal art' (2018: 288). The suggestion here seems to be for comparative analyses of sub-genres of literature. She also ties this recommendation to the sacrosanct SFL belief that the findings of language research should also feed back into the general SFL theory of the language. And we've already seen her attentiveness to the role verbal art may have in language development. Among the specific research questions she poses in this regard is where the Hasanian accent on the 'art' of verbal art fits into other SFL theoretical concepts and features: 'That is, how does "theme", "symbolic articulation", "semantic drift" ... and "latent patterning" (e.g. Butt 1988, 2016) relate to context of situation, realization, register, text structure, and/or texture?' (2018: 288).

It is impossible to disagree that contributing to the further development of global SFL theory is another essential aim for verbal art research. As we well know, linguistic theories, rather than being unchanging or impenetrable, are dynamic notions, constantly shifting and developing, as then the language system little by little does as well. Yet, as we've seen, Hasan herself has had much to say about the semiotic system of verbal art's special relation to these concepts. Moreover, I would recall here once again Matthiessen's caution about the need for extensive long-term empirical research to take place before the special register of verbal art can be said to have been truly modelled (2013a, see Chapter 2, note 7). This too is a necessary task, and one, I believe, that needs to take place prior to being able to contribute definitively to general SFL theory of register, and therefore also to that of context and realization/instantiation. This, I submit, is our foremost task, one to which I hope to have made and to continue to make a modest contribution. To this end, however, are needed numerous small and large-scale, synchronic and diachronic, corpus-assisted and comparative studies. And collaboration among scholars researching the question would undoubtedly be advantageous in this case as well. Findings in such research would then also go a long way toward answering further related queries rightly posed by Bowcher: for example, those regarding the need to extend 'locally-focused' description of theme-creation strategies in verbal art to a fuller and more globally-valid one (2018: 293).

Bowcher also deals with the future directions of verbal art pedagogy studies. She suggests the value of investigations 'into the relationship between verbal art, social codes and socialization ... for a variety of pedagogical purposes and contexts' (2018: 295). As said in Chapter 4, she notes that genre pedagogy studies have taken on this kind of research yet at the same time notes that genre pedagogy 'does not adequately deal with the nature of verbal "artistry"' (2018: 296). Many of her valuable comments and proposals on verbal art pedagogy have in fact already been commented in Chapter 4, in particular her truly inspired call for an RVAP (2018: 297), which, in its own small way, the case study recounted there might be said to be working toward.

Bowcher also calls for more interaction between Hasan's work and other approaches/ ideas (2018: 299 ff.), including APPRAISAL SYSTEMS, which of course are an integral part of the architecture of SFL. She asks whether future studies might not focus more on, for example, the relationship between the use of appraisal resources and symbolic articulation of theme. As seen in Chapter 5, many are the analyses of appraisal in literature being performed, but to the best of my knowledge only my own and Luporini's (e.g. Miller and Luporini 2018a) take up this kind of vital question, though perhaps not as explicitly or effectively as possible.

At the end of Chapter 4, for the sake of argument, I subjectively entertained certain possible drawbacks of Hasan's 'relatively rigid framework' and gave a thought to widening her toolkit, opening it up to other more student-friendly methodologies – a thought that, among others aired there, I then set aside. I believe one needs to be careful to discriminate among approaches/ideas and beware of potential interactional mismatches. Hasan herself gained significant insights from her close readings of the work of many others – among these, linguists such as Saussure, Firth, Whorf, Labov, but also social scientists concerned with language questions like Malinowski, Bernstein (with whom she collaborated), Vygotsky, Bourdieu, Rorty, and so on. Certain interactions may be fruitful, fitting, even entailed (Bernstein, for instance, and Jakobson, in my opinion), while the benefits of others to verbal art research are, even in Bowcher's estimation, in need of further clarification and testing, for instance conceptual metaphor theory.

Surely to be kept in mind is SFL's language-based approach to cognition, and to the construal of experience (Halliday and Matthiessen 1999). Moreover, the reception studies bandwagon is progressively more crowded with practices supporting subjective reader responses *minus* the kind of careful linguistic analysis that Hasan advocated; I would question the wisdom of verbal art study jostling for a place (cf. note 2 in Chapter 4).

Perhaps I also shrink from the vicissitudes of often pointless fragmentation, which is, to my mind, already too much with us. Or perhaps my viewpoint is unduly fossilized. Still, my stance takes courage from Butt's words (2016: 29), whose emphatically and bravely 'judgemental' interpersonal meanings remind me very much of Hasan's own at times!

> Hasan's stylistics ... was never swayed by the narrow focus of the Ohmann hypothesis of the generative era ... or of the later Ohmann 'speech act' suggestion ... With such partial and banal proposals, it is little wonder that so many literature specialists abandoned [the, DRM] linguistic methods of the MIT school of stylistics for the smoke and suavity of Derrida's ineffables (viz. grammatology over grammar). Nor was Hasan subject to the later fashionable extremes of some Reception theorists, who diminished or even nullified the author's role in creating literary value: as if all texts were so similar in their organizing principles that they could be treated as equal in deserving our time and analytical attention. By contrast with these 'en courant' postures, Hasan's questions were simply: what does the text mean? How does it mean what it means? And, why is the text valued as it is?

Bowcher also calls for more attention in SFTS to verbal art (i.e. to how foregrounded patternings are translated), but also to how social codes and cultural values central to a literature text's theme are rendered. She asks, in particular, how SFTS 'can contribute to a cross-cultural description of contexts of reception' but also of the context of creation of the source text. In addition, she'd hope that diachronic or synchronic descriptions of variations in world view within specific societies could also be offered (2018: 304).

I think the groundwork has begun to be laid in this case too, however. A number of the studies cited in Chapter 5 address one or more of these issues, especially those working in a solid SFTS perspective – foremost among these being Lukin and Pagano (2012), Lin (2014a, 2014b), Yu and Wu (2016) and (2017), Sellami-Baklouti (2018), and Wang and Ma (2020).

Finally, Bowcher returns to where she began, with the place of verbal art in society, this time to the importance of translation studies for investigating this as well. Much like Lin (2014a, 2014b), she too sees Hasan's work as crucial to the study of literary translation (2018: 305–306). Would the voices raised were more numerous – and also effectual.

As already noted, again and again Bowcher stresses the need for further studies linking up to what makes verbal art special: the art of verbal art, its artistry, on which Hasan placed great emphasis, as we've seen from the beginning. As noted in Chapter 5, a diffused lack of explicit scholarly concern with such artistry emerges in many of the systemic functional stylistics 'and' studies commented there, especially 'and' multimodality. As also remarked, the 'and' constituent too often inclines to prominence and the artistic element to being lost sight of. And a comparable phenomenon occurs with CL and even, though less so, with translation studies.

But there is, I suggest, a fairly straightforward explanation for this. In speaking of being able to accomplish the kind of verbal art pedagogy Hasan set such great store by – to enable her students 'to produce their own reasoned analyses of a literary work' (2011a: xv, cf. Chapter 4) – Bowcher puts her finger straight onto the sore point: the need for SFL approaches to literature to gain recognition in wider mainstream literary criticism and education circles, convincing these of the value of the SF language model and of its tools for the rigorous and replicable analysis of the linguistically-based artistry of verbal art (2018: 299). In addition to mainstream circles, however, from all that has been said it is clear that the linguistically-based *artistry* of verbal art could gain better recognition in systemic functional circles as well.

Of course Bowcher preaches to the already thoroughly converted, to those who agree that all of this *is* vitally important, a number of whom have been striving with their work to convincingly demonstrate the 'truth' of this value. However, as discussed in Chapter 2, there is a likely (conscious or un-) 'politics of exclusion' of Hasan's work on verbal art (even from mainstream stylistic toolkits that include Halliday, and even in certain systemic functional stylistics work) to be reckoned with – something Bowcher fails to do – quite reasonably: hers is a future directions chapter in a book in honour of Hasan's work on verbal art, after all.

In fact, all of her constructive proposals presume that there *is* a future for Hasan's SSS, which is a delightful presupposition, one that as a devotee I obviously sign straight up to, unreservedly. But how accurate is it? The long ongoing scenario is not encouraging; the skies not very blue. Need we fault too few and/or too unconvincing studies? Would things have been different if Hasan had not fallen victim to academic bias in favour of 'proper' linguistics and been allowed to teach linguistic stylistics (cf. Hasan 2011a: xix)? Could it at least in part be imputed to the ever-stronger taste for burgeoning toolkits? or to a possibly related preference for less challenging but fashionable tools (cf. the discussion in Chapter 1)? Whatever the reasons, a lack of an adequate number of stout-hearted, and wholehearted, SSS researchers is also a major impediment to the broader recognition Bowcher targets, a problem about which, recall, Hasan warned:

> It would be foolish to give the impression that such a research has actually been exhaustively and successfully accomplished: a project of this kind requires not just fifty years by one scholar but more than fifty scholars devoting their working life to it. (2011a: xxiii)

In closing, I propose that, while Hasan's defenders are still around to dedicate themselves to the venture, we might begin to collaborate on projects to some of the ends Bowcher proposes. This may be a way to assure that the mark Hasan's inimitable work on verbal art has made remains indelible. It might even be a way to render it more visible – thus somewhat clearing the skies.

Notes

Preliminaries

1   From the online gloss to Hasan (to appear). Available at: https://www.equinoxpub.com/home/ verbal-art-social-semiotic-perspectivethe-collected-works-ruqaiya-hasan-vol-7-ruqaiya-hasan-edited-jonathan-j-webster/ (accessed 27 June 2020).
2   As the volume elucidates, foremost among these are Lukin (e.g. 2018), Butt (e.g. Butt and Lukin 2009; Butt 2016), Webster (e.g. Lukin and Webster 2005; Webster 2015), Miller (e.g. 2010, 2017b, 2019a), and Miller and Luporini (2018a, 2018b). These SFL scholars, along with Matthiessen (e.g. 2013a, 2018), and Lin (2014a, 2014b, 2016), to varying degrees might be dubbed the custodians of the Hasanian stylistic tradition.
3   The label SSS stands for Systemic Socio-Semantic Stylistics – Ruqaiya Hasan's last formulation before her untimely passing (personal communication to Miller, 1 January 2015).

Chapter 1

1   The 3rd edition of the Dictionary came out in 2011; references here are to the 2nd.
2   Not all would agree with my description of Nowottny's stylistics. Inaccurately, I believe, Fowler confines her within the 'non-sociological New Critical tradition' and even the 'non-linguistic tradition of "practical criticism"' (1981: 46, 186). For the most part she is overlooked in contemporary stylistic literature, though there are noteworthy exceptions. Birch actually cites this same segment with observations analogous to my own (1989: 97–104, 171). Leech recognizes her positive critical input and indeed his own substantial debt to her (1969: viii, 50). Lodge (2015), and elsewhere, recalls her lectures and tutoring affectionately and approvingly, as did my own undergraduate Shakespeare lecturer in the early 1970s.
3   The meeting of these like minds has a long history. Hasan's PhD dissertation was written at the University of Edinburgh under the supervision of M.A.K. Halliday. With reference to this quotation on text description from Halliday, I admit it is preceded by a two-fold assertion I've always had trouble with, as it seems to me to be in conflict with what follows: 'Linguistics is not and will never be the whole of literary analysis, and only the literary analyst – not the linguist – can determine the place of linguistics in literary studies.' To the first statement I'd object that it would depend wholly on the linguistics, the model being adopted and, if it were context-rooted SFL/SSS, I would ask, *why not?*; to the second I can only say that I simply do not agree, contending, with Hasan, that its place is evident, and essential: 'without linguistics, the study of literature must remain a series of personal preferences, no matter how much the posture of objectivity is adopted' (1989 [1985]: 104). Halliday's apparent rejection of the move from a linguistic analysis to a literary reading is actually a major point Huisman raises against Hasan's analytical practice, in particular against the 'assumptions on which she bases her interpretation of "the theme" of a literary text' (Huisman, personal communication, 22 January 2020). More will be said on her position in Chapter 2.
4   For a valuable discussion of this work, with particular reference to theory that fed into SFL studies of verbal art, see Lukin and Webster (2005: 413–416). The authors concentrate almost exclusively on Mukařovský, however, and this choice is, I believe, linked to Hasan's opinion – cited by the authors (2005: 414) – that it was he who had produced 'the most coherent view of the nature of verbal art and its relation to language' (1989 [1985]: 122). Without debating superlatives, I would suggest that Jakobson's

work has not received the attention it deserves in SFL verbal art studies, as will be systematically argued in Chapter 3. Thus, here the intermingling ideas of these two theorists are highlighted. But, though their names are pre-eminent, many were the scholars they interacted with.

5 https://literariness.org/2016/03/17/defamiliarization/ (accessed 31 October 2019). Shklovsky set out his thought on defamiliarization in 'Art as Technique', first published in 1916 and included in Lemon and Reis (eds and trans, 1965). See also https://literariness.org/2016/03/17/roman-jakobsons-contribution-to-literary-studies-an-essay/ (accessed 31 December 2019). O'Toole (2010: 394) notes that 'the Russian work was well represented in Lemon and Reis (1965), in *Russian Poetics in Translation*, Vol. 4 (1977 [O'Toole and Shukman, eds and trans, DRM]), and pre-eminently in Victor Erlich's magisterial study *Russian Formalism: History - Doctrine*'. Erlich (1981 [1955]) is indeed dedicated, as the author declares in the Foreword to the first edition, to that 'School in Russian literary scholarship which originated in 1915–16, had its heyday in the early twenties and was suppressed about 1930.'

6 I'll mention only one such critique: Fowler's avowed 'anti-formalist approach' to stylistics, which monologically proclaims 'that linguistic formalism is of limited significance in literary studies, and educationally restrictive' (1981: 80). Not all believe such assessments are always founded (e.g. Stankiewicz 1983: 24; Caton 1987: 223–224). Erlich (1981 [1955]) is fundamental reading on how much the Formalists gave us, as well as for an even-handed avoidance of the extremes of pure praise or disparagement. Sotirova (2016a: 3–17) performs a convincing 'homage to Formalism' (14) and to the 'powerful presence' it continues to exert in current stylistic enquiry. There are even those who see Mukařovský as having offered 'a rich multi-functional view of language' (Birch and O'Toole 1988: vii). Certainly, Halliday and Hasan seem to agree. Leech (2008: 104) intriguingly entitles a section of his chapter on 'Stylistics and functionalism', 'Roman Jakobson: a formalistic functionalist'. And perhaps Jakobson's 'functional' reach was just as significant, if not as wide-ranging, as his formalist one, as I hope to show when I come back to Jakobson in Chapter 3 apropos of my proposal for a fined-tuned SSS. In any case, the too-common assumption that formalism is able to be unproblematically defined in contrast to functionalism must be rethought. The borderlines here, as is much more common, are blurred.

7 See Erlich (1981 [1955]) on the many analogies between the Russian literary scholars and these movements.

8 These Marxist-based critical theory issues are brilliantly expounded, in a diachronic perspective, by a semi-anonymous author, a certain 'Paul,' at http://herrnaphta.wordpress.com/2011/01/09/reification-and-american-literature/. See also https://literariness.org/2016/03/17/roman-jakobsons-contribution-to-literary-studies-an-essay/ (accessed 11 October 2019).

Chapter 2

1 On the aims of SFL as an appliable linguistics see, for example, Halliday (2007 [2002]: 3), Mahboob and Knight (2010: 4) and Matthiessen (2012: 436). See Lukin and Webster (2005) for useful separate summaries of Halliday and Hasan's central ideas on verbal art, and also of Butt's own contribution to systemic functional stylistics.

2 In our 'conversation', Martin interestingly rethinks one of these: a point he'd made on the need to separate out types of unpredicted foregrounding patterning. 'In retrospect I think I might adjust my position, to allow for de-automatisation between any two strata ... so whenever there is more patterning in a lower strata than is required to realize a higher one, we have foregrounding.' The significance of this 'more than what is required', to my knowledge first discussed vis-à-vis de-automatization in Martin (1992), is harnessed in Chapter 3 in arguing the place of Jakobson's parallelism in Hasan's SSS.

3 Matthiessen (2013a) – a truly serendipitous find – is unfortunately no longer available at the link provided in the references (https://it.scribd.com/document/218160408/Analysing-and-Interpreting-Works-of-Verbal-Arts. Accessed 2 April 2018). In this 'Draft' article, which Matthiessen has given me permission to quote, he addresses the registerial nature of literature as what he calls a 'recreating activity', located within a comprehensive context-based typology of registers. To my query about the paper, Matthiessen replied that '[i]t hasn't been published, but I revised and shortened it when I was asked to submit a paper to the *Indian Journal of Applied Linguistics*' (personal communication, 14 February 2018).

This is the entry labelled as 2013b in the references. Again regrettably, it does not include the valuable material sourced as 2013a in this chapter.

4   As Hasan points out, the two-fold contextual variables of narration did not originate with Halliday: 'In Malinowski's ethnographic descriptions (1935) narrative function and its dual context had been highlighted: the fact that the language of the story "referred to" a separate context – one, an imaginary one of the story itself, and another one relating to the actual process of telling the story to someone' (2009: 176).

5   With reference to note 4 to Chapter 1 above, I believe that what Halliday is describing here is precisely the kind of linguistics that indeed *is* capable of dealing with 'the whole of literary analysis'. And that 'whole' foresees an agenda that is holistic. It utterly upends the linguist's position as voiced, for instance, by Widdowson (1996: 139), according to which 'in literature, the message is text-contained, and presupposes no wider context so that everything necessary for its interpretation is to be found within the message itself ... generally speaking, we can concentrate on the text itself without worrying about distracting social appendages'. Any further comment is superfluous.

6   This aspect of Hasan's view of verbal art is compared by the authors with Halliday's own understanding of the metaphorization through grammar of 'verbal science', elaborating fascinating analogies.

7   In like manner, Matthiessen holds that the language of literature engenders a higher-order of meaning within context, a Hasanian theme, which, he insists 'can – and must – be interpreted against the context of culture' (2013a: 38). Thus, he likewise sees verbal art as a 'special' register, one, however, whose generalized characterization, he cautions, can only be properly modelled with extensive long-term empirical research.

8   For more on and around this conflict between Fowler and Simpson's positions and Hasan's, see Miller (2017b: 507–508, 510 and 2019a: 693–695, 697–700). I come back to the clash between Fowler and Hasan in Chapter 3.

9   As signalled in my Preliminaries, the gloss is visible at https://www.equinoxpub.com/home/verbal-art-social-semiotic-perspectivethe-collected-works-ruqaiya-hasan-vol-7-ruqaiya-hasan-edited-jonathan-j-webster/ (accessed 27 June 2020).

10 A propos, recall her words from her PhD dissertation, cited in Chapter 1: 'we must select a model of linguistics which has the greatest competence in handling texts of a large variety, using the same theories, methods and categories'.

11 Halliday's major analyses have been cursorily mentioned in this chapter but mainly apropos of the theoretical reflections they set forth. See Lukin (2015) for select summaries of his work, as well as Lukin (2018) for her synopsis of Hasan's discussion of Angus Wilson's short story *Necessity's Child*: 'the most detailed and comprehensive of her analyses of verbal art [thus providing] a good example of the method implied by her theoretical position' (2018: 15–16). Hasan and Miller's analysis of a contemporary poem appears in Chapter 4.

12 Omissions – in no way intended as slights – are of course unavoidable, firstly, given restricted space, but also owing to my own regrettably imperfect knowledge.

13 Even this early on, it should be evident that a good deal of Hasan's published work relating to Huisman's topic could have been drawn upon. When queried about her exclusion of Hasan, Huisman very kindly answered (personal communication, 22 January 2020) that – as pointed out in note 3 of Chapter 1 – she had issues with Hasan's analytical practice, in particular with the 'assumptions on which she bases her interpretation of "the theme" of a literary text' and what she sees as Hasan's intransigent insistence on *the* meaning of a literature text: 'a reductive structuralist move to one meaning, irrespective of the context of the individual reader'. She takes courage for her position from Halliday's own apparent reluctance to move from a linguistic analysis to a literary reading – as instantiated in that quote I take exception to in that same note 3 in Chapter 1. In any case, we have agreed to disagree! Hasan's work on literacy/education was also relevant to Huisman's topic, in particular certain papers in the third volume of her collected works, *Language and Education: Learning and Teaching in Society* (2011b). In a follow-up personal communication (23 January 2020), Huisman relates that her own work on medieval to modern literary English has not engaged with current Sydney (genre-based) work on literacy and education and concedes that her knowledge of the field has been fundamentally informed by the presentations and published work of Halliday and Matthiessen. Hasan's work on literacy and, in particular, verbal art literacy will be discussed in Chapter 4.

Chapter 3

1 Gerard Manley Hopkins SJ (28 July 1844–8 June 1889), English poet and Jesuit priest, is considered to be one of the leading Victorian poets. His thoughts on parallelism in his student papers of 1865 were hailed by Jakobson as 'a prodigious insight into the structure of poetry' (1960: 368). Indeed, Jakobson was greatly influenced by Hopkins, as even a cursory search of his name in the volume dedicated to his work, edited by Pomorska and Rudy (1987), attests. Hopkins (first published 1986; revised 2002) is a crucial text for those interested in his work.

2 'Little' is a contemporary elegy that was closely examined in the workshop Hasan and I offered at the LinC Summer School and Workshop 2010 in Cardiff: 'Semiotic Stylistics and Verbal Art'. Its analysis will be exploited in Chapter 4's illustration of an example of SSS+ pedagogy.

3 In 1917, the poem would find its more proper place in Lawrence's collection, *Look! We Have Come Through!* More 'proper', since Lawrence remarked that 'In 1912 begins the new cycle of *Look! We Have Come Through!* … 'Bei Hennef', written in May 1912, by a river in the Rhineland, starts the new cycle' (cf. Cushman 2013 [online since 1 April 2014]: paragraph 44).

4 This analysis, as well as the subsequent discussion of its context of creation, first published in Miller (2007), have been thoroughly revisited and revised.

5 Other interpretative options for restructuring these incomplete clauses would of course be possible. For instance, at the end of both interrogative clauses, 16 and 19, where I suggest 'is there', one might alternatively postulate 'do we need' or even 'could we have'. I opt for one reading simply for analytical purposes.

6 What go by the names of sound symbolism, linguistic iconism and phonosemantics, are hardly exact sciences, and yet studies into these interrelated subjects are fascinating and perhaps even revealing and reliable to some extent. For instance, Auracher et al. (2011) is an intercultural and lingual study testing the universal potential of sound iconicity for computational detection of meaning. Findings suggest that the analysis of phonemic structure could be used to assess emotional states in speakers and authors and to predict the effect on recipients.

7 Analysing the clause as embedded may raise doubts, as it seems irrational to assert that something is 'so **large** [that] I could not see it before'. However, it appears to me to complement, in a typically Lawrentian paradoxical fashion, the Reason that follows: 'Because of the **little** lights and flickers and interruptions.'

8 I reason here that 'perfect' is in itself a superlative, an absolute. There are famous exceptions to the 'rule' of course, notably the Preamble to the U.S. Constitution's 'in order to form a *more* perfect union'. 'Perfect enough' is also a currently trendy formulation for book titles, as several of the myriad hits in google reveal, but their content synopses only serve to confirm my reading of its meaning in 'Bei Hennef' as 'imperfect'.

Chapter 4

1 See Chapters 2 and 3. I am privileged to have had the opportunity to plan such a curriculum and do such teaching – something Hasan herself was never able to do officially in her institutional position, despite her passionate life-long dedication to the linguistic study of literature (2011a: xix, xxii–xxiii). I personally didn't need to combat the institution so much as disapproving colleagues, in both general linguistics and literature studies.

2 I would offer just a thought at this juncture. Although it may be true that 'More recently there has been a movement away from SFL and towards using ideas from cognitive linguistics/cognitive grammar for stylistics analysis and stylistics teaching' (Chloe Harrison, personal communication, 10 February 2020), the great attention given to readers' subjective responses to and experiences of texts in cognitive stylistics may lead to and/or perpetuate the kind of individual, intuitive verbal art reading that SFL would tend to eschew. It is beyond the scope of this chapter to compare the verbal art pedagogic practices of various stylistic sub-disciplines with SFL/SSS applications. For some examples of more or less 'competing' models one might see the edited volumes by Jeffries and McIntyre (2011) and Burke et al. (2012), as

well as the student books by Toolan (1998) and Simpson (2014 [2004]). The latter two of these includes Hallidayan SFL in their toolkits, whereas only one of the papers in the first two does (Nørgaard 2011), and the first of these excludes even Halliday (let alone Hasan) among their eleven 'Key Stylisticians and Their Contributions to the Discipline' (in 2001: 266–268).

3   The issue of the *NALDIC Quarterly* dedicated to Policy, Practice and Research in the field of English as an Additional Language (EAL) in which Dare's paper appears also hosts contributions from other system-icists who argue for the development of a shared SFG metalanguage in teaching practices. In 2016 the *NALDIC Quarterly* was replaced by the *EAL Journal*. A recent study by McCabe (2017) diligently takes the pulse of SFL language teaching research.

4   As emerges below, not all would agree that such difficulties are separable from the students' social background/class, genre theorists being first among the dissenters.

5   O'Donnell (2011: 114–116) reveals Hasan's thinking in those early years further by citing some of her illuminating personal comments from Halliday and Hasan (2006), published in a volume edited by Whittaker, O'Donnell and McCabe (accessed 30 May 2020).

6   To further clarify: recognition literacy for Hasan is concerned basically with forms whose standards of correctness students are made to learn to recognize and to conform to, mechanically, including sound-shape correspondence. Clearly, the conception of language that informs such pedagogic practice has nought to do with language as social semiotic practice.

7   Recall (as noted in Chapter 2, note 7) that Matthiessen too sees the modelling of verbal art as register as requiring extensive long-term empirical research.

8   The conflict between 'empowerment', on one hand, and the protection of linguistic and cultural identity, on the other, is also an apparently unresolvable issue in language policy debate. On the topic with reference to the 'English Only' movement in the US, see Miller (2013b).

9   No a priori distinction between the literary canon or 'artistic' literature and popular literature forms, including comics, is adhered to here, as the dividing line is a fuzzy one. When Bob Dylan was awarded the Nobel prize for literature in 2016, I was among those applauding.

10 Butt's 1983 paper cited in the quote above has been seen twice before: in Chapter 2, first where Hasan speaks of his 'happy expression "semantic drift"', an expression that is part of the title of the 1983 article. As said above, Butt's writings on the teaching of SFL stylistics are experienced-based, having also persevered in offering elective courses in it at Macquarie University, as Hasan applauds her former 'brilliant doctoral student' for doing (2011a: xix). The publication is then cited again in Chapter 2, in reporting how Butt and Lukin (2009) remark that 'it is the ensemble effect of patterns of choice from a number of systems which creates the "semantic drift" (Butt 1983)', the very merit Lukin and Webster point to in the quote above.

Chapter 5

1   Space precludes the insertion of all possible references, however deserving. This is also due to having opted for brief descriptions of the research cited, as elsewhere in previous chapters, rather than simply for less communicative lists of names/dates. Still, as usual, I append a caveat to the effect that significant lacunae are unintentional and are my own responsibility, also because of my own residual ignorance, despite sustained research. Moreover, it is beyond the scope of the chapter to deal systematically with related educational studies, though certain ones are mentioned in passing. Further, an effort to include lesser-known worthy scholars has been made. Finally, the following account on the whole eschews discussion of the divergences between scholars' allegiances to either Halliday's or the so-called Sydney School's (Martin's) SFL or of any of the more subtle but real enough distinctions in how these may see the theory and practice of, in particular, multimodality. Note 4 below offers a clue as to just how many distinctions there may be.

2   Matthiessen (2009: 37) includes O'Toole (1994) as an example of his aesthetic linguistics (see Chapter 2, meaning 'a field of investigation dealing with ... the negotiation in a community of the value of works of art'), and also as part of 'The expanding domain of artistic SFL' (Title of Matthiessen's Table 3 in 2009: 34).

3   General information on software that has been specially designed for SFL can be found at http://
www.isfla.org/Systemics/Software/index.html. The site maintainer – and creator of the UAM corpus
coding tool – is Mick O'Donnell. See this and other coding tools at http://www.isfla.org/Systemics/
Software/Coders.html.

4   The following is a brief summary of Bateman's multidimensional theoretical and methodological position on his and his colleagues' multimodal research that, when queried, he was kind enough to provide:
'The approach adopted emerged in the mid-1990s from the interaction of several development streams
where multimodal phenomena were at issue. Partially extending previous work on discourse and genre,
the overall model was essentially that of an SFL stratified along the lines proposed by Martin (1992) but
incorporating several distinct discourse-level theories. In the spirit of Kress and van Leeuwen (2006
[1996]), it was assumed that all expressive forms could be characterized as systemic resources, regardless
of modality, but that such characterizations would also need to be multistratal and include discourse.
Since all specific details beyond these general principles of stratification and paradigmatic-syntagmatic
resource organization were taken to require empirical investigation rather than being imported from
SFL meta-theory, and those empirical methods drew primarily from linguistic methodology, the
approach was labelled "multimodal linguistics" rather than being considered more narrowly a particular kind or variant of SFL. More recently, as the methodology has been strengthened in its own right
and an ever broader range of media has been addressed, the emphasis specifically on linguistics has not
always been beneficial, so we now talk increasingly of what we do simply as "multimodal semiotics", a
kind of applied semiotics conjoining Hjelmslevian, Peircean and various SFL-related elements as well as
formal and cognitive approaches to discourse' (personal communication, 16 April 2020).

5   I wouldn't have been able to provide the references myself, but Gibbons (2015: 295) does source
a similar if not identical critique: 'Whilst Kress and van Leeuwen's work in multimodality studies is
important, it has been argued that their approach is founded upon linguistic categories, and therefore
treats the devices of language and image inappropriately, as self-identical systems of meaning-making
(see Bateman, 2008; Forceville, 1999; Gibbons, 2012).' Perhaps the assessment is not fully justified, but
I am not competent to argue this. These last references are not included as entries in this volume's
bibliography.

6   Law's thesis is one of many supervised by Christian Matthiessen at the Hong Kong Polytechnic
University Faculty of Humanities. Others are mentioned below.

7   The International Conference 'Approaches to Multimodal Digital Environments: from theories to practices' took place in Rome from 20–22 June 2019. It is available in Academia at: https://www.academia.
edu/39562311/Book_of_Abstracts_International_Conference_Approaches_to_Multimodal_Digital_
Environments_from_theories_to_practices_?email_work_card=view-paper (accessed 5 April 2020). As
many know, Gunther Kress passed away on 20 June 2019 in Rome, where he had gone to deliver a ple-
nary talk to the conference.

8   In her treatment of register in SFL, Moore signals what she calls one current challenge to the Hallidayan
tradition that needs facing: its 'computational enhancement' (2017: 433).

9   The CLiC web app is the corpus stylistic web application 'Corpus Linguistics in Context', at: https://
dls.hypotheses.org/tag/corpus-tools. The Official web page for the ADHO Special Interest Group (SIG)
in Digital Literary Stylistics is Digital Literary Stylistics (SIG-DLS) (accessed 1 May 2020).

10 A caveat: the author, unhappily, writes in a less than fully intelligible English. Far be it from me to
preach standard language ideology. I taught World Englishes and argued for the recognition of indigenous varieties of English (IVEs) as fully-fledged languages for years. Nonetheless, the issue of mutual
intelligibility is a real one. There is no need to impose Standard English prescriptions, but there is a
need for the native speaking reader to feel confident of understanding an academic text written by
a NNES. Despite the difficulties with this paper, I am pleased to have discovered, and to cite, a young
Nigerian academic and staunch systemicist.

11 Matthiessen's abstract is no longer available at http://www.humaniora.sdu.dk/isfc2007/matthiessen.
htm, the url cited in Manfredi (2008: 121) and Vasconcellos (2009: 588).

References

Achugar, M. and M. Schleppegrell. 2016. Reflection literacy and the teaching of history. In W. Bowcher and J. Liang (eds), *Society in language, language in society: Essays in honour of Ruqaiya Hasan*, 357–378. London: Palgrave Macmillan.

Adams, W.C. 2015. Conducting semi-structured interviews. In K.E. Newcomer, H.P. Hatry and J.S. Wholey (eds), *Handbook of practical program evaluation* (4th edition), 492–505. Hoboken, NJ: Jossey-Bass (Wiley).

Auracher, J., S. Albers, Y. Zhai, G. Gareeva and T. Stavniychuk. 2011. P is for happiness, N is for sadness: Universals in sound iconicity to detect emotions in poetry. *Discourse Processes* 48: 1–25.

Balbert, P. 1974. *D.H. Lawrence and the psychology of rhythm: The meaning of form in* The Rainbow. The Hague: Mouton.

Baldry, A.P. and P.J. Thibault. 2006. *Multimodal transcription and text*. London: Equinox Publishing Ltd.

Banks, D. 2008. Coming to terms with the incomprehensible: Towards an analysis of a poem by J.H. Prynne. In P. Galliou and G. Le Moigne (eds), *A handful of gold, en homage au Professeur Yvon Tosser*, 11–20. Brest: Cahiers du CEIMA.

Bateman, J.A. 2013. Hallidayan systemic-functional semiotics and the analysis of the moving audio-visual image. *Text & Talk: An Interdisciplinary Journal of Language, Discourse & Communication Studies* 33(4–5): 641–663.

Bateman, J.A. and K-H. Schmidt. 2012. *Multimodal film analysis: How films mean*. Abingdon, Oxon: Routledge.

Bateman, J.A. and F.O.D. Veloso. 2013. The semiotic resources of comics in movie adaptation: Ang Lee's *Hulk* (2003) as a case study. *Studies in Comics* 4(1): 137–159.

Bateman, J.A., J. Wildfeuer and H. Tuomo. 2017. *Multimodality: Foundations, research and analysis - a problem-oriented introduction*. Berlin: De Gruyter Mouton.

Baumgarten, N. 2008. *Yeah, that's it!* Verbal reference to visual information in film texts and film translations. *Meta* 53(1): 6–25.

Bednarek, M. 2008. Teaching English literature and linguistics using corpus stylistic methods. In M. Zappavigna and C. Cloran (eds), *Bridging discourses* [electronic resource]: Proceedings of the Australian Systemic Functional Linguistics Association (ASFLA) Annual Congress, held at University of Wollongong, Wollongong, NSW, 29 June–1 July 2007, 1–13. Available at: https://opus.lib.uts.edu.au/handle/10453/11517

Bednarek, M. 2010a. Corpus linguistics and systemic functional linguistics: Interpersonal meaning, identity and bonding in popular culture. In M. Bednarek and J.R. Martin (eds), *New discourse on language: Functional perspectives on multimodality, identity, and affiliation*, 237–266. London: Continuum.

Bednarek, M. 2010b. *The language of fictional television: Drama and identity*. London: Continuum.

Bednarek, M. 2011. The stability of the televisual character: A corpus stylistic case study. In R. Piazza, M. Bednarek and F. Rossi (eds), *Telecinematic discourse: Approaches to the language of films and television series*, 185–204. Amsterdam and Philadelphia: John Benjamins.

Bednarek, M. 2014. The television title sequence: A visual analysis of *Flight of the Conchords*. In E. Djonov and S. Zhao (eds), *Critical multimodal studies of popular discourse*, 36–54. Abingdon, Oxon: Routledge.

Bednarek, M. 2015. Corpus-assisted multimodal discourse analysis of television and film narratives. In P. Baker and T. McEnery (eds), *Corpora and discourse studies*, 63–87. Houndmills, Basingstoke: Palgrave Macmillan.

Bednarek, M. 2019. The multifunctionality of swear/taboo words in television series. In J. Lachlan Mackenzie and L. Alba-Juez (eds), *Emotion in discourse*, 29–54. Amsterdam and Philadelphia: John Benjamins.

Bednarek, M. and R. Zago. 2021. Bibliography of linguistic research on fictional (narrative, scripted) television series and films/movies, version 4. Available at: https://unico.academia.edu/RaffaeleZago

Bernstein, B. 1974 [1971]. *Class, codes and control: Vol. 1: Theoretical studies towards a sociology of language.* 2nd edition. London: Routledge and Kegan Paul.

Bernstein, B. 1990. *Class, codes and control: Vol. 4: The structuring of pedagogic discourse.* London: Routledge.

Berry, R.S. 2010. *Terminology in English language teaching: Nature and use.* Bern: Peter Lang.

Biber, D. 2011. Corpus linguistics and the study of literature: Back to the future? *Scientific Study of Literature* 1(1): 15–23.

Birch, D. 1989. *Language, literature and critical practice: Ways of analysing text.* London: Routledge.

Birch, D. and L.M. O'Toole (eds). 1988. *Functions of style.* London: Pinter.

Bloch, B. 1953. Linguistic structure and linguistic analysis. In A.A. Hill (ed.), *Report of the fourth annual round table meeting on linguistics and language study*, 40–44. Washington, DC: Georgetown University (Monograph Series on Language and Linguistics 4).

Bolarinwa, O.A. 2015. Principles and methods of validity and reliability testing of questionnaires used in social and health science researches. *Nigerian Postgraduate Medical Journal* 22(4): 195–201.

Borgers, N. and J.J. Hox. 2000. Reliability of responses in questionnaire research with children. Presentation at the 5th International conference on logic and methodology, 3–6 October, Cologne, Germany. Available at: http://joophox.net/papers/p021704.pdf

Bosco, M., S.J. 2017. O'Connor's 'Pied Beauty': Gerard Manley Hopkins and the aesthetics of beauty. In M. Bosco and B. Little (eds), *Revelation and convergence: Flannery O'Connor and the Catholic intellectual tradition*, 99–117. Washington, DC: The Catholic University of America Press.

Bourke, J. 2005. The grammar we teach. *Reflections on English Language Teaching* 4: 85–97.

Bowcher, W.L. 2018. Future directions in the study of verbal art. In R. Wegener, A. Oesterle and S. Neumann (eds), *On verbal art: Essays in honour of Ruqaiya Hasan*, 278–313. Sheffield: Equinox Publishing Ltd.

Bridges, F. 2017. The inspiring life lessons 'Harry Potter' taught us. *Forbes*, 26 June 2017. Available at: https://www.forbes.com/sites/francesbridges/2017/06/26/the-inspiring-life-lessons-harry-potter-taught-us/#562ff59c1858

Bridges, J., W. Gray, G. Box and S. Machin. 2008. Discovery interviews: A mechanism for user involvement. *International Journal of Older People Nursing* 3(3): 206–210.

Burke, M. (ed.). 2014a. *The Routledge handbook of stylistics.* Abingdon, Oxon: Routledge.

Burke, M. 2014b. Rhetoric and poetics: The classical heritage of stylistics. In M. Burke (ed.), *The Routledge handbook of stylistics*, 11–30. Abingdon, Oxon: Routledge.

Burke, M., S. Csábi, L. Week and J. Zerkowitz (eds). 2012. *Pedagogical stylistics.* London: Bloomsbury.

Busse, B. and D. McIntyre. 2010. Language, literature and stylistics. In D. McIntyre and B. Busse (eds), *Language and style*, 3–14. Houndmills, Basingstoke: Palgrave Macmillan.

Butler, C. 2003. *Structure and function: A guide to three major structural-functional theories: Part 2: From clause to discourse and beyond.* Amsterdam and Philadelphia: John Benjamins.

Butt, D. 1983. Semantic drift in verbal art. *Australian Review of Applied Linguistics* 6(1): 38–48.

Butt, D. 1988. Randomness, order and the latent patterning of text. In D. Birch and L.M. O'Toole (eds), *Functions of style*, 74–97. London: Pinter.

Butt, D. 1996. Literature, culture and the classroom: The aesthetic function in our information era. In J.E. James (ed.), *The language-culture connection*, 86–106. Singapore: SEAMO Regional Language Centre.

Butt, D. 2007. Thought experiments in verbal art: Examples from Modernism. In D.R. Miller and M. Turci (eds), *Language and verbal art revisited: Linguistic approaches to the study of literature*, 68–96. London: Equinox Publishing Ltd.

Butt, D.G. 2012. On being a literature teacher: A language based perspective. In C.A. DeCoursey (ed.), *Language arts in Asia: Literature and drama in English, Putonghua and Cantonese*, 19–47. Newcastle upon Tyne: Cambridge Scholars Publishing. An analogous paper of the same title is published in R. Wegener, A. Oesterle and S. Neumann (eds). 2018. *On verbal art: Essays in honour of Ruqaiya Hasan*, 26–52. Sheffield: Equinox Publishing Ltd.

Butt, D.G. 2016. 'Construe my meaning': Performance, poetry and semiotic distance. In W.L. Bowcher and J. Liang (eds), *Society in language, language in society: Essays in honour of Ruqaiya Hasan*, 24–55. London: Palgrave Macmillan.

Butt, D.G. and A. Lukin. 2009. Stylistic analysis: Construing aesthetic organization. In M.A.K. Halliday and J.J. Webster (eds), *Continuum companion to systemic functional linguistics*, 190–215. London: Continuum.

Byrnes, H. 2009. Systemic-functional reflections on instructed foreign language acquisition as meaning-making: An introduction. *Linguistics and Education* 20(1): 1–9.

Caldwell, D. and M. Zappavigna. 2011. Visualizing multimodal patterning. In S. Dreyfus, S. Hood and M. Stenglin (eds), *Semiotic margins: Meaning in multimodalities*, 229–242. London: Continuum.

Carter, R. 2004. *Language and creativity: The art of common talk*. London: Routledge.

Carter, R. 2010. Methodologies for stylistic analysis. In D. McIntyre and B. Busse (eds), *Language and style*, 55–70. Houndmills, Basingstoke: Palgrave Macmillan.

Carter, R. and P. Stockwell (eds). 2008. *The language and literature reader*. Abingdon, Oxon: Routledge.

Catford, J.C. 1965. *A linguistic theory of translation*. Oxford: Oxford University Press.

Caton, S.C. 1987. Contributions of Roman Jakobson. *Annual Review of Anthropology* 16: 223–260.

Chen, X. 2018. Representing cultures through language and image: A multimodal approach to translations of the Chinese classic *Mulan*. *Perspectives: Studies in Translation Theory and Practice* 26(2): 214–231.

Chen, Y. 2019. *Translating film subtitles into Chinese: A multimodal study*. Singapore: Springer Nature.

Christie, F. 1989 [1985]. Foreword to the series in 'educational linguistics'. In R. Hasan, *Linguistics, language and verbal art*, v–xii. Geelong, Victoria, Australia: Deakin University Press; Oxford: Oxford University Press.

Christie, F. (ed.). 1999. *Pedagogy and the shaping of consciousness: Linguistic and social processes*. London: Continuum.

Christie, F. and L. Unsworth. 2005. Developing dimensions of an educational linguistics. In R. Hasan, C. Matthiessen and J.J. Webster (eds), *Continuing discourse on language: A functional perspective*, Vol. 1, 217–250. London: Equinox Publishing Ltd.

Christie, F., B. Devlin, P. Freebody, A. Luke, J. Martin, T. Threadgold and C. Walton. 1991. *Teaching English literacy: A project of national significance on the preservice preparation of teachers for teaching English literacy*. Australian Department of Employment, Education and Training: Darwin: Northern Territories University.

Clark, C. (ed.). 1969. *D.H. Lawrence: 'The Rainbow' and 'Women in Love': A casebook*. London: Macmillan.

Cohen, L., L. Manion and K. Morrison. 2007. *Research methods in education*. 6th edition. Abingdon, Oxon: Routledge.

Commonwealth of Australia. 2009. *The shape of the Australian curriculum.* ACT, Australia: National Curriculum Board.

Crystal, D. and D. Davy. 1969. *Investigating English style.* Bloomington, IN: Indiana University Press.

Cushman, K. 2013 [online since 1 April 2014]. The poetic voices of love poems and others. *Études Lawrenciennes* [Online] (paragraph 44). Available at: http://journals.openedition.org/lawrence/187; https://doi.org/10.4000/lawrence.187

Cummings, M. and R. Simmons. 1983. *The language of literature: A stylistic introduction to the study of literature.* Oxford: Pergamon.

Dalamu, T.O. 2019. Illuminating systemic functional grammatics (theory) as a viable tool of digital humanities. *Digital Studies/Le champ numérique* 9(1): 8(1–50).

Dare, B. 2010. Learning about language: The role of metalanguage. *NALDIC Quarterly* 8(1): 18–25. Available at: http://www.isfla.org/Systemics/Print/Papers/NaldicSFL.pdf

De Beaugrande, R. and W. Dressler. 1981. *Introduction to text linguistics.* London: Edward Arnold.

DeCoursey, C.A. (ed.). 2012a. *Language arts in Asia: Literature and drama in English, Putonghua and Cantonese.* Newcastle upon Tyne: Cambridge Scholars Publishing.

DeCoursey, C.A. 2012b. Reading literature, realizing culture: Appraising intercultural attitudes in the Hong Kong class. In C.A. DeCoursey (ed.), *Language arts in Asia: Literature and drama in English, Putonghua and Cantonese*, 48–84. Newcastle upon Tyne: Cambridge Scholars Publishing.

De Leeuw, E.D. 2005. To mix or not to mix data collection modes in surveys. *Journal of Official Statistics* 21(2): 233–255.

Denzin, N. 1978. *Sociological methods: A sourcebook.* New York: McGraw Hill.

Djonov, E. and S. Zhao (eds). 2014. *Critical multimodal studies of popular discourse.* Abingdon, Oxon: Routledge.

Don, A. 2018. The value of intertextual associations: How GM technologies are given value through association. In R. Page, B. Busse and N. Nørgaard (eds), *Rethinking language, text and context: Interdisciplinary research in stylistics in honour of Michael Toolan*, 269–285. Abingdon, Oxon: Routledge.

Douthwaite, J. 2000. *Towards a linguistic theory of foregrounding.* Edizioni dell'Orso: Alessandria.

Enkvist, N.E. 1973. *Linguistic stylistics.* The Hague: Mouton.

Erlich, V. 1981 [1955]. *Russian formalism: History - doctrine.* 4th edition. New Haven, NJ: Yale University Press.

Firth, J.R. 1957 [1951]. Modes of meaning. In F.R. Palmer (ed.), *Papers in linguistics, 1934-1951*, 190–215. Oxford: Oxford University Press.

Fischer-Starcke, B. 2010. *Corpus linguistics in literary analysis: Jane Austen and her contemporaries.* London: Continuum.

Fish, S. 1980. *Is there a text in this class? The authority of interpretative communities.* Cambridge, MA: Harvard University Press.

Fish, S. 1981. What is stylistics and why are they saying such terrible things about it? In D.C. Freeman (ed.), *Essays in modern stylistics*, 53–78. London and New York: Methuen.

Fogal, G.G. 2015. Pedagogical stylistics in multiple foreign language and second language contexts: A synthesis of empirical research. *Language and Literature* 24(1): 54–72.

Forey, G. 2020. A whole school approach to SFL metalanguage and the explicit teaching of language for curriculum learning. In S. Gardner and J. Donohue (eds), Special commemorative issue of the *Journal of English for Academic Purposes* (JEAP) 44: 1–17. Available at: https://doi.org/10.1016/j.jeap.2019.100822

Forster, E.M. 1962 [1927]. *Aspects of the novel.* Harmondsworth: Penguin Books Ltd.

Fowler, R. (ed.). 1966. *Essays on style and language.* London: Routledge.

Fowler, R. 1981. *Literature as social discourse.* London: Batsford.

Fowler, R. 1986. *Linguistic criticism.* Oxford: Oxford University Press.

Fowler, R. and F.W. Bateson. 1967. Argument II. Literature and linguistics. *Essays in Criticism* 17: 322–347.

Fowler, R. and F.W. Bateson. 1968. Argument II (continued): Language and literature. *Essays in Criticism* 18: 164–182.

Fries, P.H. 2003. The presentation of reality in James and Hemingway. In M.R. Wise and R. Brend (eds), *Language and Life*, 297–316. Amsterdam and Philadelphia: John Benjamins.

Garvin, P.L. 1964. *A Prague school reader on esthetics, literary structure and style.* Washington, DC: Georgetown University Press.

Gebhard, M., I. Chen, H. Graham and W. Gunawan. 2013. Teaching to mean, writing to mean: SFL, L2 literacy, and teacher education. *Journal of Second Language Writing* 22: 107–124.

Gibbons, A. 2015. Creativity and multimodal literature. In R.H. Jones (ed.), *The Routledge handbook of language and creativity*, 293–306. Abingdon, Oxon: Routledge.

Goatly, A. 2008. *Explorations in stylistics.* London: Equinox Publishing Ltd.

Gregory, M.J. 1974. A theory for stylistics exemplified: Donne's 'Holy Sonnet XIV'. *Language and Style* VII(2): 108–118.

Gregory, M.J. and S. Carroll. 1978. *Language and situation: Language varieties and their social contexts.* London: Routledge and Kegan Paul.

Grice, F. and A. Kramer-Dahl. 1992. Grammaticalizing the medical case history. In M.J. Toolan (ed.), *Language text and context: Essays in stylistics*, 56–90. London: Routledge.

Griffin, R. 1999. Review of *Romanticism and the Self-Conscious Poem*, by Michael O'Neill. *Criticism* 41(3): 418–422.

Hall, G. 2014. Pedagogical stylistics. In M. Burke (ed.), *The Routledge handbook of stylistics*, 239–252. Abingdon, Oxon: Routledge.

Halliday, M.A.K. 1973. *Explorations in the functions of language.* London: Arnold.

Halliday, M.A.K. 1978. *Language as social semiotic.* London: Arnold.

Halliday, M.A.K. 1985. *An introduction to functional grammar.* London: Edward Arnold (revised 2nd edition 1994; revised 3rd and 4th editions, with C.M.I.M. Matthiessen, 2004 and 2014).

Halliday, M.A.K. 1998. On the grammar of pain. *Functions of Language* 5(1): 1–32.

Halliday, M.A.K. 2001. Towards a theory of good translation. In E. Steiner and C. Yallop (eds), *Exploring translation and multilingual text production: Beyond content*, 13–18. Berlin and New York: Mouton de Gruyter.

Halliday, M.A.K. 2002 [1961]. Categories of the theory of grammar. In *Word* 17(3): 241–292. Reprinted in M.A.K. Halliday. 2002. *On grammar*, Vol. 1 of The Collected Works of M.A.K. Halliday, edited by J.J. Webster, 37–94. London: Continuum.

Halliday, M.A.K. 2002 [1964]. The linguistic study of literary texts. In H. Lunt (ed.), *Proceedings of the Ninth International Congress of Linguistics 1962.* The Hague: Mouton, 302–307. Reprinted, combined with another 1964 paper, in M.A.K. Halliday. 2002. *Linguistic studies of text and discourse*, Vol. 2 of The Collected Works of M.A.K. Halliday, edited by J.J. Webster, 5–22. London: Continuum.

Halliday, M.A.K. 2002 [1970]. Language structure and language function. In J. Lyons (ed.), *New horizons in linguistics*, 140–165. Harmondsworth: Penguin Books Ltd. Reprinted in M.A.K. Halliday. 2002. *On grammar*, Vol. 1 of The Collected Works of M.A.K. Halliday, edited by J.J. Webster, 173–195. London: Continuum.

Halliday, M.A.K. 2002 [1971]. Linguistic function and literary style: An inquiry into the language of William Golding's *The Inheritors*. In S. Chatman (ed.), *Literary style: A symposium*, 330–365. New York and Oxford: Oxford University Press. Reprinted in M.A.K. Halliday. 2002. *Linguistic studies of text and discourse*, Vol. 2 of The Collected Works of M.A.K. Halliday, edited by J.J. Webster, 88–125. London: Continuum.

Halliday, M.A.K. 2002 [1977]. Text as semantic choice in social contexts. In T.A. van Dijk and J.A. Petröfi (eds), *Grammars and descriptions*, 176–225. Berlin: Walter de Gruyter. Reprinted in M.A.K. Halliday. 2002. *Linguistic studies of text and discourse*, Vol. 2 of The Collected Works of M.A.K. Halliday, edited by J.J. Webster, 23–81. London: Continuum.

Halliday, M.A.K. 2002 [1982]. The de-automatization of grammar: From Priestley's 'An Inspector Calls'. In J.M. Anderson (ed.). *Language form and linguistic variation: Papers dedicated to Angus McIntosh*, 129–159. Amsterdam and Philadelphia: John Benjamins. Reprinted in M.A.K. Halliday. 2002. *Linguistic studies of text and discourse*, Vol. 2 of The Collected Works of M.A.K. Halliday, edited by J.J. Webster, 126–148. London: Continuum.

Halliday, M.A.K. 2002 [1985]. Dimensions of discourse analysis. In T.A. van Dijk (ed.), *The handbook of discourse analysis, Vol.2. Dimensions of discourse*, 29–56. London: Academic Press. Reprinted in M.A.K. Halliday. 2002. *On grammar*, Vol. 1 of The Collected Works of M.A.K. Halliday, edited by J.J. Webster, 261–286. London: Continuum.

Halliday, M.A.K. 2002 [1988]. Poetry as scientific discourse: The nuclear sections of Tennyson's 'In Memoriam'. In D. Birch and L.M. O'Toole (eds), *Functions of style*, 31–44. London and New York: Pinter. Reprinted in M.A.K. Halliday. 2002. *Linguistic studies of text and discourse*, Vol. 2 of The Collected Works of M.A.K. Halliday, edited by J.J. Webster, 149–167. London: Continuum.

Halliday, M.A.K. 2002 [1996]. *On grammar and grammatics*. In R. Hasan, C. Cloran and D.G. Butt (eds), *Functional descriptions: Theory in practice*, 1–38. Amsterdam and Philadelphia: John Benjamins. Reprinted in M.A.K. Halliday. 2002. *On grammar*, Vol. 1 of The Collected Works of M.A.K. Halliday, edited by J.J. Webster, 384–417. London: Continuum.

Halliday, M.A.K. 2003 [2001]. Is the grammar neutral? Is the grammarian neutral? In J. de Villiers and R.J. Stainton (eds), *Communication in linguistics*, Vol. 1: Papers in honour of Michael Gregory, 179–204. Toronto: Editions du Gref. Reprinted in M.A.K. Halliday. 2003. *On language and linguistics*, Vol. 3 of The Collected Works of M.A.K. Halliday, edited by J.J. Webster, 271–292. London: Continuum.

Halliday, M.A.K. 2005 [1956]. The linguistic basis of a mechanical thesaurus, and its application to English preposition classification. *Mechanical Translation* 3(3): 81–88. Reprinted in M.A.K. Halliday. 2005. *Computational and quantitative studies*, Vol. 6 of The Collected Works of M.A.K. Halliday, edited by J.J. Webster, 20–36. London: Continuum.

Halliday, M.A.K. 2005 [1991a]. Towards probabilistic interpretations. In E. Ventola (ed.), *Functional and systemic linguistics: Approaches and uses* (Trends in Linguistics Studies and Monographs 55), 39–62. Berlin and New York: Mouton de Gruyter. Reprinted in M.A.K. Halliday. 2005. *Computational and quantitative studies*, Vol. 6 of The Collected Works of M.A.K. Halliday, edited by J.J. Webster, 42–62. London: Continuum.

Halliday, M.A.K. 2005 [1991b]. Corpus studies and probabilistic grammar. In K. Aijmer and B. Altenberg (eds), *English corpus linguistics: Studies in honour of Jan Svartvik*, 30–43. London and New York: Longman. Reprinted in M.A.K. Halliday. 2005. *Computational and quantitative studies*, Vol. 6 of The Collected Works of M.A.K. Halliday, edited by J.J. Webster, 63–75. London: Continuum.

Halliday, M.A.K. 2005 [1992]. Language as system and language as instance: The corpus as a theoretical construct. In J. Svartvik (ed.), *Directions in corpus linguistics: Proceedings of Nobel Symposium 82, Stockholm, 4-8 August 1991*, 61–77. Berlin: Mouton de Gruyter. Reprinted in M.A.K. Halliday. 2005. *Computational and quantitative studies*, Vol. 6 of The Collected Works of M.A.K. Halliday, edited by J.J. Webster, 76–92. London: Continuum.

Halliday, M.A.K. 2006. Afterwords. In G. Thompson and S. Hunston (eds), *System and corpus: Exploring connections*, 293–299. London: Equinox Publishing Ltd.

Halliday, M.A.K. 2007 [2002]. Applied linguistics as an evolving theme. Originally presented by Halliday on the occasion of his being awarded the first Gold Medal by the International

Association of Applied Linguistics (AILA). Published in M.A.K. Halliday. 2007. *Language and education*, Vol. 9 of The Collected Works of M.A.K. Halliday, edited by J.J. Webster, 1–19. London: Continuum.

Halliday, M.A.K. 2009. *Language and education*. Vol. 9 of The Collected Works of M.A.K. Halliday, edited by J.J. Webster. London: Continuum.

Halliday, M.A.K. 2013 [2009]. The gloosy ganoderm. Systemic functional linguistics and translation. *Chinese Translators Journal* 1: 17–26, Nanjing University Press. Reprinted in M.A.K. Halliday. 2013. *Halliday in the 21st century*, Vol. 11 of The Collected Works of M.A.K. Halliday, edited by J.J. Webster, 105–126. London: Bloomsbury Academic.

Halliday, M.A.K. 2013 [2012]. Pinpointing the choice. Meaning and the search for equivalents in a translated text. In A. Mahboob and N.K. Knight (eds), *Appliable linguistics*, 13–24. London: Continuum. Reprinted in M.A.K. Halliday. 2013. *Halliday in the 21st century*, Vol. 11 of The Collected Works of M.A.K. Halliday, edited by J.J. Webster, 143–154. London: Bloomsbury Academic.

Halliday, M.A.K. and D.G. Butt. 2019. Language and science, language in science, and linguistics as science. In G. Thompson, W.L. Bowcher, L. Fontaine and J.Y. Liang (eds), *The Cambridge handbook of systemic functional linguistics*, 620–650. Cambridge: Cambridge University Press.

Halliday, M.A.K. and R. Hasan. 1976. *Cohesion in English*. London: Longman.

Halliday, M.A.K. and R. Hasan. 1989 [1985]. *Language, text and context: Aspects of language in a social semiotic perspective*. Geelong, Victoria: Deakin University Press; Oxford: Oxford University Press.

Halliday, M.A.K. and R. Hasan. 2006. Retrospective on SFL and literacy. In R. Whittaker, M. O'Donnell and A. McCabe (eds), *Language and literacy: Functional approaches*, 15–44. London: Continuum.

Halliday, M.A.K. and C.M.I.M. Matthiessen. 1999. *Construing experience through meaning: A language-based approach to cognition*. London: Cassell.

Halliday, M.A.K. and C.M.I.M. Matthiessen. 2014. *Halliday's introduction to functional grammar*. 4th edition. Abingdon, Oxon: Routledge.

Halliday, M.A.K. and C. Yallop. 2007. *Lexicology: A short introduction*. London: Continuum.

Halliday, M.A.K., A. McIntosh and P. Strevens. 1964. *The linguistic sciences and language teaching*. London: Longman.

Harman, R. 2017. Bringing it all together: Critical take(s) on systemic functional linguistics. In R. Harman (ed.), *Bilingual learners and social equity: Critical approaches to systemic functional linguistics*, 243–254. Springer International Publishing AG (Educational Linguistics book series, Vol. 33).

Harman, R. and K.J. Burke. 2020. *Culturally sustaining systemic functional linguistics praxis: Embodied inquiry with multilingual youth*. Abingdon, Oxon: Routledge.

Hasan, R. 1964. A linguistic study of contrasting linguistic features in the style of two contemporary English prose writers. Unpublished PhD thesis. University of Edinburgh. Available at: http://hdl.handle.net/1842/16409

Hasan, R. 1967. Linguistics and the study of literary texts. *Etudes de Linguistique Appliquée* 5: 106–121.

Hasan, R. 1971. Rime and reason in literature. In Chatman S. (ed.), *Literary style: A symposium*, 299–329. London: Oxford University Press.

Hasan, R. 1975. The place of stylistics in the study of verbal art. In H. Ringbom (ed.), *Style and text*, 49–62. Amsterdam: Skriptor.

Hasan, R. 1978. Text in the systemic-functional model. In W. Dressler (ed.), *Current trends in text linguistics*, 228–246. Berlin: Walter de Gruyter.

Hasan, R. 1988. The analysis of one poem: Theoretical issues in practice. In D. Birch and L.M. O'Toole (eds), *Functions of style*, 45–73. London and New York: Pinter.

Hasan, R. 1989 [1985]. *Linguistics, language and verbal art*. Geelong, Victoria, Australia: Deakin University Press; Oxford: Oxford University Press.

Hasan, R. 1996a. Teaching literature across cultures. In J.E. James (ed.), *The language-culture connection*, 34–63. Singapore: SEAMO Regional Language Centre.

Hasan, R. 1996b. *Ways of saying: Ways of meaning. Selected papers of Ruqaiya Hasan*, edited by C. Cloran, D.G. Butt and G. Williams. London and New York: Cassell.

Hasan, R. 2007. Private pleasure, public discourse: Reflections on engaging with literature. In D.R. Miller and M. Turci (eds), *Language and verbal art revisited: Linguistic approaches to the study of literature*, 13–40. London: Equinox Publishing Ltd.

Hasan, R. 2009. The place of context in a systemic functional model. In M.A.K. Halliday and J.J. Webster (eds), *Continuum companion to systemic functional linguistics*, 166–189. London: Continuum.

Hasan, R. 2011a. A timeless journey: On the past and future of present knowledge. In *Selected works of Ruqaiya Hasan on applied linguistics*, xiv–xliii. Beijing: Foreign Language Teaching and Research Press.

Hasan, R. 2011b. *Language and education: Learning and teaching in society*. Vol. 3 of The Collected Works of Ruqaiya Hasan, edited by J.J. Webster. London: Equinox Publishing Ltd.

Hasan, R. 2011c [1996]. Literacy, everyday talk and society. In R. Hasan and G. Williams. *Literacy in society*, 377–424. London and New York: Longman. Reprinted in R. Hasan. 2011b. *Language and education: Learning and teaching in society*, Vol. 3 of The Collected Works of Ruqaiya Hasan, edited by J.J. Webster, 169–206. London: Equinox Publishing Ltd.

Hasan, R. forthcoming [1984]. Coherence and cohesive harmony. In J. Flood (ed.), *Understanding reading comprehension*, 181–219. Delaware: International Reading Association. To be reprinted in R. Hasan, *Unity in discourse: Texture and structure*, Vol. 6 of The Collected Works of Ruqaiya Hasan, edited by J.J. Webster and G. Williams. Sheffield: Equinox Publishing Ltd.

Hasan, R. To appear. *Verbal art: A sociosemiotic perspective*. Vol. 7 of The Collected Works of Ruqaiya Hasan, edited by J.J. Webster and D.G. Butt. Sheffield: Equinox Publishing Ltd.

Hassall, C. 1959. *A biography of Edward Marsh*. New York: Harcourt, Brace and Co.

Hatim, B. 2009. Translating text in context. In J. Munday (ed.), *The Routledge companion to translation studies* (revised edition), 36–53. Abingdon, Oxon: Routledge.

Hatim, B. and I. Mason. 1990. *Discourse and the translator*. London: Longman.

Hatzfeld, H.A. 1953. *A critical bibliography of the new stylistics (1900-1952)*. Chapel Hill: University of North Carolina Press.

Hawkins, E. 1999. Foreign language study and language awareness. *Language Awareness* 8: 124–142.

Hiippala, T. 2015. A bibliography of multimodal research: 1980s–2015. Available at: https://zenodo.org/record/32450#.XpW2pJlS9PY

Hopkins, G.M. First published 1986; revised 2002. *Gerard Manley Hopkins: The major works: Including all the poems and selected prose*. C. Phillips (ed.), Oxford World's Classics. Oxford and New York: Oxford University Press.

Hough, G. 1969. *Style and stylistics*. London: Routledge and Kegan Paul.

House, J. 1997. *Translation quality assessment: A model revisited*. Tübingen: Narr.

House, J. 2001. How do we know when a translation is good? In E. Steiner and C. Yallop (eds), *Exploring translation and multilingual text production: Beyond content*, 127–160. Berlin and New York: De Gruyter.

Huang, G.W. 2014. Analyzing the reporting clause in translating Confucius's *Lun Yu* (*The Analects*). In Y. Fang and J.J. Webster (eds), *Developing systemic functional linguistics: Theory and application*, 256–270. London: Equinox Publishing Ltd.

Hudson, R. 2008. Linguistic theory. In B. Spolsky and F.M. Hult (eds), *The handbook of educational linguistics*, 53–65. Oxford: Blackwell Publishing.

Huisman, R. 2016. Talking about poetry – using the model of language in Systemic Functional Linguistics to talk about poetic texts [online]. *English in Australia* 51(2): 7–19. Available at: https://search.informit.com.au/documentSummary;dn=433028696266165;res=IELHSS

Huisman, R. 2019. The discipline of English Literature from the perspective of SFL register. *Language, Context and Text* 1(1): 102–120.

Hymes, D.H. 1967. Phonological aspects of style: Some English sonnets. In S. Chatman and S.R. Levin (eds), *Essays on the language of literature*, 33–53. Boston: Houghton Mifflin.

Ingram, A. 1990. *The language of D.H. Lawrence*. London: Macmillan.

Jakobson, R. 1960. Closing statement: Linguistics and poetics. In T.A. Sebeok (ed.), *Style in language*, 350–377. Cambridge, MA: MIT Press.

Jakobson, R. 1966. Grammatical parallelism and its Russian facet. *Language* 42(2): 399–429.

Jakobson, R. 1968. Poetry of grammar and grammar of poetry. *Lingua* 21: 597–609.

Jakobson, R. 1985 [1921]. Novejsaja russkaja poezija. Nabrosok pervyi. Viktor Khlebnikov (Новьйшая русская поезия). Prague: Tipografija Politica. Translated as Modern Russian Poetry: Velimir Khlebnikov. In S. Rudy (ed.), *Roman Jakobson: Select writings*, 299–344. 's-Gravenhage: Mouton.

Jeffries, L. 2010. *Critical stylistics: The power of English*. Houndmills, Basingstoke: Palgrave Macmillan.

Jeffries, L. and D. McIntyre. 2010. *Stylistics*. Cambridge: Cambridge University Press.

Jeffries, L. and D. McIntyre (eds). 2011. *Teaching stylistics*. Houndmills, Basingstoke: Palgrave Macmillan.

Ji, Y. and D. Shen. 2004. Transitivity and mental transformation: Sheila Watson's *The Double Hook*. *Language and Literature* 13(4): 335–348.

Johnson, J.H. 2010. A corpus-assisted study of *parere/sembrare* in Grazia Deledda's *Canne al Vento* and *La Madre*: Constructing point of view in the Source Texts and their English translations. In J. Douthwaite and K. Wales (eds), *Stylistics and co. (unlimited) – the range, methods and applications of stylistics*, special issue of *Textus* 23(1): 283–302.

Katan, D. 2009 [2001]. Translation as intercultural communication. In J. Munday (ed.), *The Routledge companion to translation studies* (revised edition), 74–92. Abingdon, Oxon: Routledge.

Katan, D. 2014 [2004]. *Translating cultures: An introduction for translators, interpreters and mediators*. 2nd edition. Abingdon, Oxon: Routledge.

Kennedy, C. 1982. Systemic grammar and its use in literary analysis. In R. Carter (ed.), *Language and literature: An introductory reader in stylistics*, 83–99. London: Unwin Hyman.

Kress, G. and T. van Leeuwen. 2001. *Multimodal discourse: The modes and media of contemporary communication*. London: Arnold.

Kress, G.R. and T. van Leeuwen. 2006 [1996]. *Reading images: The grammar of visual design*. 2nd edition. Abingdon, Oxon: Routledge.

Krishnamurthy, R. 2006. Collocations. In K. Brown (ed. in chief), *Encyclopedia of language & linguistics* (2nd edition), 596–600. Oxford: Elsevier Science.

Kunz, K. and E. Teich. 2017. Translation studies. In T. Barlett and G. O'Grady (eds), *The Routledge handbook of systemic functional linguistics*, 547–560. Abingdon, Oxon: Routledge.

Kunz, K., S. Degaetano-Ortlieb, E. Lapshinova-Koltunski, K. Menzel and E. Steiner. 2017. GECCo – An empirically-based comparison of English-German cohesion. In G. De Sutter, M-A. Lefer and I. Delaere (eds), *Empirical translation studies: New methodological and theoretical traditions*, 265–312. Berlin and New York: De Gruyter Mouton.

Larsen-Freeman, D. 2009. Teaching and testing grammar. In M.H. Long and C.J. Doughty (eds), *The handbook of language teaching*, 518–542. Oxford: Blackwell Publishing.

Law, L. 2017. House M.D. and creativity: A corpus linguistic systemic functional multimodal discourse analysis approach. Unpublished PhD thesis. The Hong Kong Polytechnic University.

Law, L. 2020. Creativity and multimodality: An analytical framework for creativity in multimodal texts (AFCMT). *Linguistics and Human Sciences (LHS)* 14(1–2): 36–69.

Lawrence, D.H. 1913. *Love poems and others.* London: Duckworth and Co.

Lawrence, D.H. 1917. *Look! We have come through!* London: Chatto and Windus.

Lawrence, D.H. 1960 [1920]. *Women in love.* New York: Viking.

Lawrence, D.H. 1960 [1922]. *Fantasia of the unconscious* (1960 edition published together with *Psychoanalysis of the unconscious*). New York: Viking.

Lawrence, D.H. 1961 [1915]. *The rainbow.* New York: Viking Compass.

Lawrence, D.H. 1971 [1928]. Hymns in a man's life. In W. Roberts and H.T. Moore (eds), *Phoenix II*, 597–601. New York: Viking Compass.

Lawrence, D.H. 1971 [1936]. Foreword to *Women in Love.* In W. Roberts and H.T. Moore (eds), *Phoenix II*, 275–276. New York: Viking Compass.

Lawrence, D.H. 1974 [1924]. Climbing down Pisgah. In E. McDonald (ed.), *Phoenix: The posthumous papers of D.H. Lawrence*, 740–744. New York: Viking Compass.

Lawrence, D.H. 1974 [s.a.]. The novel and the feelings. In E. McDonald (ed.), *Phoenix: The posthumous papers of D.H. Lawrence*, 755–760. New York: Viking Compass.

Lawrence, D.H. 1981. Letters. In G. Zytaruk and J.T. Bolton (eds), *The letters of D.H. Lawrence.* Volume 2: 1913–16. Cambridge: Cambridge University Press.

Lawrence, D.H. 1994 [1919]. Poetry of the present (Introduction to the American edition of *New poems*). Reprinted in V. de Sola Pinto and W. Roberts (eds), *The complete poems of D.H. Lawrence*, 181–186. Harmondsworth: Penguin Classics.

Lawrence, D.H. 1994 [1928]. Foreword to collected poems. In V. de Sola Pinto and W. Roberts (eds), *The complete poems of D.H. Lawrence*, 849–852. Harmondsworth: Penguin Classics.

Lecercle, J-J. 1993. The current state of stylistics. *The European English Messenger* 2(1): 14–18.

Leech, G.N. 1965. 'This bread I break': Language and interpretation. *Review of English Literature* 6: 66–75.

Leech, G.N. 1969. *A linguistic guide to English poetry.* Harlow: Longman.

Leech, G.N. 2008. *Language in literature: Style and foregrounding.* Abingdon, Oxon: Routledge.

Leech, G.N. and M.H. Short. 2007 [1981]. *Style in fiction: A linguistic introduction to English fictional prose.* London: Longman.

Lemke, J.L. 1995. *Textual politics.* London: Taylor & Francis.

Lemon, L.T. and M.J. Reis (eds and trans). 1965. *Russian formalist criticism: Four essays.* Lincoln and London: University of Nebraska Press.

Lin, B. 2010. Old houses, linguistics and literature in schools: What stylistics can offer. *Linguistics and the Human Sciences (LHS)* 3(2): 191–219.

Lin, B. 2012. The lang-lit connection in language education. In C.A. DeCoursey (ed.), *Language arts in Asia: Literature and drama in English, Putonghua and Cantonese*, 145–161. Newcastle upon Tyne: Cambridge Scholars Publishing.

Lin, B. 2014a. Stylistics in translation. In P. Stockwell and S. Whiteley (eds), *The Cambridge handbook of stylistics*, 573–589. Cambridge: Cambridge University Press.

Lin, B. 2014b. Using SFL in an appliable stylistics: Exploring verbal artistry and its implications for poetic translation. *Linguistics and the Human Sciences (LHS)* 10(1): 29–48.

Lin, B. 2016. Functional stylistics. In V. Sotirova (ed.), *The Bloomsbury companion to stylistics*, 57–77. London and New York: Bloomsbury Academic.

Lodge, D. 2015. *Quite a good time to be born. A memoir: 1935-1975.* London: Harvill Secker.

Louw, B. and M. Milojkovic. 2014. Semantic prosody. In P. Stockwell and S. Whiteley (eds), *The Cambridge handbook of stylistics*, 263–280. Cambridge: Cambridge University Press.

Love, K., C. Sandiford, M. Macken-Horarik and L. Unsworth. 2014. From 'bored witless' to 'rhetorical nous': Teacher orientation to knowledge about language and strengthening student persuasive writing. *English in Australia* 49(3): 43–56.

Luke, A. 1996. Genres of power? Literacy education and the production of capital. In R. Hasan and G. Williams (eds), *Literacy in society*, 308–338. London: Longman.

Lukin, A. 2003. Grammar and the study of poetry. In J.E. James (ed.), *Grammar in the language classroom*, 228–246. Singapore: SEAMO Regional Language Centre.

Lukin, A. 2008. Reading literary texts: Beyond personal responses. In Z. Fang and M.J. Schleppegrell (eds), *Reading in secondary content areas: A language-based pedagogy*, 84–103. Ann Arbor, MI: University of Michigan Press.

Lukin, A. 2015. A linguistics of style: Halliday on literature. In J.J. Webster (ed.), *The Bloomsbury companion to M.A.K. Halliday*, 348–366. London and New York: Bloomsbury Publishing.

Lukin, A. 2018. Language, linguistics and verbal art: The contribution of Ruqaiya Hasan to the study of literature. In R. Wegener, A. Oesterle and S. Neumann (eds), *On verbal art: Essays in honour of Ruqaiya Hasan*, 6–25. Sheffield: Equinox Publishing Ltd.

Lukin, A. and A. Pagano. 2012. Context and double articulation in the translation of verbal art. In J. Knox (ed.), *To boldly proceed: Papers from the 39th International Systemic Functional Linguistics Congress*, 123–128. Sydney: UTS. Available at: https://researchers.mq.edu.au/en/publications/context-and-double-articulation-in-the-translation-of-verbal-art

Lukin, A. and A. Pagano. 2016. Inner and outer worlds: Speech and thought presentation in Mansfield's *Bliss*. *Journal of Literary Semantics* 45(2): 97–116.

Lukin, A. and J.J. Webster. 2005. Systemic functional linguistics and the study of literature. In R. Hasan, C.M.I.M. Matthiessen and J.J. Webster (eds), *Continuing discourse on language: A functional perspective*, 413–456. London: Equinox Publishing Ltd.

Lukin, A., A. Moore, M. Herke, R. Wegener and C. Wu. 2011. Halliday's model of register revisited and explored. *Linguistics and the Human Sciences* (*LHS*) 4(2): 187–213.

Luporini, A. 2019. Corpus-assisted systemic socio-semantic stylistics: Exploring 'white' and 'red' in Jean Rhys' *Wide Sargasso Sea*. *L'analisi linguistica e letteraria* XXVII(1): 5–28. Available at: http://www.analisilinguisticaeletteraria.eu/fascicolo-1-2019/

Ma, Y. and B. Wang. 2020. *Translating Tagore's* Stray Birds *into Chinese: Applying systemic functional linguistics to Chinese poetry translation*. Abingdon, Oxon: Routledge.

Mahboob, A. and N. Knight. 2010. Appliable linguistics: An introduction. In A. Mahboob and N. Knight (eds), *Appliable linguistics*, 1–12. London: Continuum.

Malinowski, B. 1935. An ethnographic theory of language. *Coral gardens and their magic*, Vol. II (Part IV). London: Allen and Unwin.

Macken-Horarik, M. 2008. A 'good enough' grammatics: Developing an effective metalanguage for school English in an era of multiliteracies. In C. Wu, C.M.I.M. Matthiessen and M. Herke (eds), *Proceedings of the ISFC 35: Voices around the world*, 43–48. Sydney: 35th ISFC Organizing Committee.

Macken-Horarik, M. and M. Adoniou. 2008. Genre and register in multiliteracies. In B. Spolsky and F.M. Hult (eds), *The handbook of educational linguistics*, 367–382. Oxford: Blackwell Publishing.

Macken-Horarik, M. and L. Unsworth. 2014. New challenges for literature study in primary school English: Building teacher knowledge and know-how through systemic functional theory. *Onomázein: Revista semestral de linguistica, filogia y traduccion*, Numero Especial IXth ALSFAL Congress, 230–251.

Macken-Horarik, M., K. Love and L. Unsworth. 2011. A grammatics 'good enough' for school English in the 21st century: Four challenges in realising the potential. *Australian Journal of Language and Literacy* 34(1): 9–23.

Macken-Horarik, M., K. Love, C. Sandiford and L. Unsworth. 2018. *Functional grammatics: Re-conceptualizing knowledge about language and image for school English*. Abingdon, Oxon: Routledge.

Macken-Horarik, M., C. Sandiford, K. Love and L. Unsworth. 2015. New ways of working 'with grammar in mind' in School English: Insights from systemic functional grammatics. *Linguistics and Education* 31: 145–158.

Mahlberg, M. and V. Wiegand. 2020. Literary stylistics. In S. Adolphs and D. Knight (eds), *The Routledge handbook of English language and digital humanities*, 306–327. Abingdon, Oxon: Routledge.

Mahlberg, M., M. Hoey, M. Stubbs and W. Teubert. 2007. *Text, discourse and corpora: Theory and analysis*. London: Continuum.

Maiorani, A. 2015. Revisiting Hitchcock: An alternative multimodal reading of interactive patterns in *Psycho*. In S. Starc, C. Jones and A. Maiorani (eds), *Meaning making in text: Multimodal and multilingual functional perspectives*, 134–151. London: Palgrave Macmillan.

Manfredi, M. 2008. *Translating text and context: Translation studies and systemic functional linguistics. Volume 1: Translation theory*. Bologna: Dupress (Quaderni del CeSLiC, Functional Grammar Studies for Non-Native Speakers of English).

Manfredi, M. 2012. Description vs prescription in translation teaching: A bridgeable gulf? In F. Dalziel, S. Gesuato and M.T. Musacchio (eds), *A lifetime of English studies: Essays in honour of Carol Taylor Torsello*, 545–553. Padova: Il Poligrafo.

Manfredi, M. 2014. *Translating text and context: Translation studies and systemic functional linguistics. Volume 2: From theory to practice*. Bologna: Asterisco (Quaderni del CeSLiC, Functional Grammar Studies for Non-Native Speakers of English).

Manfredi, M. 2019. Functional grammar as a helpful tool for translator training. In M. Berré, B. Costa, A. Kefer, C. Letawe, H. Reuter and G. Vanderbauwhede (eds), *La formation grammaticale du traducteur: Enjeux didactiques et traductologiques*, 95–109. Villeneuve d'Ascq, France: Presses universitaires du Septentrion (PUS), (TRADUCTOLOGIE).

Marco, J. 2000. Register analysis in literary translation: A functional approach. *Babel* 46(1): 1–19.

Martin, J.R. 1992. *English text: System and structure*. Amsterdam and Philadelphia: John Benjamins.

Martin, J.R. 2012 [1985]. The language of madness: Method or disorder? *Language and the Inner Life*. Canberra: Faculty of Military Studies, Duntroon (Department of English Occasional Papers (4): 4–35. Reprinted in J.R. Martin. 2012. *Text analysis*, Vol. 5 of The Collected Works of J.R. Martin, edited by W. Zhenhua, 46–78. Shanghai: Shanghai Jiao Tong University Press.

Martin, J.R. 2012 [1996]. Evaluating disruption: Symbolising theme in junior secondary narrative. In R. Hasan and G. Williams (eds), *Literacy in society*, 124–171. London and New York: Longman. Reprinted in J.R. Martin. 2012. *Text analysis*, Vol. 5 of The Collected Works of J.R. Martin, edited by W. Zhenhua, 213–248. Shanghai: Shanghai Jiao Tong University Press.

Martin, J.R. 2012 [2008]. Intermodal reconciliation: Mates in arms. In L. Unsworth (ed.), *New literacies and the English curriculum: Multimodal perspectives*. London: Continuum. 112–148. Reprinted in J.R. Martin. 2012. *Text analysis*, Vol. 5 of The Collected Works of J.R. Martin, edited by W. Zhenhua, 305–328. Shanghai: Shanghai Jiao Tong University Press.

Martin, J.R. and P.R.R. White. 2005. *The language of evaluation: Appraisal in English*. Houndmills, Basingstoke: Palgrave Macmillan.

Martinec, R. 2000. Construction of identity in Michael Jackson's *Jam*. *Social Semiotics* 10(3): 313–329.

Mastropierro, L. 2017. *Corpus stylistics in* Heart of Darkness *and its Italian translations*. London: Bloomsbury.

Mastropierro, L. and M. Mahlberg. 2017. Key words and translated cohesion in Lovecraft's *At the Mountains of Madness* and one of its Italian translations. *English Text Construction* 10(1): 78–105. Available at: https://benjamins.com/catalog/etc.10.1.05mas

Matthiessen, C.M.I.M. 2001. The environments of translation. In E. Steiner and C. Yallop (eds), *Exploring translation and multilingual text production: Beyond content*, 41–124. Berlin and New York: De Gruyter.

Matthiessen, C.M.I.M. 2007. Multilinguality: Translation – a 'feverish' phase in SFL. Presentation at the International Systemic Functional Linguistics Conference 2007, 16–20 July, Odense, Denmark.

Matthiessen, C.M.I.M. 2009. Ideas & new directions. In M.A.K. Halliday and J.J. Webster (eds), *Continuum companion to systemic functional linguistics*, 12–58. London: Continuum.

Matthiessen, C.M.I.M. 2012. Systemic functional linguistics as appliable linguistics: Social accountability and critical approaches. *D.E.L.T.A.* 28(Especial): 435–471.

Matthiessen, C.M.I.M. 2013a. Analysing and interpreting works of verbal art as acts of meaning instantiating the meaning potential of language in context, 1–58. Draft paper no longer available at: https://it.scribd.com/document/218160408/Analysing-and-Interpreting-Works-of-Verbal-Arts

Matthiessen, C.M.I.M. 2013b. Talking and writing about literature: Some observations based on systemic functional linguistics. *The Indian Journal of Applied Linguistics* 39(2): 5–49.

Matthiessen, C.M.I.M. 2014. Choice in translation: Metafunctional considerations. In K. Kunz, E. Teich, S. Hansen-Schirra, S. Neumann and P. Daut (eds), *Caught in the middle: Language use and translation: A festschrift for Erich Steiner on the occasion of his 60th birthday*, 271–333. Saarbrücken: Saarland University.

Matthiessen, C.M.I.M. 2018. Subliminal construal of world order clause by clause: Hierarchy of control in *Noah's Ark*. *Linguistics and the Human Sciences (LHS)* 1(2–3): 250–283.

McCabe, A. 2017. Systemic functional linguistics and language teaching. In T. Bartlett and G. O'Grady (eds), *The Routledge handbook of systemic functional linguistics*, 591–604. Abingdon, Oxon: Routledge.

McIntyre, D. 2011. The place of stylistics in the English curriculum. In L. Jeffries and D. McIntyre (eds), *Teaching stylistics*, 9–29. Houndmills, Basingstoke: Palgrave Macmillan.

Mickan, P. 2019. Language and education: Learning to mean. In G. Thompson, W.L. Bowcher, L. Fontaine and J.Y. Liang (eds), *The Cambridge handbook of systemic functional linguistics*, 537–560. Cambridge: Cambridge University Press.

Miller, D.R. 1998. Insegnando la lingua speciale del testo letterario: l'approccio sociosemiotico. In M. Pavese and G. Bernini (eds), *L'apprendimento linguistico all'Università: le lingue speciali*, 271–293. Bulzoni: Roma.

Miller, D.R. 2007. Construing the 'primitive' primitively: Grammatical parallelism as patterning and positioning strategy in D.H. Lawrence. In D.R. Miller and M. Turci (eds), *Language and verbal art revisited: Linguistic approaches to the study of literature*, 41–67. London: Equinox Publishing Ltd.

Miller, D.R. 2010. The Hasanian framework for the study of 'verbal art' revisited ... and reproposed. In J. Douthwaite and K. Wales (eds), *Stylistics and co. (unlimited) – the range, methods and applications of stylistics*, special issue of *Textus* 23(1): 29–51.

Miller, D.R. 2013a. Another look at social semiotic stylistics: Coupling Hasan's 'verbal art' framework with 'the Mukařovský-Jakobson theory'. In C.A.M. Gouveia and M.F. Alexandre (eds), *Languages, metalanguages, modalities, cultures: Functional and socio-discoursive perspectives*, 121–40. Lisbon: BonD.

Miller, D.R. 2013b. The 'English Only' movement in the USA: Its attitudes, politics and discursive practices ... and the sundry questions it raises. In R. Cagliero and A. Belladelli (eds), *American English(es): Linguistic and socio-cultural perspectives*, 62–88. Cambridge: Cambridge Scholars.

Miller, D.R. 2016a. Jakobson's place in Hasan's Social Semiotic Stylistics: 'Pervasive parallelism' as symbolic articulation of theme. In W. Bowcher and J. Liang (eds), *Society in language, language in society: Essays in honour of Ruqaiya Hasan*, 59–80. London: Palgrave Macmillan.

Miller, D.R. 2016b. On negotiating the hurdles of corpus-assisted appraisal analysis in verbal art. In S. Gardner and S. Alsop (eds), *Systemic functional linguistics in the digital age*, 211–228. Sheffield: Equinox Publishing Ltd.

Miller, D.R. 2017a. *Language as purposeful: Functional varieties of text.* 2nd edition. Bologna: AMSActa/ AlmaDL (Quaderni del CeSLiC, Functional Grammar Studies for Non-Native Speakers of English).

Miller, D.R. 2017b. Language and verbal art. In T. Bartlett and G. O'Grady (eds), *The Routledge handbook of systemic functional linguistics*, 506–519. Abingdon, Oxon: Routledge.

Miller, D.R. 2019a. Language and literature. In G. Thompson, W.L. Bowcher, L. Fontaine and J.Y. Liang (eds), *The Cambridge handbook of systemic functional linguistics*, 689–713. Cambridge: Cambridge University Press.

Miller, D.R. 2019b. Methodological triangulation for monitoring teaching practices. Presentation at the European Systemic Functional Linguistics Conference 2019, 3–5 July, Leiria, Portugal.

Miller, D.R. and A. Luporini. 2015. Social semiotic stylistics and the corpus: How do-able is an automated analysis of verbal art? In A. Duguid, A. Marchi, A. Partington and C. Taylor (eds), *Gentle obsessions: Literature, linguistics and learning. In honour of John Morley*, 235–250. Roma: Artemide Edizioni.

Miller, D.R. and A. Luporini. 2018a. Software-assisted systemic socio-semantic stylistics – appraising tru* in J.M. Coetzee's *Foe*. In R. Wegener, A. Oesterle and S. Neumann (eds), *On verbal art: Essays in honour of Ruqaiya Hasan*, 53–79. Sheffield: Equinox Publishing Ltd.

Miller, D.R. and A. Luporini. 2018b. Systemic socio-semantic stylistics (SSS) as appliable linguistics: The cases of literary criticism and language teaching/learning. In A. Sellami-Baklouti and L. Fontaine (eds), *Perspectives from systemic functional linguistics: An appliable theory of language*, 229–248. Abingdon, Oxon: Routledge.

Miller, D.R. and A. Luporini. 2018c. Systemic socio-semantic stylistics: un metodo per insegnare la lingua e la cultura del/nel testo letterario. In B. Ivancic, P. Puccini, M.J. Rodrigo Mora and M. Turci (eds), *Il testo letterario nell'apprendimento linguistico: esperienze a confronto*, 61–74. Bologna: AMSActa/AlmaDL (Quaderni del CeSLiC, Atti di Convegni CeSLiC – 6).

Miller, D.R. and A. Luporini. 2020. Guiding towards register awareness in an undergraduate EFL curriculum in Italy: The special case of verbal art. *Register Studies* 2(2): 209–240.

Miller, D.R. and M. Turci (eds). 2007. *Language and verbal art revisited: Linguistic approaches to the study of literature.* London: Equinox Publishing Ltd.

Mills, K. and L. Unsworth. 2017. Multimodal literacy. In G. Noblit (ed.), *Oxford research encyclopedia of education*, 1–45. New York: Oxford University Press.

Moore, A. 2017. Register analysis in systemic functional linguistics. In T. Barlett and G. O'Grady (eds), *Routledge handbook of systemic functional linguistics*, 418–437. Abingdon, Oxon: Routledge.

Mouka, E., I.E. Saridakis and A. Fotopoulou. 2015. Racism goes to the movies: A corpus-driven study of cross-linguistic racist discourse annotation and translation analysis. In C. Fantinuoli and F. Zanettin (eds), *New directions in corpus-based translation studies*, 35–70. Berlin: Language Science Press.

Munday, J. 2008. *Style and ideology in translation: Latin American writing in English.* Abingdon, Oxon: Routledge.

Munday, J. 2012. *Evaluation in translation: Critical points of translator decision making.* Abingdon, Oxon: Routledge.

Munday, J. 2015. Engagement and graduation resources as markers of translator/interpreter positioning. *Target* 27(3): 406–421.

Munday, J. 2016 [2001]. *Introducing translation studies: Theories and applications.* 4th edition. Abingdon, Oxon: Routledge.

Mukařovský, J. 1977. *The word and verbal art: Selected essays by Jan Mukařovský*. Edited and translated by J. Burbank and P. Steiner. London: Yale University Press.

Mukařovský, J. 1978. *Structure, sign and function: Selected essays by Jan Mukařovský*. Edited and translated by J. Burbank and P. Steiner. London: Yale University Press.

Mukařovský, J. 2014 [1932]. Jazyk spisovný a jazyk básnický [Standard language and poetic language]. In B. Havránek and M. Weingart (eds), *Spisovná čeština a jazyková kultura* [*Standard Czech and the cultivation of language*], 123–149. Prague: Melantrich. In English in J. Chovanec. 2014. *Chapters from the history of Czech functional linguistics*, 41–53. Brno: Masarykova Univerzita. Available at: https://digilib.phil.muni.cz/bitstream/handle/11222.digilib/131565/Books_2010_2019_071-2014-1_7.pdf?sequence=1

Newmark, P. 1991. *About translation*. Clevedon, Philadelphia and Adelaide: Multilingual Matters.

Nørgaard, N. 2003. *Systemic functional linguistics and literary analysis: A Hallidayan approach to Joyce – A Joycean approach to Halliday*. Odense, Denmark: University Press of Southern Denmark.

Nørgaard, N. 2011. Teaching multimodal stylistics. In L. Jeffries and D. McIntyre (eds), *Teaching stylistics*, 221–238. Houndmills, Basingstoke: Palgrave Macmillan.

Nørgaard, N. 2014. Multimodality and stylistics. In M. Burke (ed.), *The Routledge handbook of stylistics*, 471–484. Abingdon, Oxon: Routledge.

Nørgaard, N. 2018. *Multimodal stylistics of the novel: More than words*. Abingdon, Oxon: Routledge.

Nørgaard, N., B. Busse and R. Montoro. 2010. *Key terms in stylistics*. London: Continuum.

Nowottny, W. 1962. *The language poets use*. University of London: The Athlone Press.

O'Donnell, M. 2011. From teaching literature to exploring ideological development: The life and works of Ruqaiya Hasan. *Nexus* 2011(1): 114–124. (Asociación Española De Estudios Anglo-Norteamericanos). Available at: http://www.wagsoft.com/Papers/HasanBio-2011.pdf

O'Halloran, K.A. 2007. The subconscious in James Joyce's 'Eveline': A corpus stylistic analysis which chews on the 'Fish hook'. *Language and Literature* 16(3): 227–244.

O'Halloran, K.L. 2004. Visual semiosis in film. In K.L. O'Halloran (ed.), *Multimodal discourse analysis*, 109–130. London: Continuum.

O'Halloran, K.L. 2008. Systemic functional-multimodal discourse analysis (SF-MDA): Constructing ideational meaning using language and visual imagery. *Visual Communication* 7: 443–475. https://doi.org/10.1177/1470357208096210

O'Halloran, K.L., S. Tan and P. Wignell. 2019. SFL and multimodal discourse analysis. In G. Thompson, W.L. Bowcher, L. Fontaine and J.Y. Liang (eds), *The Cambridge handbook of systemic functional linguistics*, 433–461. Cambridge: Cambridge University Press.

Ohmann, R. 1967. Literature as sentences. In S. Chatman and S.R. Levin (eds), *Essays on the language of literature*, 231–238. Boston, MA: Houghton Mifflin.

Ong, W.J. 1967. *The Presence of the Word*. New Haven, NJ: Yale University Press.

Ong, W.J. 1982. *Orality and literacy: The technologizing of the word*. London and New York: Methuen.

Othman, W. 2017. Explicitational enhancement in translation. In S. Neumann, R. Wegener, J. Fest, P. Niemietz and N. Hützen (eds), *Challenging boundaries in linguistics: Systemic functional perspectives*, 283–306. Bern: Peter Lang.

Othman, W. 2020. An SFL-based Model for Investigating Explicitation-Related Phenomena in Translation. *Meta* 65(1): 193–210.

O'Toole, L.M. 1982. *Structure, style and interpretation in the Russian short story*. New Haven, NJ: Yale University Press.

O'Toole, L.M. 1994. *The language of displayed art*. London: Leicester University Press.

O'Toole, L.M. 2010. Review of *Language and verbal art revisited: Linguistic approaches to the study of literature*, D.R. Miller and M. Turci (eds), Equinox. *Linguistics and the Human Sciences* (*LHS*) 3(3): 393–398.

O'Toole, L.M. 2018. *The hermeneutic spiral and interpretation in literature and the visual arts*. Abingdon, Oxon: Routledge.

O'Toole, L.M. and A. Shukman (eds and trans). 1977. *Russian poetics in translation*, Vols 1–8. Oxford: Holdan Books Ltd.

Otto, R. 1958 [1917]. *Das Heilige*. Breslau: Trewendt und Granier. *The idea of the holy* (trans. J.W. Harvey). London: Oxford University Press.

Pagano, A.S., G.P. Figueredo and A. Lukin. 2015. Measuring proximity between source and target texts: An exploratory study. In A. Tuzzi, M. Benešová and J. Macutek (eds), *Recent contributions to quantitative linguistics*, 103–114. Berlin: De Gruyter Mouton.

Pagano, A.S., G.P. Figueredo and A. Lukin. 2016. Modelling proximity in a corpus of literary retranslations: A methodological proposal for clustering texts based on systemic-functional annotation of lexicogrammatical features. In M. Ji (ed.), *Empirical translation studies: Interdisciplinary methodologies explored*, 93–127. Sheffield: Equinox Publishing Ltd.

Page, R., B. Busse and N. Nørgaard (eds). 2018. *Rethinking language, text and context: Interdisciplinary research in stylistics in honour of Michael Toolan*. Abingdon, Oxon: Routledge.

Painter, C., J.R. Martin and L. Unsworth. 2013. *Reading visual narratives: Image analysis of children's picture books*. London: Equinox Publishing Ltd.

Painter, C., J.R. Martin and L. Unsworth. 2014. Reading visual narratives: Image analysis of children's picture books. *Functions of Language* 21(3): 333–341.

Pérez-González, L. 2007. Appraising dubbed conversation: Systemic functional insights into the construal of naturalness in translated film dialogue. *The Translator* 13(1): 1–38.

Piazza, R., M. Bednarek and F. Rossi (eds). 2011. *Telecinematic discourse: Approaches to the language of films and television series*. Amsterdam and Philadelphia: John Benjamins.

Pomorska, K. and S. Rudy (eds). 1987. *Roman Jakobson: Language in literature*. Cambridge, MA and London: The Belknap Press of Harvard University.

Rodrigues-Júnior, A.S. and L. Barbara. 2013. Linguistic constructions of appraisal in the novel *The Picture of Dorian Gray* and its Brazilian translation and adaptations: An exploratory analysis. *Revista Brasileira de Lingüística Aplicada* 13(1): 259–285.

Rosa, A.A. 2013. The power of voice in translated fiction: Or, following a linguistic track in translation studies. In C. Way, S. Vandepitte, R. Meylaerts and M. Bartłomiejczyk (eds), *Tracks and treks in translation studies*, 223–245. Amsterdam and Philadelphia: John Benjamins.

Rose, D. 2016. Engaging children in the pleasures of literature and verbal art. *English in Australia* [online] 51(2): 52–62. Available at: https://search.informit.com.au/documentSummary;dn=433103228151198;res=IELHSS

Rossi, F. and M-G. Sindoni. 2016. The phantoms of the opera: Toward a multidimensional interpretative framework of analysis. In M-G. Sindoni, J. Wildfeuer and K.L. O'Halloran (eds), *Mapping multimodal performance studies*, 61–84. Abingdon, Oxon: Routledge.

Rothery, J. 1996. Making changes: Developing an educational linguistics. In R. Hasan and G. Williams (eds), *Literacy in society*, 86–123. London and New York: Longman.

Ryan, F., M. Coughlan and P. Cronin. 2009. Interviewing in qualitative research: The one-to-one interview. *International Journal of Therapy and Rehabilitation* 16(6): 309–314.

Salameh, M.Y.A.B. 2010. Stylistic manipulations in Henry James' novel *The Portrait of a Lady*. Unpublished PhD thesis. Department Of Linguistics, Aligarh Muslim University, Aligarh (India). Available at: http://hdl.handle.net/10603/11247

Schleppegrell, M.J. 2004. *The language of schooling: A functional linguistics perspective*. Mahwah, NJ and London: Lawrence Erlbaum Associates Publishers. Available at: http://www.iltec.pt/TeL4ELE/Schleppegrell.pdf, edition published in the Taylor & Francis e-Library, 2008.

Schleppegrell, M.J. 2013. The role of metalanguage in supporting academic language development. *Language Learning* 63(Suppl. 1): 153–170.

Schleppegrell, M.J. 2020 [2018]. The knowledge base for language teaching: What is the English to be taught as content? *Language Teaching Research* 24(1): 17–27. Article first published online: 2 July 2018: 1–11; Issue published: 1 January 2020.

Schulze, J.M. 2016. Enhancing pre-service teachers' knowledge of language through systemic functional linguistics. *International Journal of Education and Social Science* 3(8): 8–17.

Scott, M. 1996–2020. WordSmith tools: Through 2004 version, Oxford: Oxford University Press; 2008 version, Liverpool: Lexical Analysis Software; 2012, 2016, 2020 versions, Stroud: Lexical Analysis Software. Available at: https://lexically.net/publications/citing_wordsmith.htm

Sellami-Baklouti, A. 2018. Maintenance versus shift in literary translation: SFL perspectives on the translation of user-related varieties in socio-cultural contexts. In A. Sellami-Baklouti and L. Fontaine (eds), *Perspectives from systemic functional linguistics*, 121–139. Abingdon, Oxon: Routledge.

Shklovsky, V. 1965 [1916]. Art as technique. In L.T. Lemon and M.J. Reis (eds and trans), *Russian formalist criticism: Four essays*, 3–24. Lincoln, NB and London: University of Nebraska Press.

Simpson, P. 2014 [2004]. *Stylistics*. 2nd edition. Abingdon, Oxon: Routledge.

Sindoni, M-G., J. Wildfeuer and K.L. O'Halloran (guest eds). 2016a. *Journal of Social Semiotics* 26(4): The languages of performing arts: Semiosis, communication and meaning-making. Introduction available at: https://www.tandfonline.com/doi/full/10.1080/10350330.2016.1189733

Sindoni, M-G., J. Wildfeuer and K.L. O'Halloran (eds). 2016b. *Multimodal semiotics of theatrical performances*. Abingdon, Oxon: Routledge.

Sotirova, V. 2016a. Introduction. In V. Sotirova (ed.), *The Bloomsbury companion to stylistics*, 3–17. London and New York: Bloomsbury Academic.

Sotirova, V. (ed.). 2016b. *The Bloomsbury companion to stylistics*. London and New York: Bloomsbury Academic.

Stankiewicz, E. 1983. Roman Jakobson: Teacher and scholar. In *A tribute to Roman Jakobson 1896–1982*, 17–26. Berlin and New York: De Gruyter.

Steiner, E. 1988. The interaction of language and music as semiotic systems: The example of the folk ballad. In J.D. Benson, M.J. Cummings and W.S. Greaves (eds), *Linguistics in a systemic perspective*, 393–441. Amsterdam and Philadelphia: John Benjamins.

Steiner, E. 2004. *Translated texts: Properties, variants, evaluations*. Bern: Peter Lang.

Steiner, E. 2005. Halliday and translation theory — enhancing the options, broadening the range, and keeping the ground. In R. Hasan, C.M.I.M. Matthiessen and J.J. Webster (eds), *Continuing discourse on language: A functional perspective*, Vol. 1, 481–500. London: Equinox Publishing Ltd.

Steiner, E. 2015a. Halliday's contributions to a theory of translation. In J.J. Webster (ed.), *The Bloomsbury companion to M.A.K. Halliday*, 412–426. London: Bloomsbury.

Steiner, E. 2015b. Contrastive studies of cohesion and their impact on our knowledge of translation (English-German). *Target* 27(3): 351–369.

Steiner, E. and C. Yallop (eds). 2001. *Exploring translation and multilingual text production: Beyond content*. Berlin and New York: De Gruyter.

Stockwell, P. and S. Whiteley (eds). 2014. *The Cambridge handbook of stylistics*. Cambridge: Cambridge University Press.

Stubbs, M. 2009. Memorial article: John Sinclair (1933–2007): The search for units of meaning: Sinclair on empirical semantics. *Applied Linguistics* 30(1): 115–137.

Swain, E. 2014. Translating metaphor in literary texts: An intertextual approach. In D.R. Miller and E. Monti (eds), *Tradurre figure/translating figurative language*, 241–254. Bologna: Bononia University Press.

Tajvidi, G.R. and S.H. Arjani. 2017. Appraisal theory in translation studies: An introduction and review of studies of evaluation in translation. *Journal of Research in Applied Linguistics* 8(2): 3–30.

Tan, S., P. Wignell and K.L. O'Halloran. 2016a. From book to stage to screen: Semiotic transformations of Gothic horror genre conventions. *Journal of Social Semiotics* 26(4): 404–423.

Tan, S., Wignell P. and K.L. O'Halloran. 2016b. Multimodal semiotics of theatrical performances. In M-G. Sindoni, J. Wildfeuer and K.L. O'Halloran (eds), *Mapping multimodal performance studies*, 14–38. Abingdon, Oxon: Routledge.

Taylor, C. 1990. *Aspects of language and translation: Contrastive approaches for Italian/English translators*. Udine: Campanotto Editore.

Taylor, C.J. 1993. Systemic linguistics and translation. In T. Gibson and C. Stainton (eds), *Occasional papers in systemic linguistics* 7: 87–103. Nottingham: University of Nottingham.

Taylor, C. 1998. *Language to language*. Cambridge: Cambridge University Press.

Taylor, C.J. 2003. Multimodal transcription in the analysis, translation and subtitling of Italian films. *The Translator* 9(2): 191–205.

Taylor, C. 2004. Multimodal text analysis and subtitling. In E. Ventola, C. Charles and M. Kaltenbacher (eds), *Perspectives on multimodality*, 153–172. Amsterdam and Philadelphia, PA: John Benjamins.

Taylor, C. 2008. Predictability in film language: Corpus-assisted research. In C. Taylor Torsello, K. Ackerley and E. Castello (eds), *Corpora for university language teachers*, 167–181. Bern: Peter Lang.

Taylor, C. 2017. Reading images (including moving ones). In T. Bartlett and G. O'Grady (eds), *The Routledge handbook of systemic functional linguistics*, 575–590. Abingdon, Oxon: Routledge.

Taylor, C. and A. Baldry. 2001. Computer assisted text analysis and translation: A functional approach in the analysis and translation of advertising texts. In E. Steiner and C. Yallop (eds), *Exploring translation and multilingual text production: Beyond content*, 277–305. Berlin and New York: De Gruyter.

Taylor Torsello, C. 1992. *Linguistica Sistemica e Educazione Linguistica*. Unipress: Padua.

Taylor Torsello, C. 1996. Grammatica e traduzione. In G. Cortese (ed.), *Tradurre i linguaggi settoriali*, 87–119. Torino: Edizioni Libreria Cortina.

Taylor Torsello, C. 2007. Projection in literary and non-literary texts. In D.R. Miller and M. Turci (eds), *Language and verbal art revisited: Linguistic approaches to the study of literature*, 115–148. London: Equinox Publishing Ltd.

Taylor Torsello, C. 2016. Woolf's lecture/novel/essay: *A Room of One's Own*. In D.R. Miller and P. Bayley (eds), *Hybridity in systemic functional linguistics: Grammar, text and discursive context*, 240–267. Sheffield: Equinox Publishing Ltd.

Thibault, P.J. 1991. *Social semiotics as praxis: Text, social meaning making, and Nabokov's Ada*. Minnesota, MI: University of Minnesota Press.

Thompson, G. and S. Hunston (eds). 2006. *System and corpus: Exploring connections*. London: Equinox Publishing Ltd.

Toolan, M.J. 1988. *Narrative: A critical linguistic introduction*. London: Routledge.

Toolan, M.J. 1990. *The stylistics of fiction: A literary-linguistic approach*. London: Routledge.

Toolan, M.J. (ed.). 1992. *Language, text and context: Essays in stylistics*. London: Routledge.

Toolan, M.J. 1998. *Language in literature: An introduction to stylistics*. London: Arnold.

Toolan, M.J. 2009. *Narrative progression in the short story: A corpus stylistic approach*. Amsterdam: John Benjamins.

Toolan, M.J. 2014. Stylistics and film. In M. Burke (ed.), *The Routledge handbook of stylistics*, 455–470. Abingdon, Oxon: Routledge.

Toury, G. 1995. *Descriptive translation studies – and beyond*. 1st edition. Amsterdam and Philadelphia: John Benjamins.

Turci, M. 2007. The meaning of dark* in Joseph Conrad's *Heart of Darkness*. In D.R. Miller and M. Turci (eds), *Language and verbal art revisited: Linguistic approaches to the study of literature*, 97–114. London: Equinox Publishing Ltd.

Turci, M. 2014. Multimodality and illustrations: A comparative study of the English and Italian illustrated first editions of *The Jungle Book* by Rudyard Kipling. In A. Maiorani and C. Christie (eds), *Multimodal epistemologies: Towards an integrated framework*, 174–187. Abingdon, Oxon: Routledge.

Turner, G.W. 1973. *Stylistics*. Harmondsworth: Penguin Books Ltd.

Unsworth, L. (ed.). 2008. *New literacies and the English curriculum: Multimodal perspectives*. London: Continuum.

Unsworth, L. 2008. Comparing and composing digital re-presentations of literature: Multimedia authoring and meta-communicative knowledge. In L. Unsworth (ed.), *New literacies and the English curriculum: Multimodal perspectives*, 186–212. London: Continuum.

Unsworth, L. 2014. Point of view in picture books and animated film adaptations: Informing critical multimodal comprehension and composition pedagogy. In E. Djonov and S. Zhao (eds), *Critical multimodal studies of popular discourse*, 202–216. Abingdon, Oxon: Routledge.

Unsworth, L. and M. Macken-Horarik. 2015. Interpretive responses to images in picture books by primary and secondary school students: Exploring curriculum expectations of a 'visual grammatics'. *English in Education* 49(1): 56–78.

van de Ven, I. 2010. The literary work as stranger: The disrupting ethics of defamiliarization and the literariness of literature: A search for ethical effects of literary aesthetics in a post-critical landscape. Research Master thesis, Utrecht University. Available at: https://dspace.library. uu.nl/handle/1874/179771

van Leeuwen, T. 1999. *Speech, music, sound*. London: Macmillan.

Vasconcellos, M.L. 2009. Systemic functional translation studies (SFTS): The theory travelling in Brazilian environments [Estudos sistêmico funcionais em tradução (TSFs): a teoria viajando no contexto brasileiro]. *D.E.L.T.A.* 25(Especial): 585–607.

Veloso, F. 2012. Comic books and the construction of reality: A critical approach in the classroom. In C.A. DeCoursey (ed.), *Language arts in Asia: Literature and drama in English, Putonghua and Cantonese*, 85–102. Newcastle upon Tyne: Cambridge Scholars Publishing.

Vygotsky, L. 1978. *Mind in society: The development of higher psychological process*. Edited and translated (revising) by M. Cole, V. John-Steiner, S. Scribner and E. Souberman. Cambridge, MA: Harvard University Press.

Wales, K. 2001 [1990]. *A dictionary of stylistics*. 2nd edition. Harlow: Pearson Education Ltd.

Wales, K. 2012. A celebration of style: Retrospect and prospect, *Language and Literature* 2(1): 9–11.

Wales, K. 2014. The stylistic tool-kit: Methods and sub-disciplines. In P. Stockwell and S. Whiteley (eds), *The Cambridge handbook of stylistics*, 32–45. Cambridge: Cambridge University Press.

Wang, B. and Y. Ma. 2020. *Lao She's Teahouse and its two English translations: Exploring Chinese drama translation with systemic functional linguistics*. Abingdon, Oxon: Routledge.

Wang, B. and Y. Ma. 2021. *Systemic functional translation studies: Theoretical insights and new directions*. Sheffield: Equinox Publishing Ltd.

Wang, Y. 2018. A contextual investigation of Chinese translations of detective stories – mismatched Holmes. *Linguistics and Human Sciences (LHS)* 14(1–2): 123–150.

Warner, M. 2005. Angels and engines: Apocalypse and its aftermath, from George W. Bush to Philip Pullman. *TLS* no. 5382/3. 19 and 26 August: 14–17.

Weber, J.J. (ed.). 1996. *The stylistics reader: From Roman Jakobson to the present*. London and New York: Arnold.

Webster, J.J. 2001. Thumboo's *David*. In C.K. Tong, A. Pakir, K.C. Ban and H.B.H. Goh (eds), *Ariels: Departures and returns. Essays for Edwin Thumboo*, 75–88. Oxford: Oxford University Press.

Webster, J.J. 2015. *Understanding verbal art: A functional linguistic approach*. Berlin and Heidelberg: Springer-Verlag.

Wellek, R. 1960. Closing statement (retrospects and prospects from the viewpoint of literary criticism). In T.A. Sebeok (ed.), *Style in language*, 417–418. Cambridge, MA: MIT Press.

White, P.R.R. 2003. Beyond modality and hedging: A dialogic view of the language of intersubjective stance. In S. Sarangi and J. Wilson (eds), *Text* 23(2): 259–284.

White, P.R.R. 2016. Constructing the 'stranger' in Camus' *L'Etranger*: Registerial and attitudinal variability under translation. *The Journal of Translation Studies* 17(4): 75–106.

Whitworth, J. 2012 [2010]. Little. First published in *TLS*, 2010. Also in the collection, *Girlie Gangs*, 2012. London: Enitharmon Press.

Widdowson, H.G. 1996. Stylistics: An approach to stylistic analysis. In J.J. Weber (ed.), *The stylistics reader: From Roman Jakobson to the present*, 138–156. London and New York: Arnold.

Williams, G. 2004. Ontogenesis and grammatics: Functions of metalanguage in pedagogical discourse. In G. Williams and A. Lukin (eds), *The development of language: Functional perspectives on species and individuals*, 241–267. London: Continuum.

Williams, G. 2016. Reflection literacy in the first years of schooling: Questions of theory and practice. In W. Bowcher and J. Liang (eds), *Society in language, language in society: Essays in honour of Ruqaiya Hasan*, 333–356. London: Palgrave Macmillan.

Wimsatt, W.K. and M. Beardsley. 1949. The affective fallacy. *Sewanee Review* 57(1): 31–55.

Wiratno, T. 2012. Teaching English language and literature integratively by using language-based approach: An Indonesian university context. In C.A. DeCoursey (ed.), *Language arts in Asia: Literature and drama in English, Putonghua and Cantonese*, 178–196. Newcastle upon Tyne: Cambridge Scholars Publishing.

Wolfer, D. and B. Harrison-Lever. 2005. *Photographs in the mud*. Fremantle, WA: Fremantle Arts Centre Press.

Yallop, C. 2001. The construction of equivalence. In E. Steiner and C. Yallop (eds), *Exploring translation and multilingual text production: Beyond content*, 229–246. Berlin and New York: De Gruyter.

Yu, H. and C. Wu. 2016. Recreating the image of Chan master Huineng: The roles of MOOD and MODALITY. *Functional Linguistics* 3(4): 1–21.

Yu, H. and C. Wu. 2017. Recreating the image of Chan master Huineng: The role of personal pronouns. *Target* 29(1): 64–86.

Zurru, E. 2010. Breaking the crystal shoes: A multimodal stylistic analysis of the character of Cinderella in the *Shrek* saga. In J. Douthwaite and K. Wales (eds), *Stylistics and co. (unlimited) - the range, methods and applications of stylistics*, special issue of *Textus* 23(1): 235–262.

Zyngier, S. and O. Fialho. 2016. Pedagogical stylistics: Charting outcomes. In V. Sotirova (ed.), *The Bloomsbury companion to stylistics*, 208–230. London: Bloomsbury.

Zyngier, S., O. Fialho and P.A.D.P. Rios. 2007. Revisiting literary awareness. In G. Watson and S. Zyngier (eds), *Literature and stylistics for language learners*, 194–209. Houndmills, Basingstoke: Palgrave Macmillan.

Websites

Mambrol, N. 2016. https://literariness.org/2016/03/17/defamiliarization/ and https://literariness.org/2016/03/17/roman-jakobsons-contribution-to-literary-studies-an-essay/

The corpus stylistic web application 'Corpus Linguistics in Context', at https://dls.hypotheses.org/tag/corpus-tools

The Official Web page for the ADHO Special Interest Group (SIG) in Digital Literary Stylistics, at Digital Literary Stylistics (SIG-DLS), at: https://www.openedition.org/19079?lang=en

Reification and American Literature, by herrnaphta (Paul). 2011. https://herrnaphta.wordpress.com/2011/01/09/reification-and-american-literature/

Name Index

Subject Index

CPSIA information can be obtained
at www.ICGtesting.com
Printed in the USA
JSHW051726171121
20498JS00002B/97